IMAGES
of America

SAN JUAN

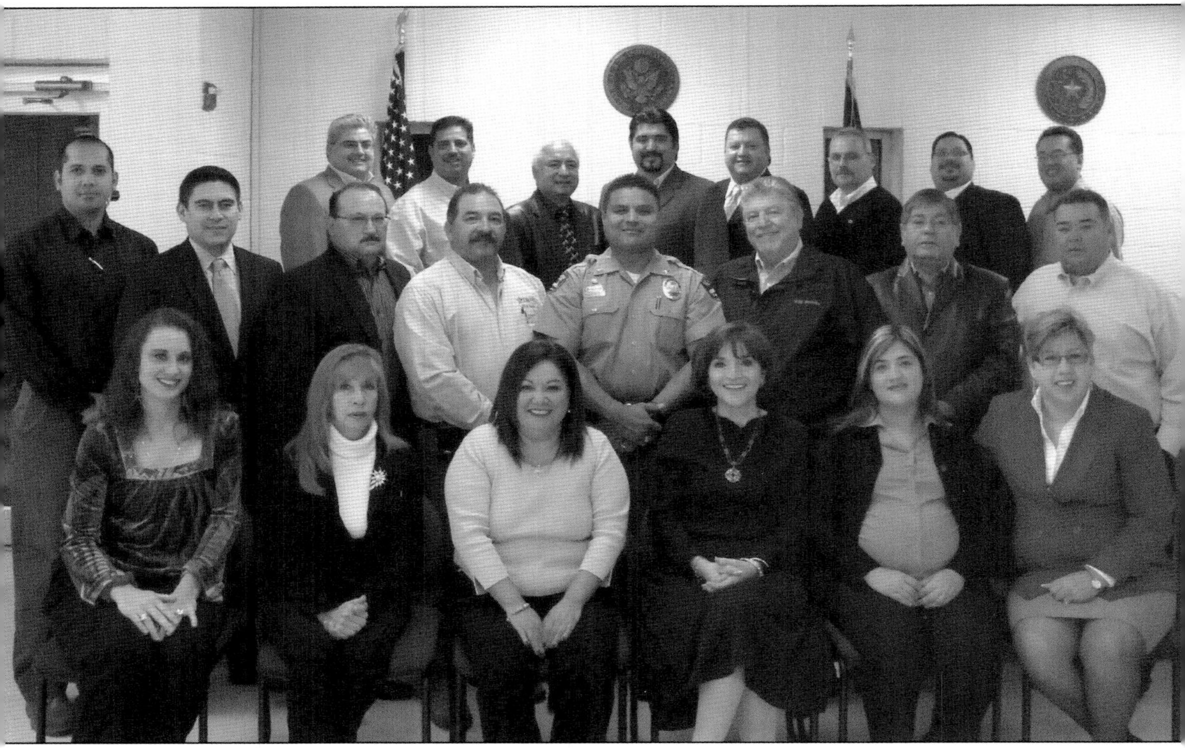

The 2009 city leadership of San Juan, Texas, is captured in this photograph. They are, from left to right, (first row) Miki McCarthy (San Juan Economic Development Corporation executive director), Carmen Gonzalez (purchasing director), Melissa Gonzalez (grant writer), Yolanda Jackson (human resources coordinator), Sujei Mireles (municipal court), Christina Walker (assistant to the city manager); (second row) Trini Cantu (utilities director), Jesse Zambrano (San Juan Economic Development Corporation board president), Emilio Garcia (planning director), Eddie Tapia (San Juan Economic Development Corporation board vice president), Juan Gonzalez (police chief), Ruben Rojas (streets and sanitation director), Ramiro Lopez (finance director), Roel Garza (parks and recreation director); (third row) Jerry Muñoz (city attorney), Eddie Suarez (commissioner), Lupe Rodriguez (mayor pro tempore), Pedro Contreras (mayor), Bob Garza (commissioner), Tirso Garza (interim city manager), Armando Garza (commissioner), and Bobby Rodriguez (city secretary). (Courtesy of City of San Juan)

On the Cover: The San Juan Hotel, shown here in the mid-1940s, has been one of San Juan's landmark buildings since it opened in 1920. A center for lodging, dining, and entertainment, many have enjoyed the hotel and its amenities throughout the years. (Courtesy of Museum of South Texas History.)

IMAGES *of America*
SAN JUAN

Roseann Bacha-Garza and
San Juan Economic Development Corporation

ARCADIA
PUBLISHING

ISBN 978-0-7385-6681-8

Published by Arcadia Publishing
Charleston, South Carolina

Printed in the United States of America

Library of Congress Control Number: 2009937656

For all general information contact Arcadia Publishing at:
Telephone 843-853-2070
Fax 843-853-0044
E-mail sales@arcadiapublishing.com
For customer service and orders:
Toll-Free 1-888-313-2665

Visit us on the Internet at www.arcadiapublishing.com

To the San Juan Economic Development Corporation Board of Directors:
Thank you for granting this opportunity to create
a wonderful gift to our fine city.

CONTENTS

ACKNOWLEDGMENTS

The San Juan Economic Development Corporation would like to extend a sincere thanks to the wonderful citizens of San Juan for their contributions and participation in this project. Early in 2009, we asked former and current residents to come forward with photographs and memories to help us navigate through our deep and rich history. As we prepare for our upcoming centennial celebration, we are now better equipped to tell our story from different perspectives. We were so fortunate to get such an overwhelming response. There were so many people who participated in the research for this book that we feel it would be impossible to thank them all individually. Thanks to everyone involved, we now have the benefit of hindsight as it relates to city government, local law enforcement, industry, education, commerce, and livelihood. As you read through this book, you will see these individuals credited for the photographs they contributed below each caption. In addition to the photographs, the memories they shared with us were a great help in creating each chapter introduction and each photograph caption.

We especially would like to thank the Centennial Committee, which was made up of local leaders and residents who helped gather information and collect photographs for the purpose of this book. We would like to offer them our sincere thanks for all of their assistance with this project. They are as follows: Dr. Fernando Castillo (chairman), Estela Salazar (vice chairman), Juan Maldonado (secretary/treasurer), Estella Rojas (member), Romeo Jimenez (member), Kathleen Carrizal-Frye (member), and Arturo Ramirez (member).

Dr. Sonia Hernandez, San Juan native and assistant professor of history at the University of Texas-Pan American, was both a positive influence and kind enough to proofread the historical introduction.

Finally, we would like to thank the following institutions for their research assistance: Basilica of Our Lady of San Juan Del Valle National Shrine Archives (Esteban Martinez), Hidalgo County Historical Commission (Adela Ortega and Glenn Housley), Museum of South Texas History Archives (Barbara Stokes and Steve Lomas), and University of Texas Pan American Special Collections Library (George Gause and Janette Garcia).

FOREWORD

The San Juan Economic Development Corporation (EDC) welcomes you to experience the vibrant culture and diversity of the city of San Juan as we celebrate 100 years of its existence. The San Juan EDC proudly presents this book as a gift to the city of San Juan and all its residents. This book also serves as an invitation to come visit San Juan. It was a collaborative effort of many individuals from the community who have shared their personal history. We hope you enjoy learning about our people, our historical places, and many wonderful tales about San Juan's development.

While 100 years covers plenty of ground, we have woven a tapestry of history that encompasses many unique stories. The first chapter, "Dawn of San Juan," chronicles San Juan's development and its variety of cultural heritages from both sides of the border between the United States and Mexico. From the early discovery of new lands, the awarding of Spanish land grants, and land excursions leading to the city's founding, San Juan has witnessed much growth and prosperity.

The second chapter, "On the Farm," discusses the pioneer farmers who helped develop the agricultural industry in San Juan. Farming provided food, work, and industry to the families already residing here as well as new settlers arriving to this fertile promised land.

Chapter three, "Vital Local Enterprise," shares the awakening of entrepreneurship by the city's early pioneers. Opportunities were abundant for all hardworking individuals. The town's boom was directly related to the expansion of the railroad into the city. The main street atmosphere of both Nebraska Street and U.S. Highway 83 evolved from this expansion.

The fourth chapter, "Education and Religion," focuses on schools, teachers, and city leaders who advanced education throughout the community. This chapter also shares the rich history of many religious institutions that draw worshipers and pilgrims to San Juan to this day.

"Leadership and Heroism" fills the pages of chapter five, which delves into how the city has flourished since the Great Depression and beyond. We document important moments in San Juan's history. This chapter also highlights the significant contributions of local war heroes and local law enforcement.

San Juan has a wealth of contributions accomplished by its Hispanic leaders, residents, and social activists. Chapter six, "Hispanic Legacy," demonstrates the impact these individuals have made on the community.

Chapter seven, "Community Pride," expands on the civic achievements of many different organizations and individuals.

This book concludes with the eighth chapter dedicated to "Friends and Family." This chapter showcases the many rites of passage and awards experienced by San Juan residents. We are delighted to have provided you with a brief pictorial insight into the history of the city of San Juan. We wish a happy centennial to the city of San Juan and all its residents.

—Miki McCarthy

INTRODUCTION

Life along the southern tip of Texas existed long before the founding of the city of San Juan. Indigenous people lived in the Rio Grande Valley prior to the arrival of the Spanish conquistadores in the mid-1700s. During the middle of the 18th century, the king of Spain granted land to Jose Maria Balli and Narciso Cavazos along the banks of the Rio Grande. There were two particular portions of land referred to as *porciones* that formed the territory called San Juan, Texas.

Longtime local families share a unique history that is characteristic of the border region. As time marched on, different generations of local family lineages have lived under six different government flags. With the most recent change in government in 1848, the border between the United States and Mexico crossed over descendants of these original settlers. Many of them remained steadfast in their conviction that their land was exactly that. They held fast to their claims and remained in a territory that was governed by yet another government. As time went on, their land was divided among family heirs, and eventually subdivided further and sold either to individuals, or in large parcels to land developers.

Settlers along the Texas border with Mexico had formidable character and determination. This frontier territory represented an opportunity for success, prosperity in land ownership, and a general rebirth for newcomers. Railroad junctions dotted the landscape between Brownsville and Roma, determining the pattern of settlement as the St. Louis, Brownsville, and Mexican Railroad was laid. Land promoters purchased large tracts of land, marketing the dream of endless possibilities as cotton, sugar, and citrus fields eventually covered thousands of acres. Northern settlers arrived by train excursions into the Rio Grande Valley with a desire to create a new life in a new land. They rested in hotels and clubhouses, taking their pick of the lots available for purchase. Settling along the Rio Grande, pioneers built strong foundations, fostering economic and agricultural development in the progression of small-town life. Hard times were ahead of these ambitious souls. Some did not succeed and returned to their home territories. Others stayed and created a fruitful life, and many of their descendants live in San Juan today.

The story of the city of San Juan also includes settlers from south of the border. The Mexican Revolution of 1910 created difficult times and infused a desire to start over in the neighboring country. Hardworking Mexicans immigrated to Texas in search of a better life. Crossing the Rio Grande, men established themselves within the community and sent for the rest of their family members when financially stable. Jobs were available clearing land and working on new farms. Entrepreneurial opportunities abounded as these new citizens established themselves as merchants, barbers, teachers, and other valuable members of the community. They also brought many customs from their homeland and maintained those traditions while building their future.

As San Juan became embedded in the footprint of the Rio Grande Valley, centers of transportation and communication connected residents with the outside world. Conveniently located at the crossroads of the route to San Antonio and the Oblate Trail, San Juan evolved as a logical stop for newcomers to the valley. Railway stations, such as the San Juan Depot, provided passengers with a convenient location for purchasing railway tickets and for local businesses to ship and receive merchandise. The San Juan Hotel, strategically located across from the train depot, accepted guests for overnight stays. Naturally commercial centers surfaced and businesses such as general merchandise stores, local banks, cafés, and the local post office became the center of town life. Schools and churches were established to serve the educational and religious needs of the community.

For a long time in San Juan, there was an obvious divide between the Mexican American population on the north side of the railroad tracks and the white population on the south side. In the 1920s and 1930s, there was an unwritten social regulation whereby the Mexican population understood that they were not welcome on the south side of the tracks. There were separate theaters, separate grocery stores, separate schools, and the like, which catered to the needs of the two ethnic groups. Today's residents look back on those times and clearly remember the way it was. While it should not be dismissed or minimized, perhaps the time has come to view this history based on a series of achievements rather than a community of conflict.

As time went on, the population within the town continued to grow. Farming became an increasingly successful industry in San Juan, and more people immigrated to the area to work. Irrigation became the lifeblood of the farming industry with the Hidalgo County Water District No. 2 having its headquarters in San Juan. Packing sheds sprang up along the railroad tracks to store local produce. Grain elevators and cotton gins also emerged to serve the needs of local farmers. Trucking and shipping companies began operations in order to get local produce to markets outside the Rio Grande Valley. This growth positively affected Main Street businesses catering to the community. Local grocers delivered supplies and products directly to farmers on the river in order to better serve farmworkers' needs. More schools and churches were established to fulfill a growing populace.

Local government provided an opportunity for strong community residents to serve as local leaders. Former city mayors, commissioners, and other civil servants all can remember their time in office and proudly list their achievements. Religious leaders have also been present throughout the years with many religious institutions serving different denominations. Not only does San Juan proudly serve as the home to the Basilica of Our Lady of San Juan del Valle National Shrine, it is also home to several other churches, such as St. John's Lutheran Church, The Peoples Covenant Church, and First Baptist Church to name a few.

As San Juan stands on the shoulders of its forefathers, its population today has achieved a good living as a result of the early settlers' hard work ethic and industrious entrepreneurship. While some residents venture outward to make their way, many maintain their roots in San Juan, focusing their efforts with dignity on family, work, and community. An uninterrupted connection with the present and the future is combined with a meaningful past.

The people of San Juan share a vibrant history, enabling each generation to prosper successfully while maintaining the traditions that make them who they are. Heralded as "The Spirit of the Rio Grande Valley," San Juan approaches its centennial celebration in 2010, which will provide an opportunity to pause and reflect upon the role people play as individual citizens committed to a more prosperous San Juan.

—Roseann Bacha-Garza

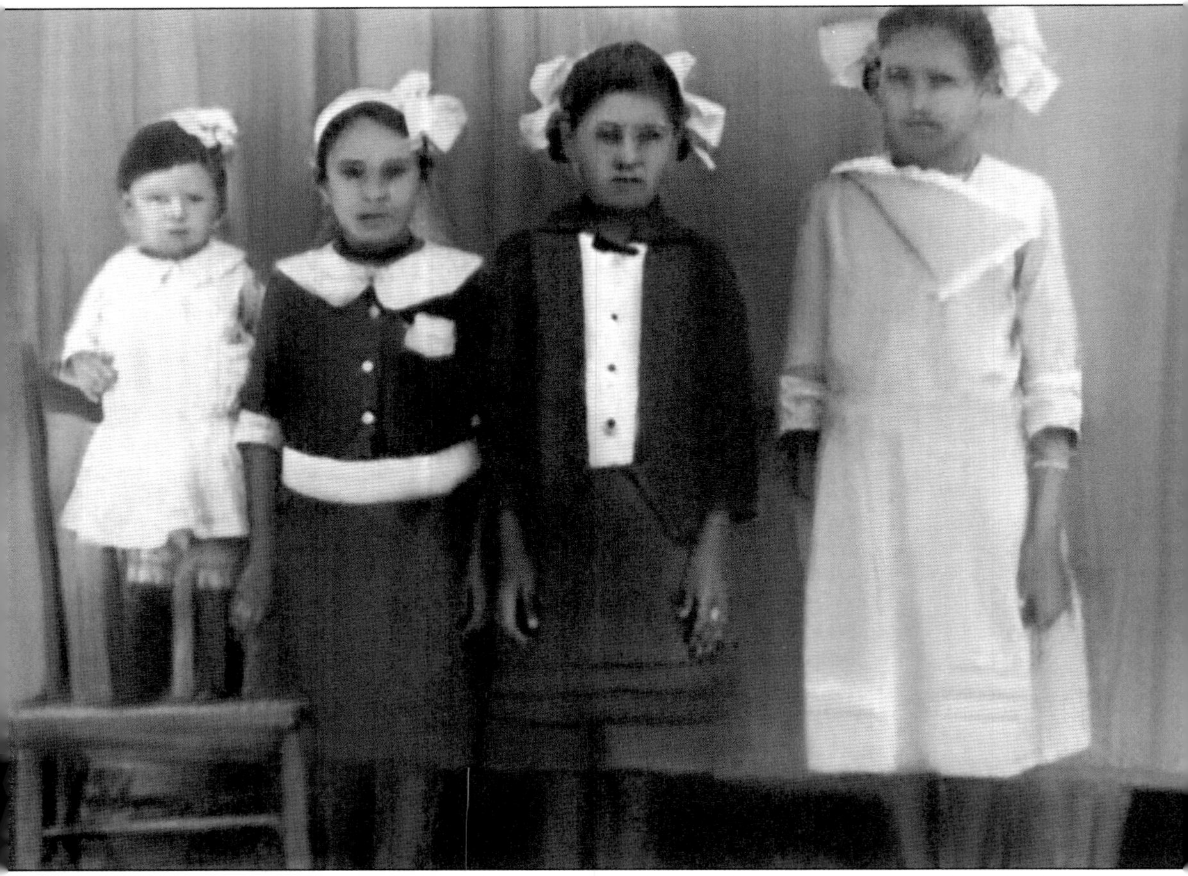

The Trevino sisters line up in this 1915 photograph. Featured from left to right are Manuela, Aeropaja, San Juanita, and Josefina. Manuela Trevino Alanis, born in 1913, is currently one of the oldest living residents of San Juan, turning 97 years old in 2010. (Courtesy of Manuela T. Alanis.)

One

The Dawn of San Juan

Life along the southern tip of Texas existed long before the founding of the city of San Juan. Indigenous people lived in the Rio Grande Valley prior to the arrival of the Spanish conquistadores in the mid-1700s. With the railroad expansion into the area in the late 1800s, international trade and agriculture was commonplace. Clubhouses emerged for the purpose of entertaining future landowners. Land developers such as the Standard Land Company and C. H. Swallow romanced eager families from northern and midwestern states to purchase land. Plots of land were subdivided and sold. In 1911, land cost $40 per acre. By 1914, the price had increased to $200 per acre.

In the late 1890s, John Closner established San Juan Plantation, which had a sugar mill, farmhouses, and a church dedicated to St. John the Baptist. In addition to an 800-acre sugar cane crop, the plantation eventually encompassed over 45,000 acres. In 1910, Closner sold 406 acres of his property to the San Juan Townsite Company to found the original town. Folklore tells the story that San Juan was named after John Closner, known as "Don Juan" to his Spanish-speaking farmworkers.

When rail transit into San Juan arrived in 1904, banks, general merchandise stores, pharmacies, and cafés opened on U.S. Highway 83 and Nebraska Street, creating commerce. Formal brick structures emerged as the downtown area took shape. San Juan was officially incorporated in 1917. San Juan was also one of the first towns in the Rio Grande Valley to have a telephone company. By 1919, the San Juan Telephone Company was established with 8,000 shares available for the purchase price of $50 per share. San Juan found itself conveniently placed at the crossroads of railway and highway. As the chamber of commerce materialized, positive publicity dubbed San Juan the "Friendly City."

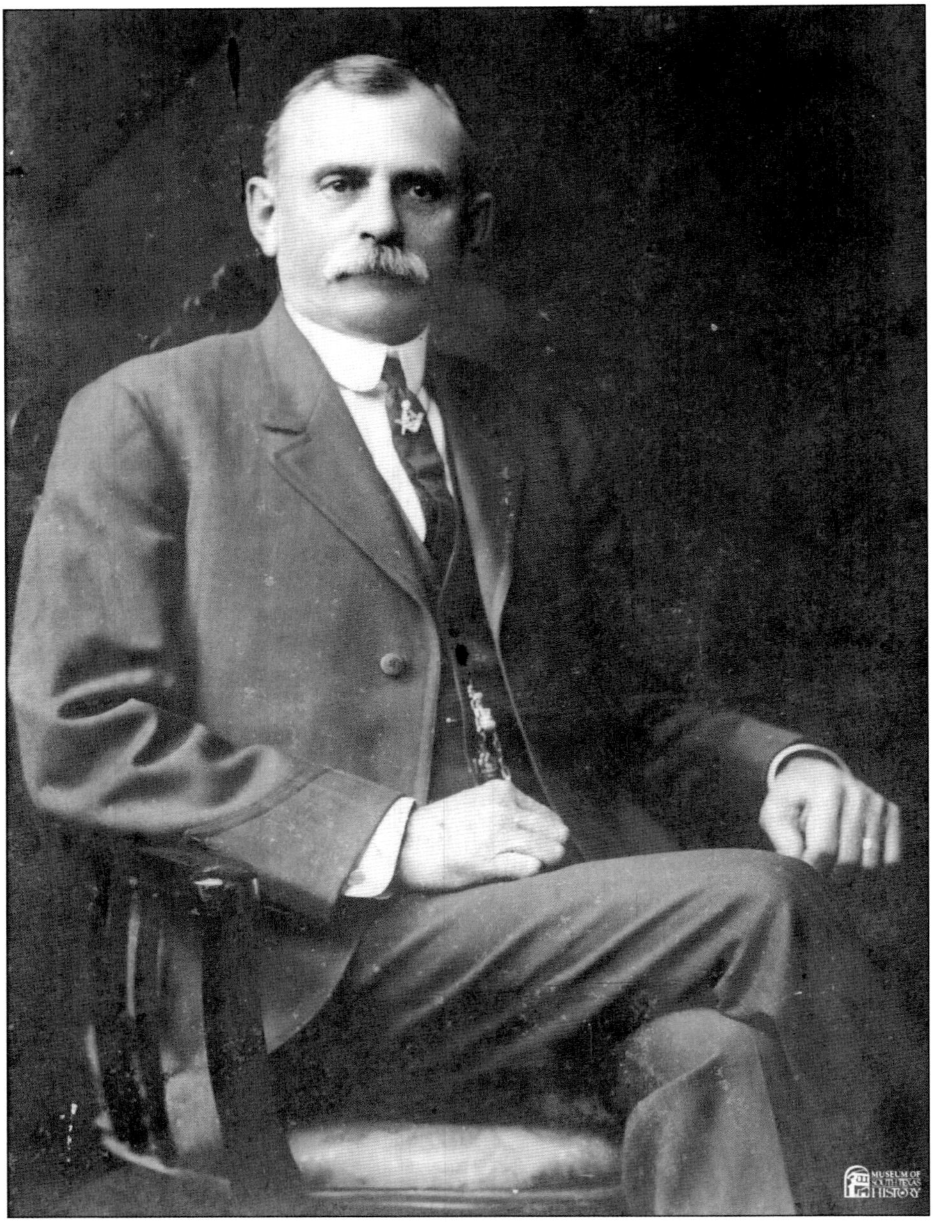

John Closner arrived in the Rio Grande Valley in 1883 from Wisconsin. Working on the railroad south of the border, he established roots in the valley and was elected county sheriff and county tax assessor. He capitalized on opportunities to buy condemned land for nonpayment of taxes, paying approximately 50¢ per acre. Once he purchased land, he began farming crops. By 1895, he initiated the first irrigation system in the area by establishing a pumping plant along the river. Later on, he served as a partner in the establishment of the Louisiana-Rio Grande Canal Company. Working closely with the railroad companies, Closner created a transportation crossroads on his property that placed San Juan as one of the more desirable locations along the tracks. In 1910, Closner sold 406 acres of his land to the San Juan Townsite Company, and thus the town of San Juan was founded. (Courtesy of Museum of South Texas History.)

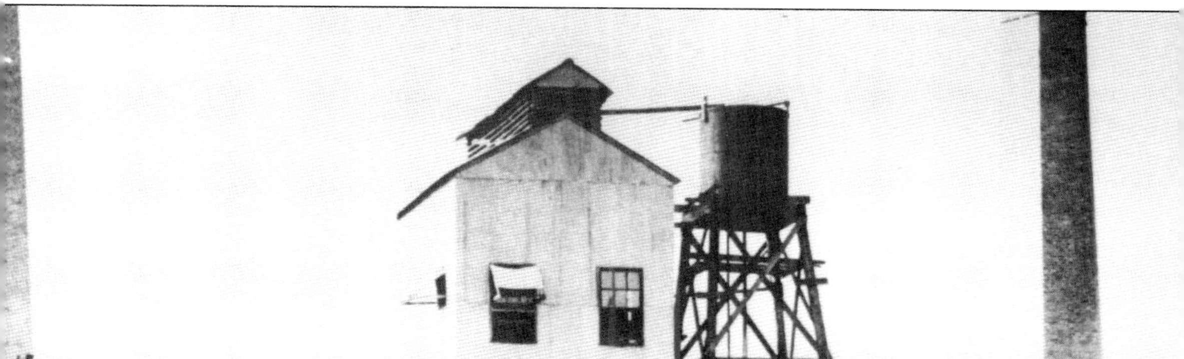

The 7,000-acre San Juan Plantation was officially established by 1904. Although Closner had farmed for 20 years prior to that time, he later amassed 45,000 total acres of land. Employing the local Hispanic labor force, he cleared the majority of his land, which was covered with mesquite trees and chaparral brush. Irrigation canals were dug by hand with the assistance of mules. Known in its early years as the San Juan Hacienda, a school was built on the plantation and the earliest St. John the Baptist Church was established. Crops such as cotton, sugar cane, alfalfa, and onions were grown on the plantation. (Courtesy of Museum of South Texas History.)

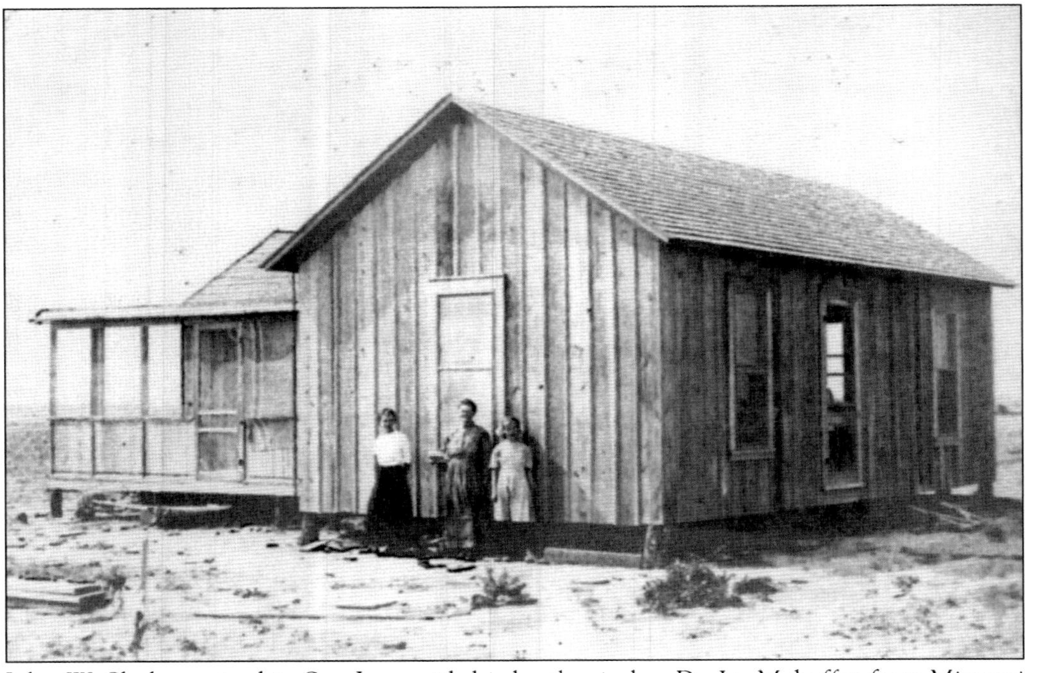

John W. Shulze arrived in San Juan with his brother-in-law Dr. Ira Mahaffay from Missouri in 1907. Returning to San Juan in 1911 with his family, they built their home on M Road. In this 1912 photograph from left to right are Lillian, Mary Ellen, and Ruth Schulze. (Courtesy of Mary Stotler.)

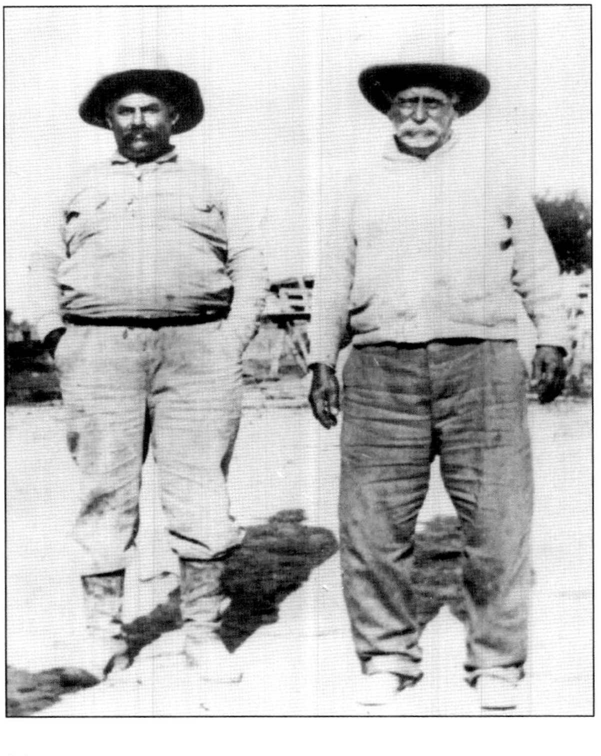

Gavino Bravo (left) and his father Don Esteban Bravo, pictured here around 1910, were members of one of the earliest families to come to the area. Esteban bought 22 acres south of Military Highway in San Juan, and the acreage was later divided amongst his seven sons. Gavino Bravo was the father of Erasmo C. Bravo, San Juan's first Hispanic patrolman and constable. (Courtesy of Erasmo Bravo family.)

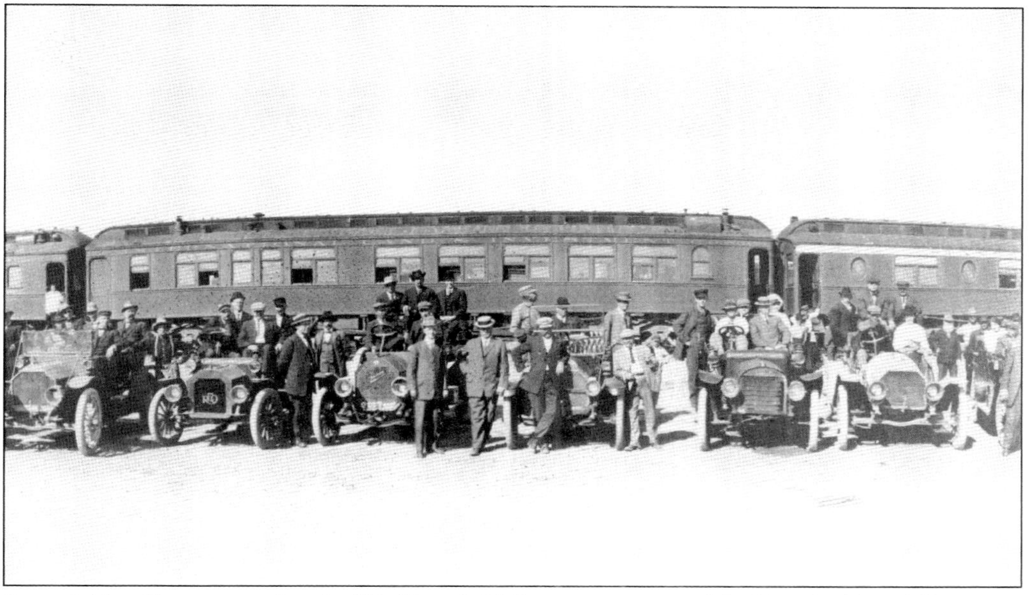

Potential land buyers travel to the Rio Grande Valley as customers of the Standard Land Company. This photograph, taken in December 1911, shows the excursion party that stopped at the San Juan Depot. Fred L. Schafroth and Robert Riley were on this train. (Courtesy of Museum of South Texas History.)

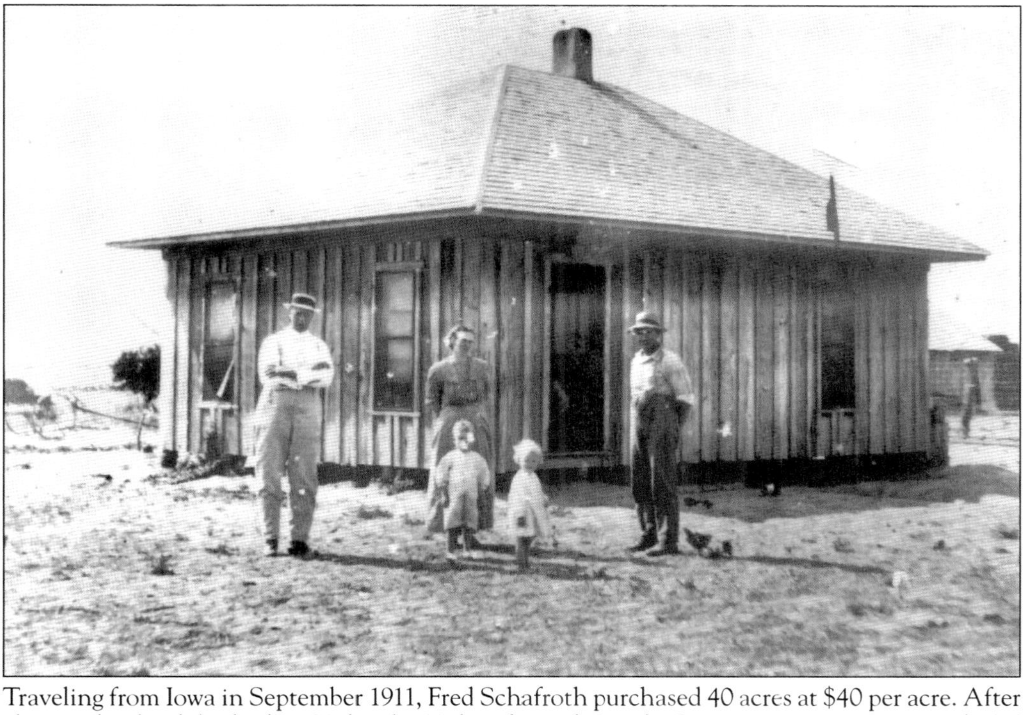

Traveling from Iowa in September 1911, Fred Schafroth purchased 40 acres at $40 per acre. After clearing his land, he built a 20-foot-by-22-foot frame house by January 1912, approximately 3.5 miles north of San Juan on M Road. From left to right are Robert Riley and Elsie, Harold, Thelma, and Fred Schafroth. (Courtesy of Robert D. Schafroth.)

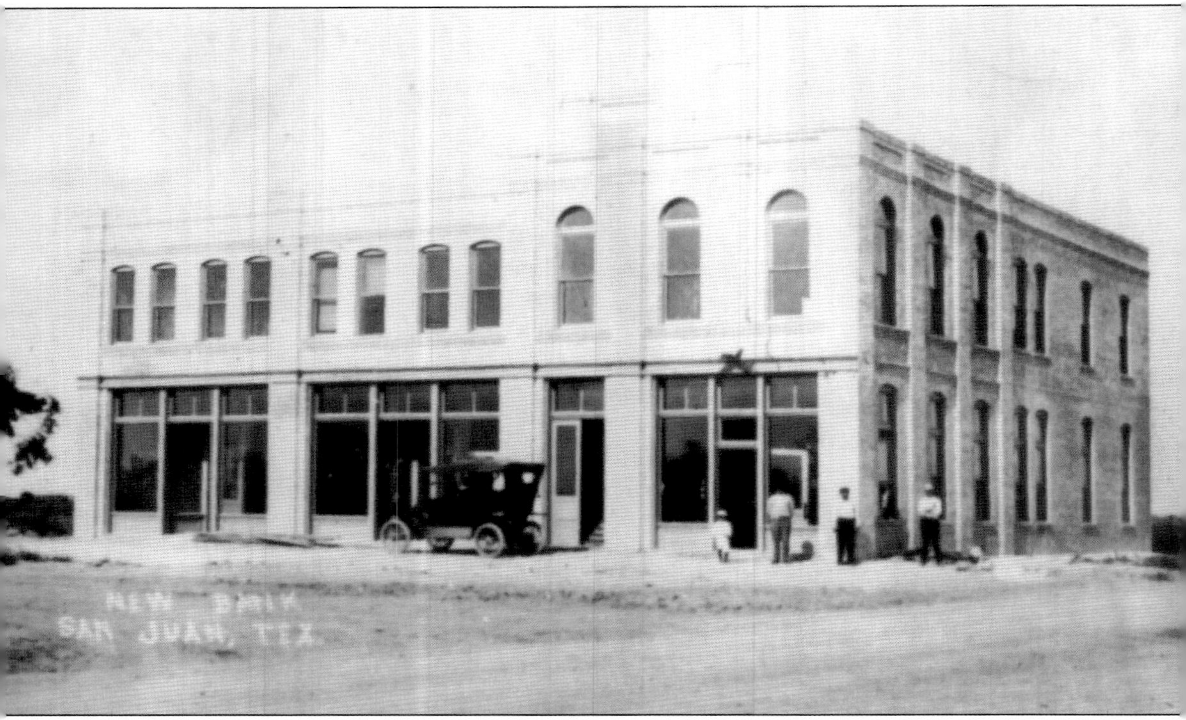

Constructed on the original town site, this formidable two-story brick building was completed on July 17, 1911. The architecture was common for commercial buildings of its time, with double brick construction on all exterior walls and large plate-glass windows on the front of the first floor. F. C. Platt and Albert Ewers bought the bank in 1912 and operated it in the same building until 1918. It was home to several businesses over the years, including the Hidalgo Water Improvement District No. 2 offices and San Juan Public Library, and was partially demolished in 1982. (Courtesy of Edna Platt Walsh estate.)

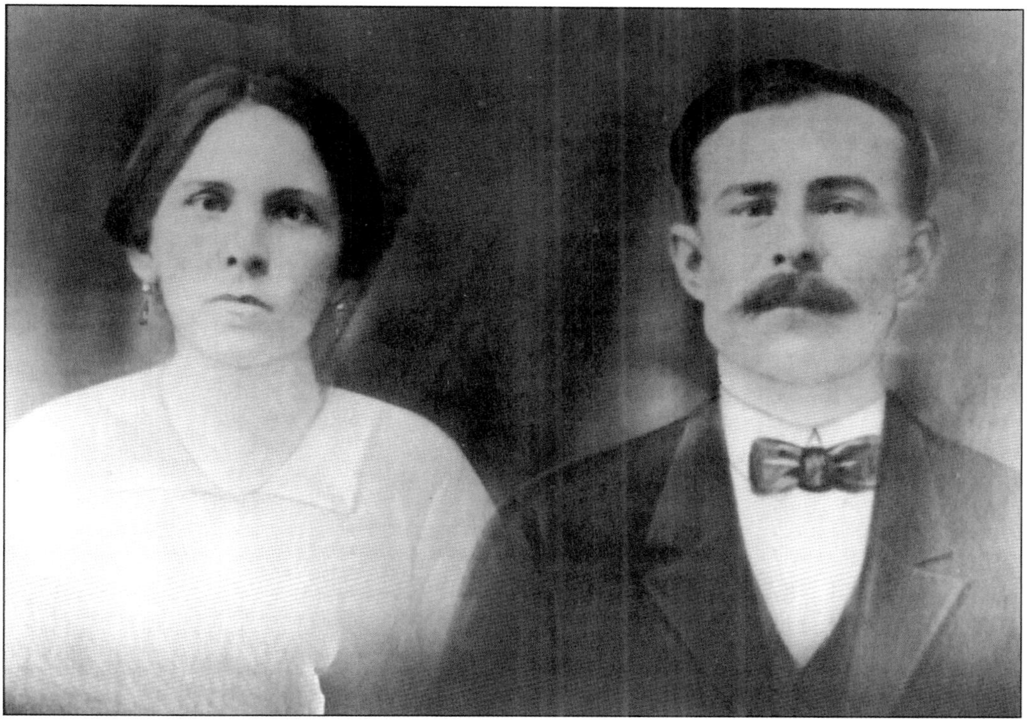

Petra Alvarado and Donato Jimenez moved to San Juan in the 1920s. Jiminez, a harvester of crops, was born in 1887 in Mexico, where he married his wife, Petra. The couple had a son, Toribio, in 1918, and the family moved to San Juan in the 1920s. (Courtesy of Romeo Jimenez.)

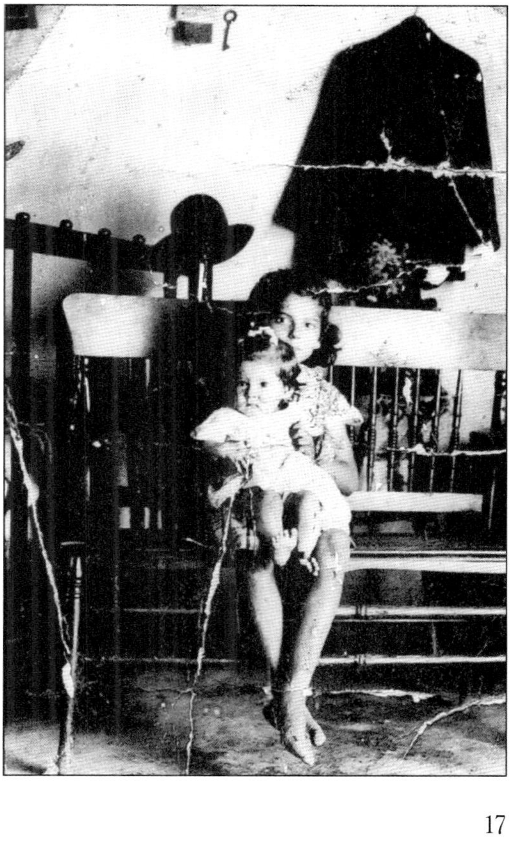

Beatrice Suarez sits on the lap of her sister Rafaela in 1920, the year they immigrated to San Juan from La Cascara, Mexico, with their parents Desiderio Suarez and Maria Del Refugio Cavazos. (Courtesy of Romeo Jimenez.)

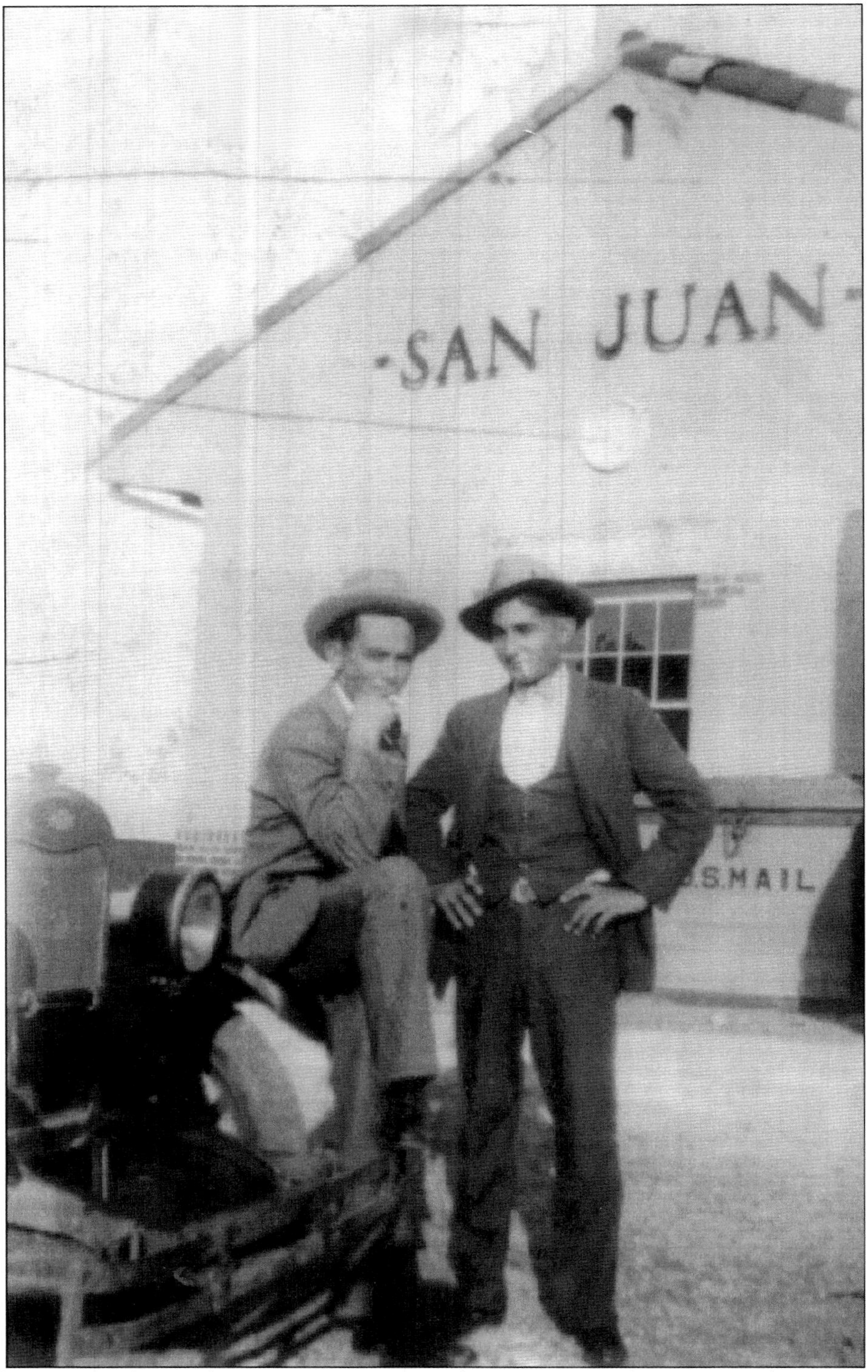

Frank Guerra and Miguel Garza Pena, prominent businessmen in the grocery industry, stand in front of San Juan Depot. (Courtesy of Alicia G. Salinas.)

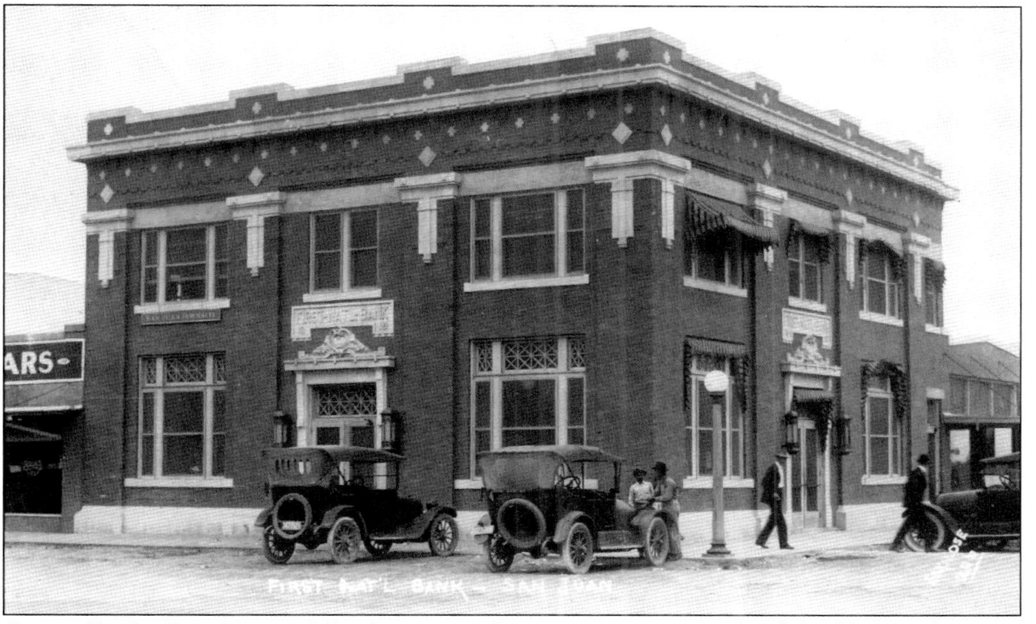

Originally the First National Bank in 1919, the concrete two-story bank building and annex, depicted above, was constructed at a cost of $49,000. This structure graced the intersection at U.S. Highway 83 and Standard Avenue, serving as the center of activity in San Juan in the 1920s. The building was also occupied by O. S. V. Ross of the San Juan Townsite Company and O. C. Aldrich. The offices and switchboard of the San Juan Telephone Company were also located in this building. Frank Griffith owned the company and installed all of the phone lines. Originally the towns of Pharr, San Juan, and Alamo were combined as one exchange. Later on, the telephone company offices moved to Pharr. It was sold to the Rio Grande Valley Telephone Company in 1926. Pictured below is a San Juan Telephone Company share of stock from December 1919. (Above photograph courtesy of Estella Rojas; below, Joe Hetrick.)

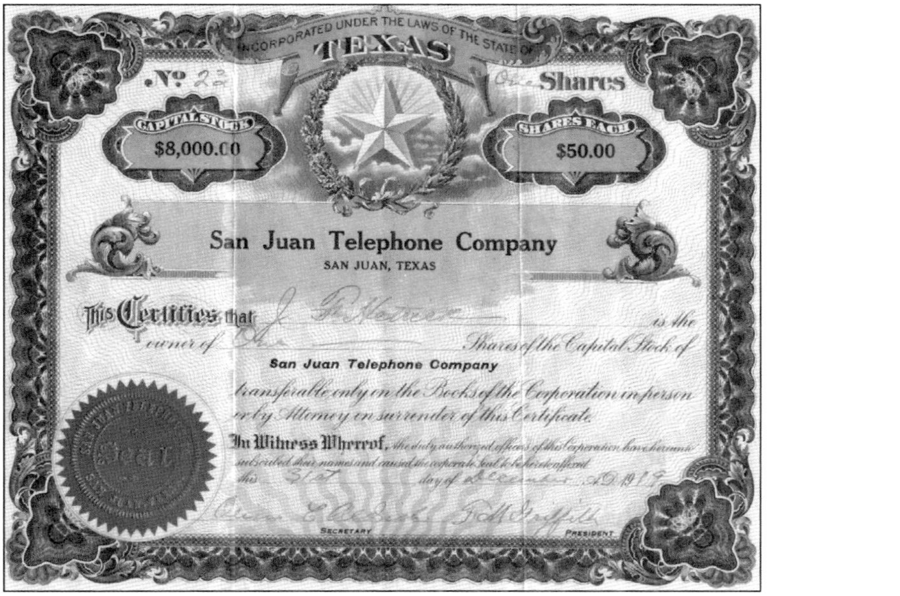

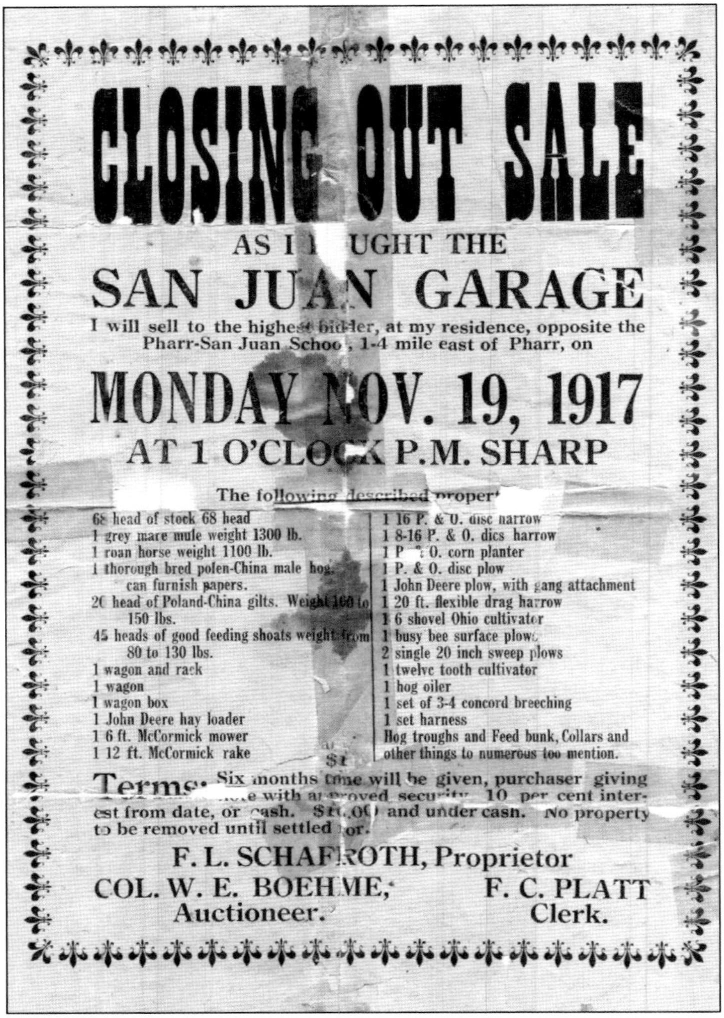

CLOSING OUT SALE

AS I [illegible]UGHT THE

SAN JUAN GARAGE

I will sell to the highest bidder, at my residence, opposite the Pharr-San Juan School, 1-4 mile east of Pharr, on

MONDAY NOV. 19, 1917

AT 1 O'CLOCK P.M. SHARP

The following described propert[illegible]

68 head of stock 68 head	1 16 P. & O. disc harrow
1 grey mare mule weight 1300 lb.	1 8-16 P. & O. dics harrow
1 roan horse weight 1100 lb.	1 P[illegible] O. corn planter
1 thorough bred polen-China male hog, can furnish papers.	1 P. & O. disc plow
20 head of Poland-China gilts. Weight 160 to 150 lbs.	1 John Deere plow, with gang attachment
45 heads of good feeding shoats weight from 80 to 130 lbs.	1 20 ft. flexible drag harrow
1 wagon and rack	1 6 shovel Ohio cultivator
1 wagon	1 busy bee surface plow
1 wagon box	2 single 20 inch sweep plows
1 John Deere hay loader	1 twelve tooth cultivator
1 6 ft. McCormick mower	1 hog oiler
1 12 ft. McCormick rake	1 set of 3-4 concord breeching
	1 set harness
	Hog troughs and Feed bunk, Collars and other things to numerous too mention.

Terms: Six months time will be given, purchaser giving [illegible] with approved security 10 per cent interest from date, or cash. $[illegible] and under cash. No property to be removed until settled for.

F. L. SCHAFROTH, Proprietor

COL. W. E. BOEHME, Auctioneer. F. C. PLATT Clerk.

During World War I, Fred Schafroth unfortunately lost much of his livestock to a disease called Glanders, causing his farming business to fail. As seen in the flier at left, he auctioned his farming equipment and surviving livestock in order to raise money to open the San Juan Garage in 1917. Below, Fred Schafroth used this advertisement to generate business for his San Juan Garage. (At left, courtesy of Ronald and Dorothy Beamsley; below, Robert D. Schafroth.)

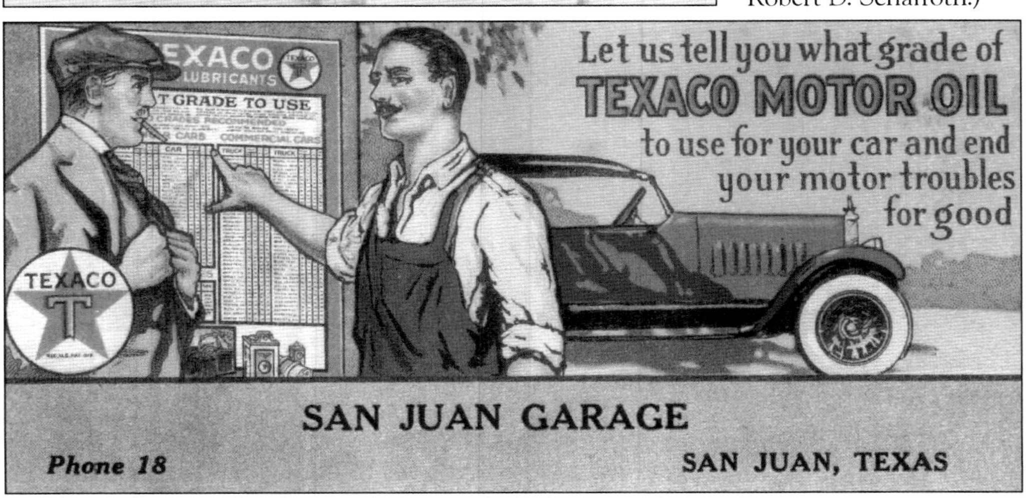

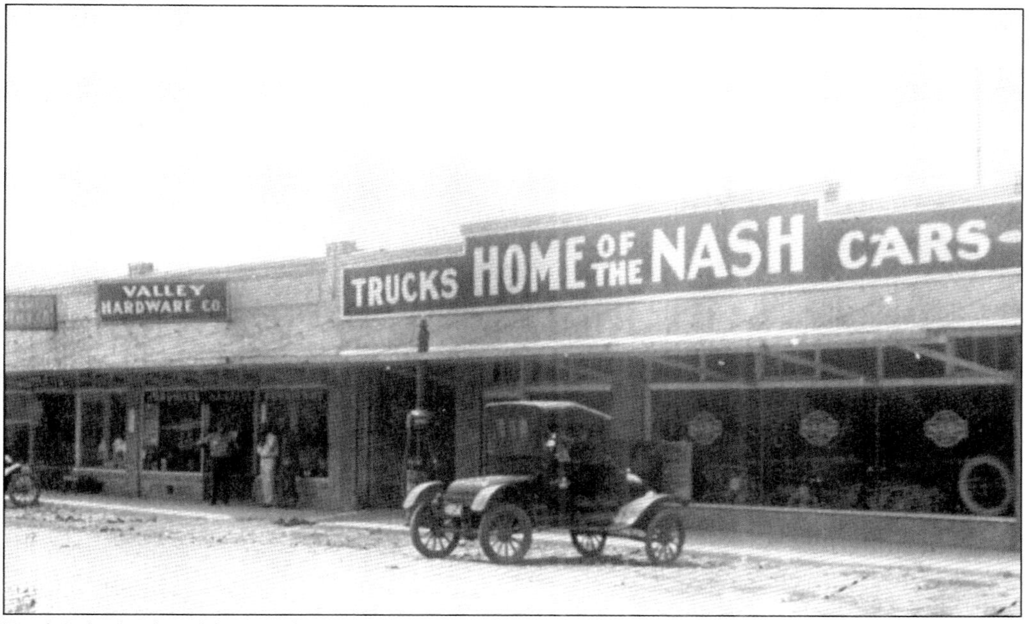

Fred Schafroth sold cars, drove prospective buyers in land excursion party tours, and ran his San Juan Garage. This 1920 photograph shows the exterior view of his Nash Valley Sales auto dealership along U.S. Highway 83. The slogan of this auto dealership was "The Valley Home of the Nash." (Courtesy of Robert D. Schafroth.)

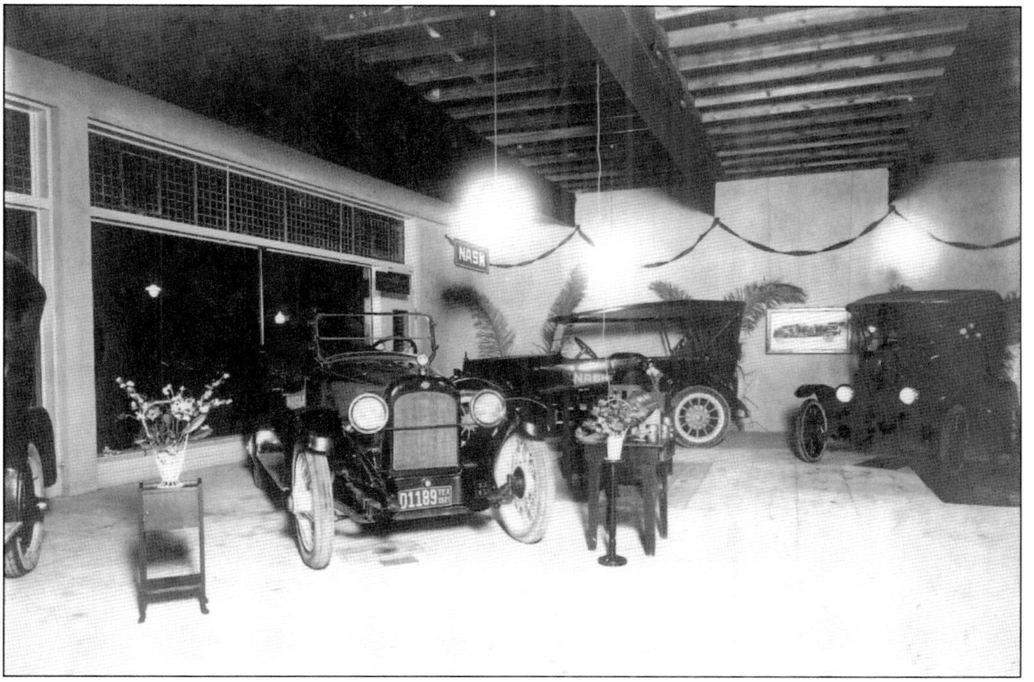

An interior view of F. L. Schafroth Nash Valley Sales in 1921 features the 1920 Nash Sport Touring Car, which came equipped with wire wheels and an imitation alligator cover. (Courtesy of Robert D. Schafroth.)

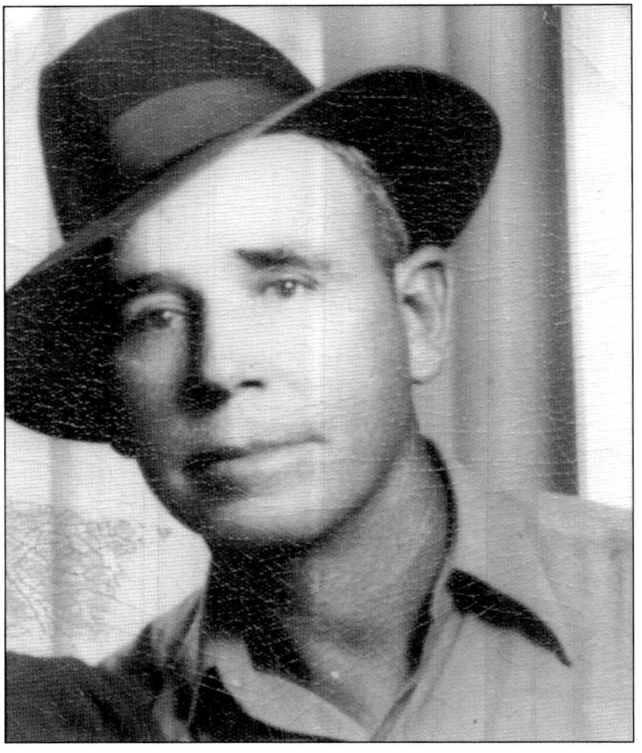

Eusebio Maldonado, pictured here in the 1920s, was born on La Hacha Ranch in Fronton, Texas, which is located in Starr County. Known as Chevo, he moved to San Juan in the early 1930s along with many other families from that area. He married Felicitas Guerra and started a family. Initially he earned his living by building fences, and then he went into farming. (Courtesy of Juanita Flores.)

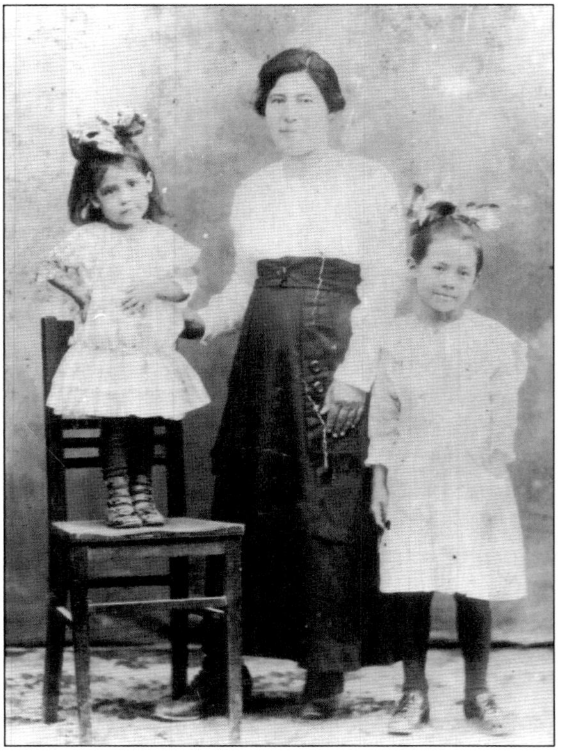

Midwife Anselma Garza Sloss poses with her daughters Aurora Gonzalez Garcia (left) and Maria Gonzalez Salazar in 1920. Known to Hispanics as a *partera*, or midwife, she delivered hundreds of babies in San Juan. Day or night, in her home or in the homes of others, she would perform her service to the community when called upon. (Courtesy of Estela Salazar.)

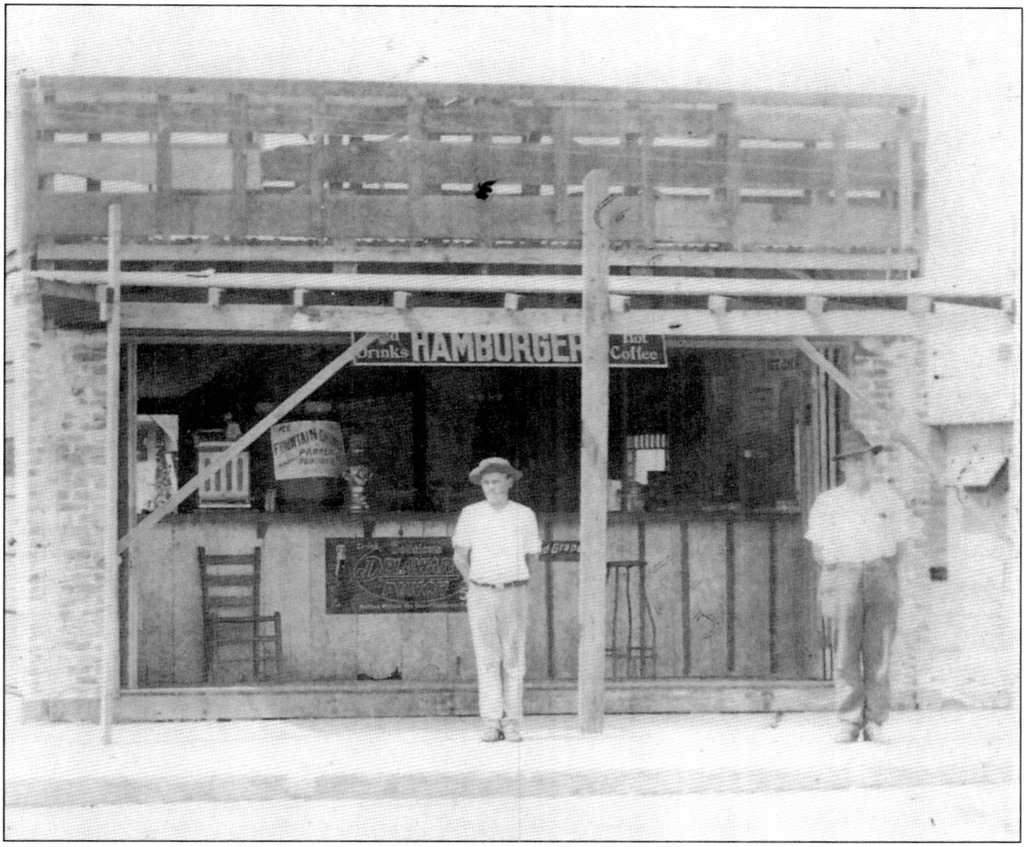

Harold Schafroth (left) and R. L. Savage, San Juan's first mayor, pose in the summer of 1924 in front of Thelma and Harold Schafroth's hamburger stand, located between the San Juan Hotel and San Juan Garage. Open from 10:00 a.m. until midnight, hamburgers sold for 10¢ each, or three for a quarter. They also sold pies, ice cream, soda, candy, cigarettes, and "near beer"—a malt beverage containing little or no alcohol that was legal under Prohibition. (Courtesy of Robert D. Schafroth.)

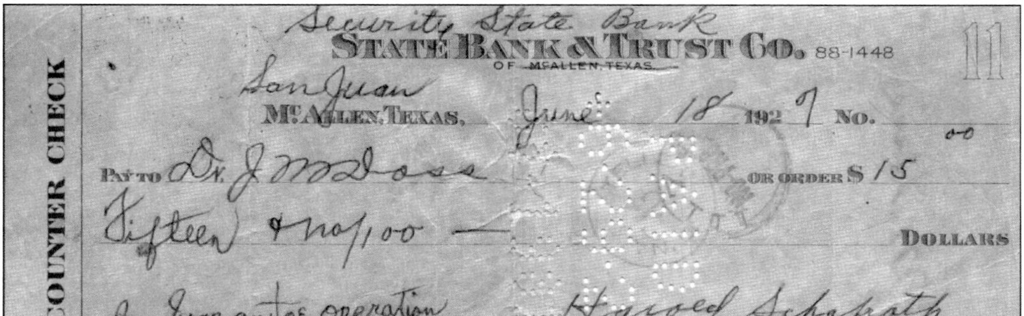

This Security State Bank of San Juan counter check dated June 18, 1927, was a $15 payment to Dr. J. M. Doss from Harold Schafroth for a toe operation. Schafroth accidentally shot himself in the foot while in his 1927 Chevy Coupe. (Courtesy of Robert D. Schafroth.)

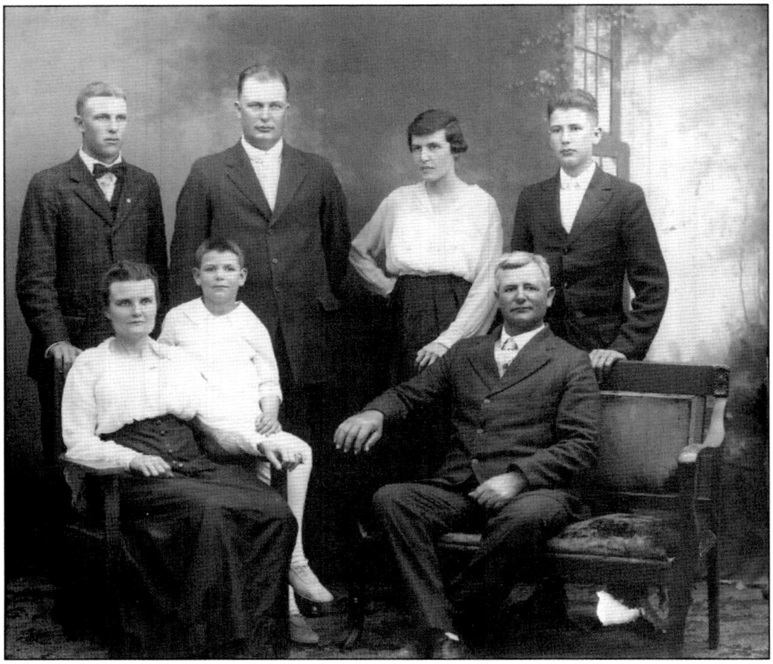

The Hetrick family poses for a family portrait in 1921. Pictured are, from left to right, (first row) Bird Cline Hetrick, Paul Hetrick, and Joseph Franklin Hetrick; (second row) J. Floyd Hetrick, Harry Hetrick, Hazel Hetrick, and Lyle Hetrick. Originally from Kansas, the Hetricks arrived in San Juan in 1914 and bought property off of Stewart Road. (Courtesy of Joe Hetrick.)

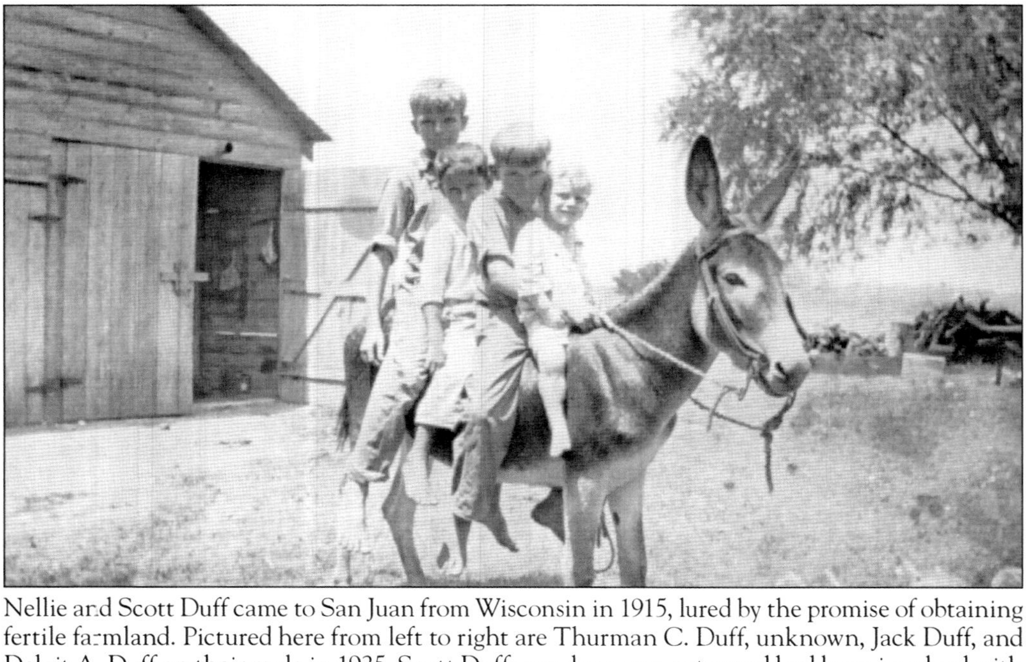

Nellie and Scott Duff came to San Juan from Wisconsin in 1915, lured by the promise of obtaining fertile farmland. Pictured here from left to right are Thurman C. Duff, unknown, Jack Duff, and Deloit A. Duff on their mule in 1925. Scott Duff was also a carpenter and had been involved with the building of the McAllen Post Office in 1935. (Courtesy of Karen Duff.)

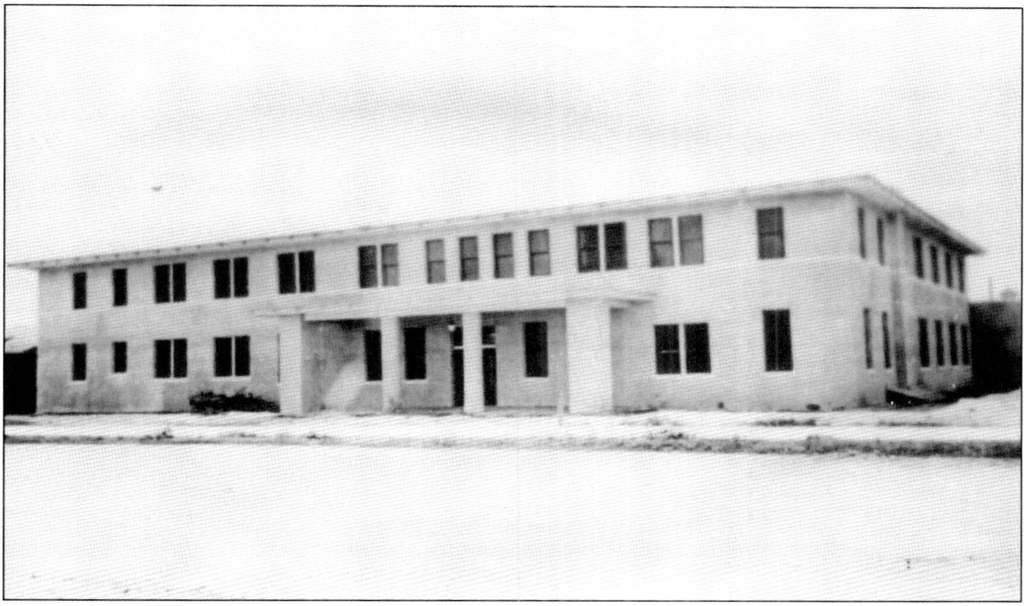

The original San Juan Hotel was constructed in 1920. First known as the Reilly Hotel, Mr. and Mrs. Owen Reilly provided excellent service to the guests of this 25-room hotel. Harold Schafroth used to earn $3.50 every Wednesday night shining the salesmen's shoes out on the front porch. It was a custom for the traveling salesmen working in the area to meet at the San Juan Hotel every Wednesday night, and it was a popular place for businessmen and tourists traveling to the area. In 1928, the exterior was updated with a new Spanish flair by Frederich Trimble, with relief carvings at the center front roofline and new terra cotta roof tiles as pictured below. In the 1960s, the Bryan family operated the hotel, closing it by the mid-1960s. In 1986, the Sigle family renovated and reopened it. It currently stands abandoned once again, but plans are in the works by local attorney Gus Acevedo to renovate and reopen this historic landmark by the fall of 2010. (Both courtesy of Hidalgo County Historical Commission.)

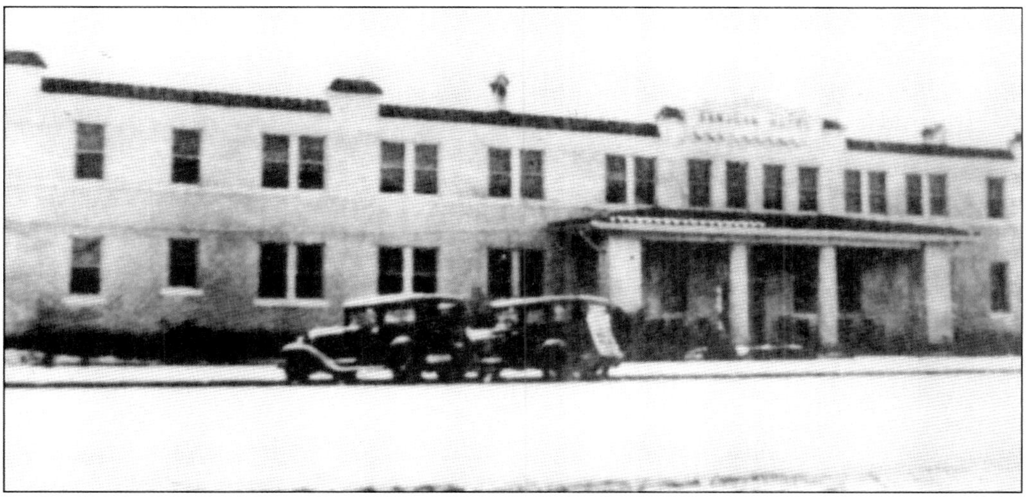

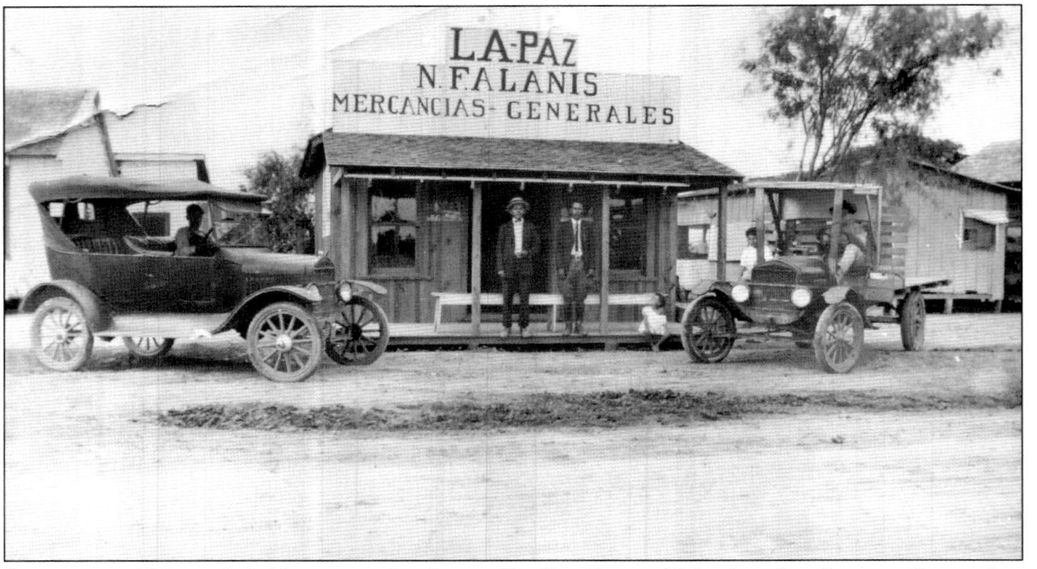

Santiago and Natividad Alanis stand in front of La Paz General Merchandise Store in September 1925. The store, owned by Natividad and Felipe Alanis, was located on Railroad Street east of Nebraska Street. A decade later, Santiago and his wife, Manuela Trevino Alanis, opened the Alanis General Merchandise Store on the corner of Fourth (formerly Alonzo) and Nebraska Streets. (Courtesy of Manuela T. Alanis.)

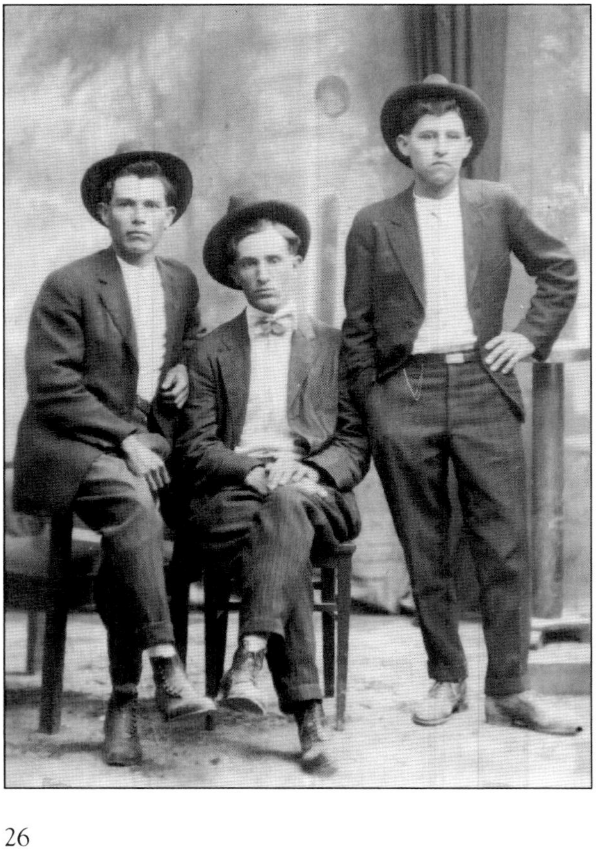

Formally dressed and ready seize the day, Teofilo Treviño (left), Sylvano Serna (center), and Agustin Treviño pose for a photograph in the late 1920s. Teofilo was the father of Korean War hero Sgt. Leonel Treviño. (Courtesy of Agustin and Elodia Treviño.)

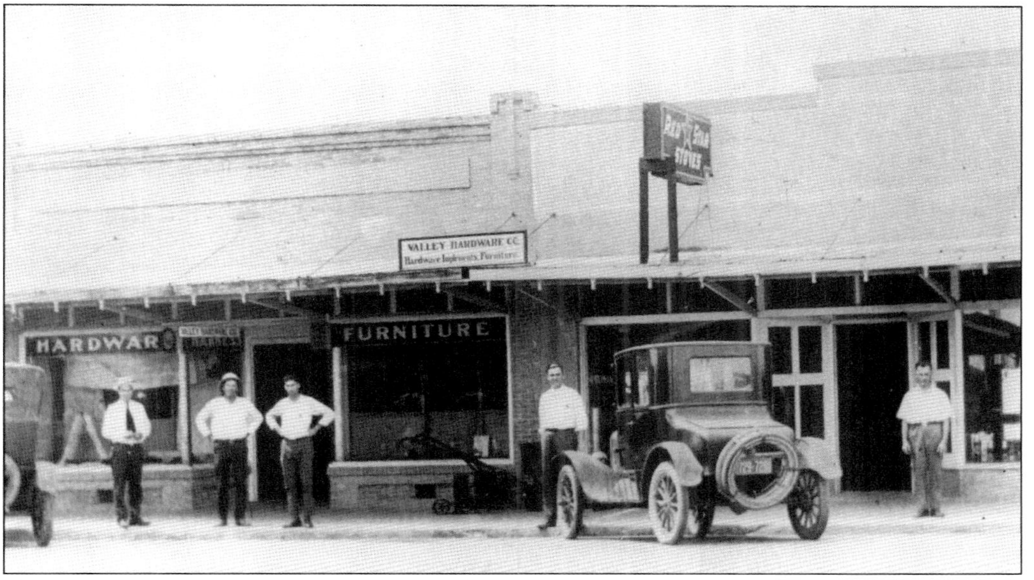

The Valley Hardware Store, shown around 1924, was located on U.S. Highway 83 next to the Nash Dealership. Pictured above from left to right are John R. Lemen, Charles Cheney, L. C. Bill Lemen, Stewart Simpson, and Marvin Rhenhart. Early publicity promoting San Juan businesses touted this store as one of the most beautiful of its kind in the area. Starter furniture kits, which contained the essentials needed to start a family home in the Rio Grande Valley, were popular items in this store and included items such as a stove, bed, dresser, dining table, and four chairs. Also taken around 1924 is the photograph below showing the interior of the Valley Hardware Store. (Both courtesy of Bill Lemen.)

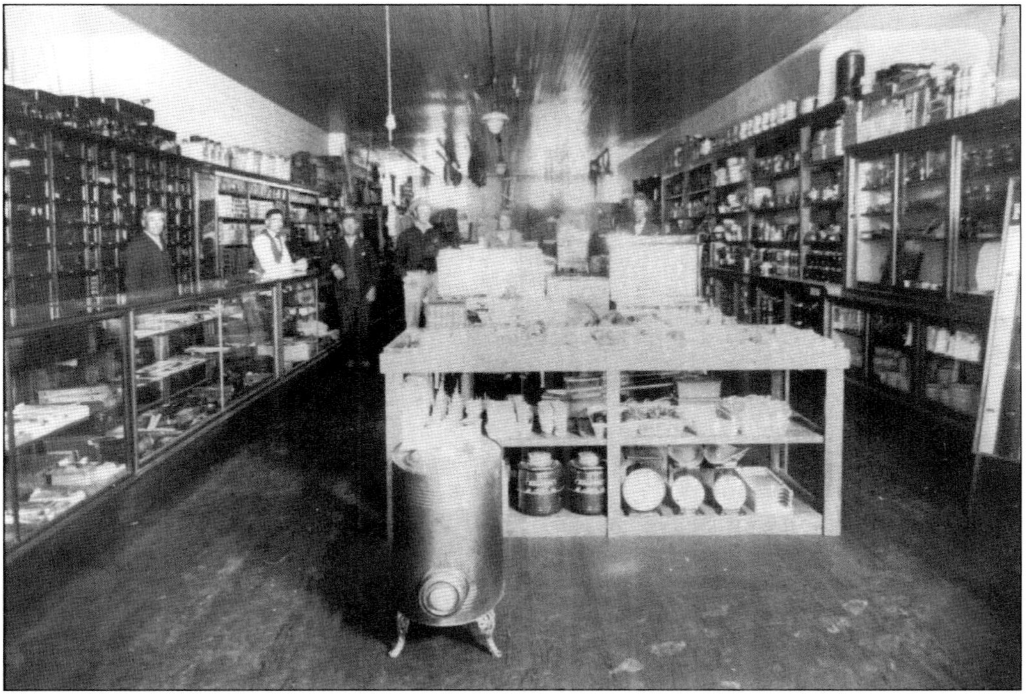

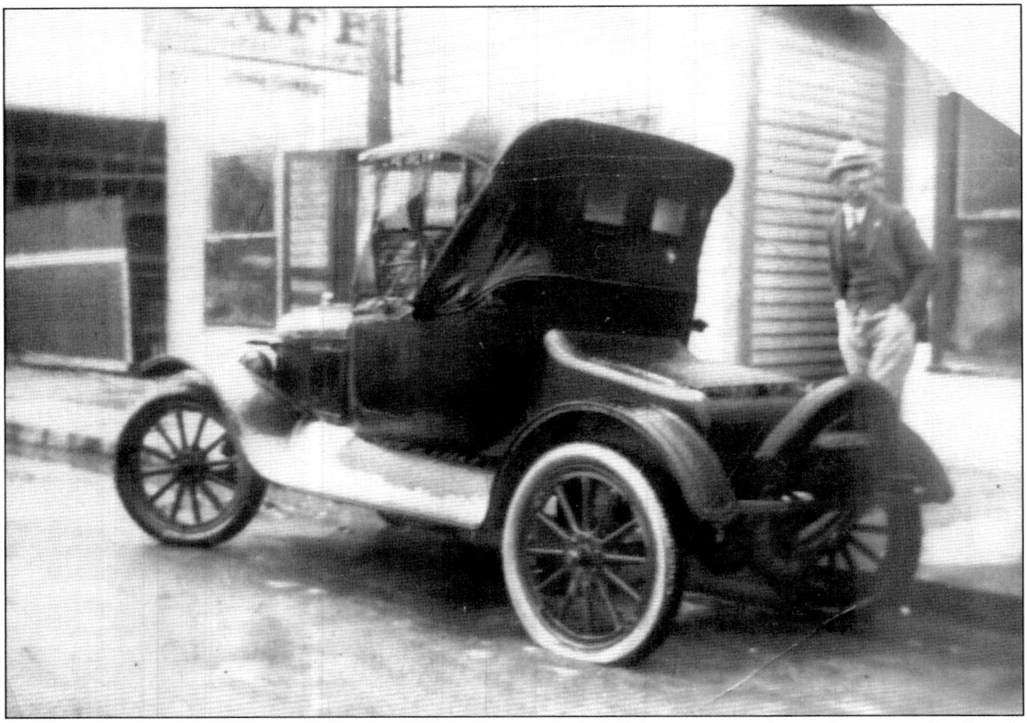

Snow on the ground in front of La Fleur's Café in 1924 heralds an unusual weather treat for South Texas. (Courtesy of Robert Kristek.)

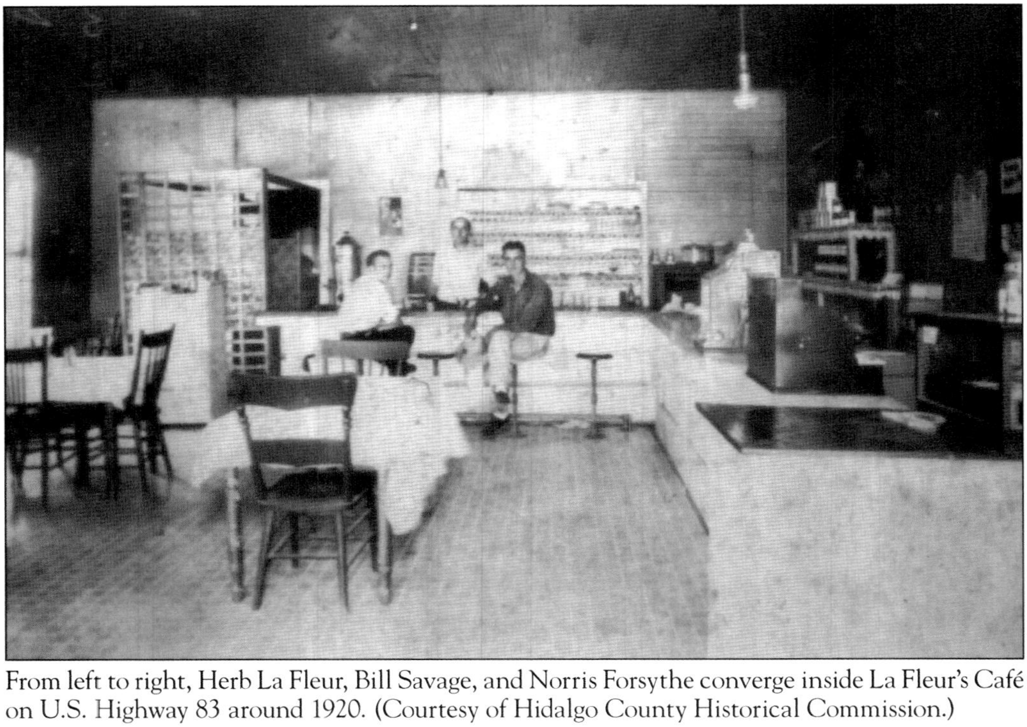

From left to right, Herb La Fleur, Bill Savage, and Norris Forsythe converge inside La Fleur's Café on U.S. Highway 83 around 1920. (Courtesy of Hidalgo County Historical Commission.)

Two

On the Farm

Farming has been part of daily life in the Rio Grande Valley since the original indigenous tribes settled in the area centuries ago. Once the Spaniards colonized the area in the mid-1700s, families established small ranches along the Rio Grande River and acquired the necessities to sustain life by raising crops and livestock. Original Spanish land grantees Jose Maria Balli and Narciso Cavazos were the landowners of the property that encompasses what we know of today as San Juan, Texas. As time went on, the land was divided among family heirs and eventually subdivided further and sold either to individuals or in large parcels to land developers.

As the railroad was established and the town site founded, more investors from the Midwest United States arrived with visions of successful year-round farming. Early advertisements publicized an agricultural town that quadrupled its size between the years of 1918 and 1920. There was an expectation that property values would quickly increase with the rapid growth in population. One of the first developers to purchase land in the area of San Juan was John Closner. He and other early investors were instrumental in building the vast irrigation system that still exists today. Great pumps installed at the river's edge saturated thousands of acres of fertile farmland.

Farming in San Juan has faced severe challenges. Many local farmers narrowly survived the freezes of 1949, 1951, 1961, 1983, and 1989. Hurricanes hit the area several times throughout the years, and the Rio Grande often flooded, drowning the crops that were planted nearby. Although cotton was a popular crop early on, other crops of citrus fruits and vegetables were also successful. San Juan developed a farm-to-market network of packing sheds and cotton gins, all conveniently located at the crossroads of rail and roadways. Valley produce was easily shipped not only to surrounding communities but to northern markets such as San Antonio.

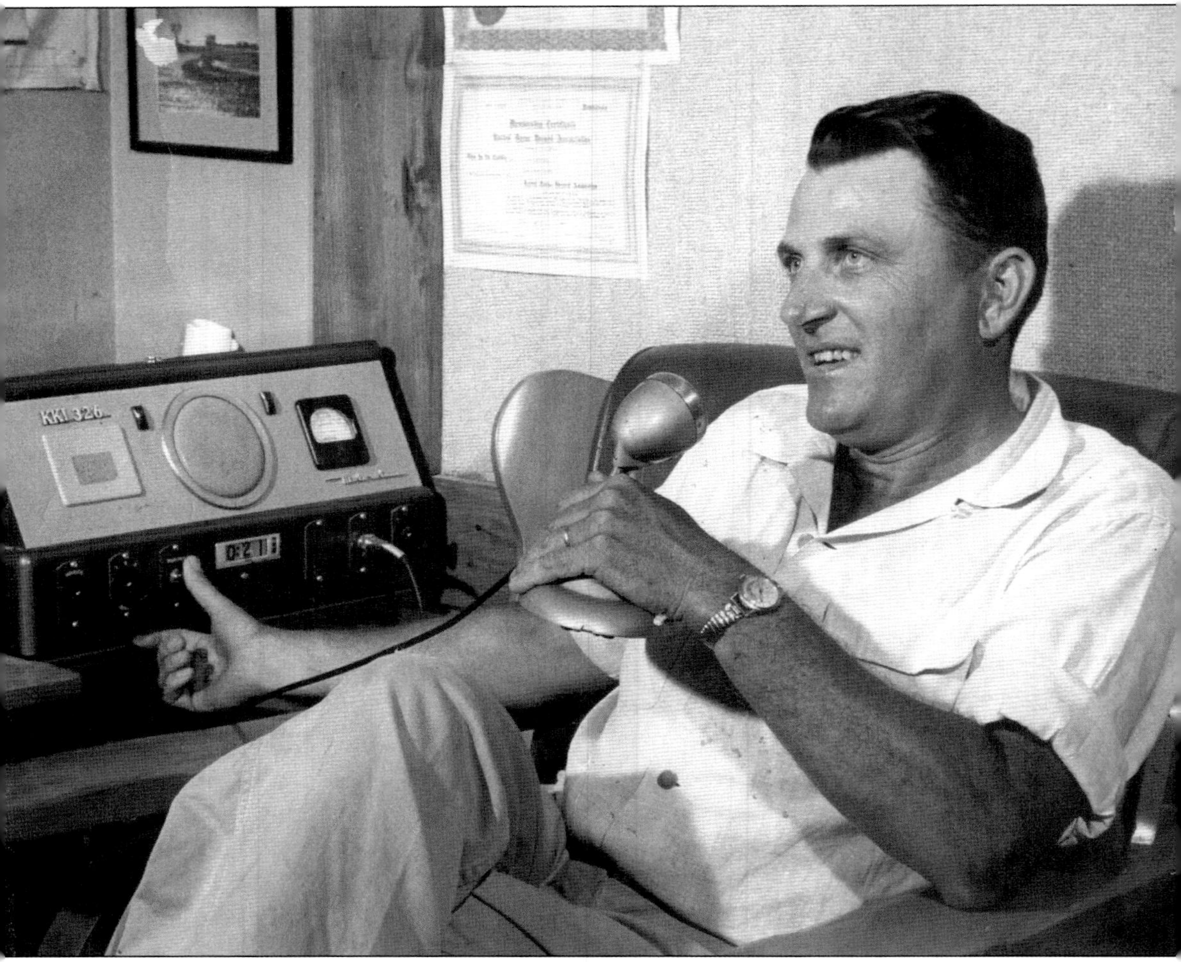

Carl Schuster, busy in his Rio Fresh office in 1948, was intrigued by the idea of conquering a new frontier. The Rio Grande Valley was a challenging territory that had the promise of becoming a riverside paradise. Leaving behind the beautiful mountain scenery of the Austrian Alps, he was inspired with confidence to create a tropical oasis of his own by taming the thickets of San Juan. He arrived in the fall of 1933 and began to work with his uncles Fred and Max Krenmueller on their 160-acre farm. He ventured out on his own eight years later, purchasing his first 25 acres in Alamo, as well as various other plots in Pharr and San Juan. He settled permanently in San Juan and in 1941 he married Wilma Reis from McAllen, with whom he started a family and continued to expand his farming business. (Courtesy of Schuster family.)

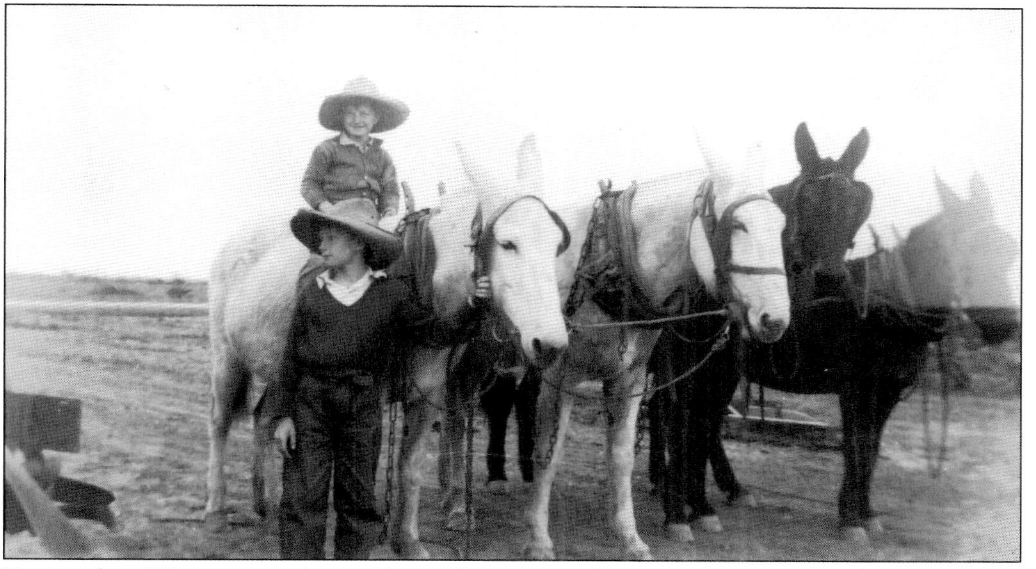

During the 1930s, prior to the purchase of mechanized tractors, horses and mules served their purpose. These mules, known as Cat and Vedo, played a vital role for the Krenmueller family in the cultivation of their farmland. Teddy Abel is on the mule and Fred Abel is standing. (Courtesy of Trudy Forthuber.)

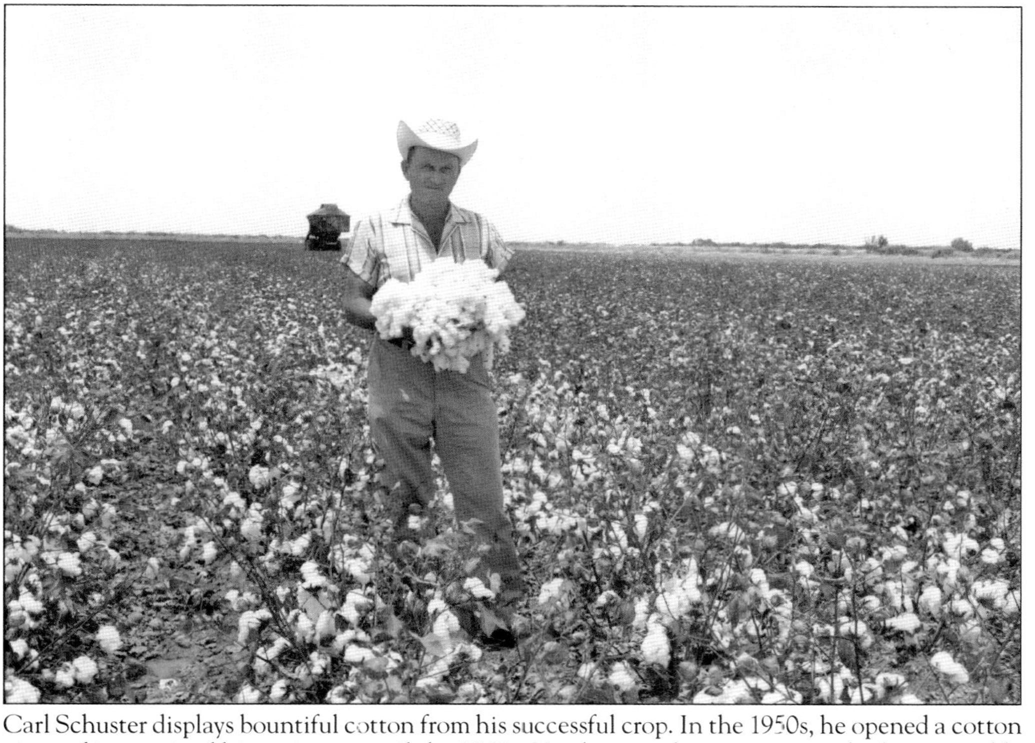

Carl Schuster displays bountiful cotton from his successful crop. In the 1950s, he opened a cotton gin, and it remained his mainstay until the 1960s. He also raised grain, corn, and other vegetable crops. He concentrated mostly on vegetables, although he later produced some sugar cane on his farm. (Courtesy of Schuster family.)

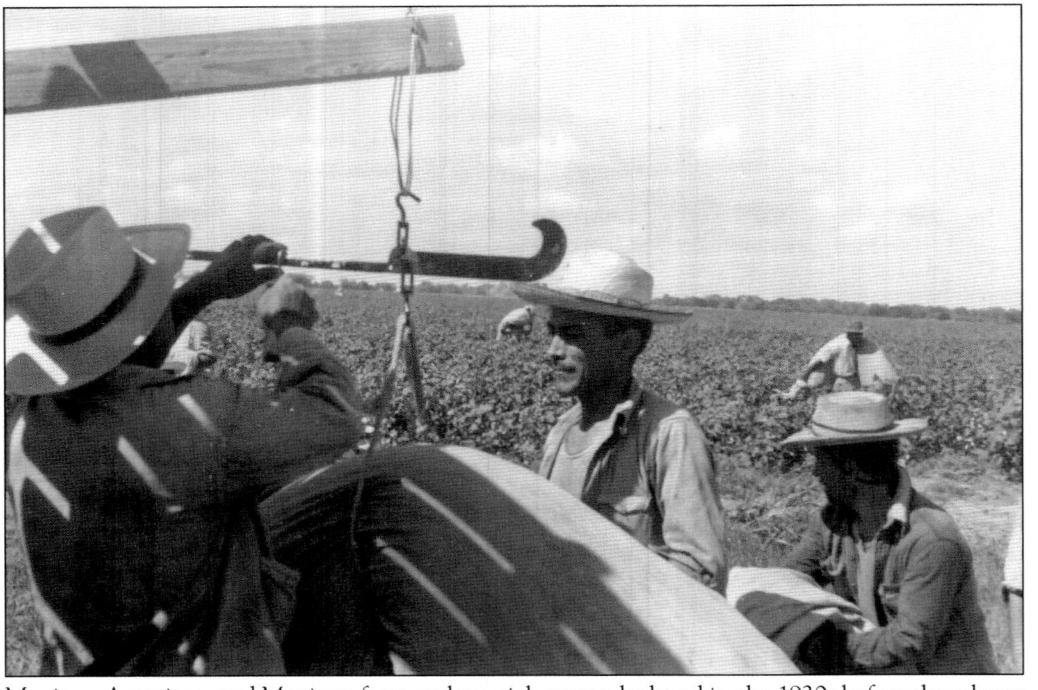

Mexican American and Mexican farmworkers pick cotton by hand in the 1930s before the advent of cotton-picking machines. (Courtesy of Trudy Forthuber.)

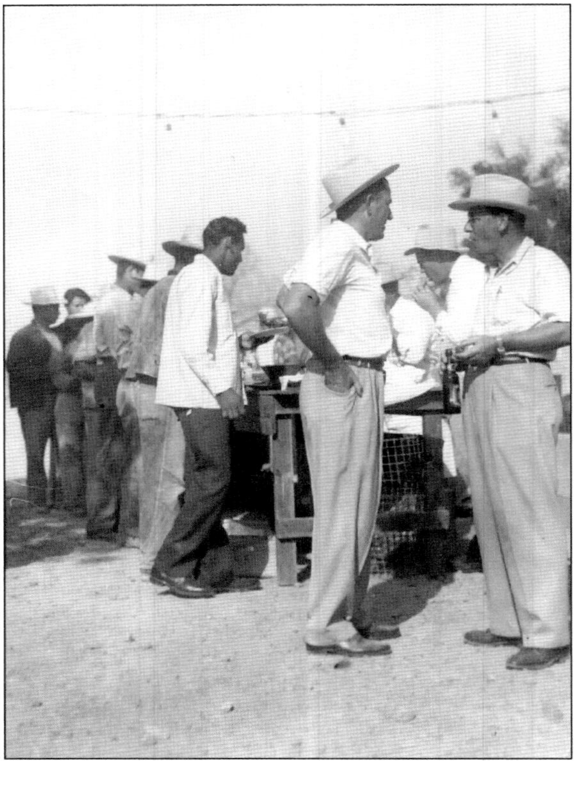

Carl Schuster (second from right) exhibited a fondness for his employees and often provided barbeque meals for them. Having learned Spanish from the workers, he enjoyed mingling during these company picnics. (Courtesy of Schuster family.)

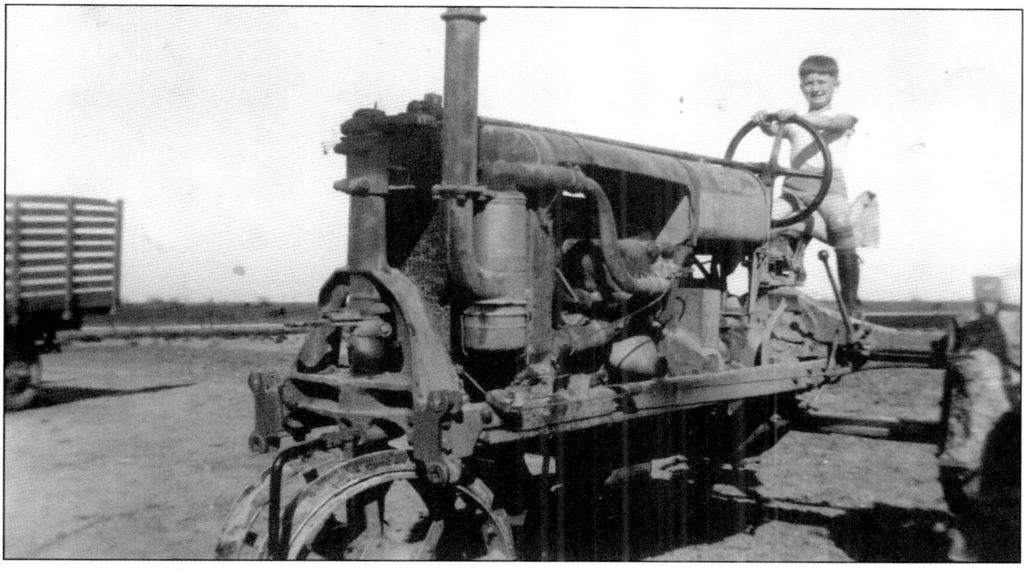

A young Carl Schuster rides the first tractor on his uncles' Krenmueller's Farm in the late 1930s. The Krenmuellers purchased the first tractor for farming the area. Working their farm at the time, Carl was given the responsibility of being the new tractor's only driver. The young and old worked alongside one another. (Courtesy of Schuster family.)

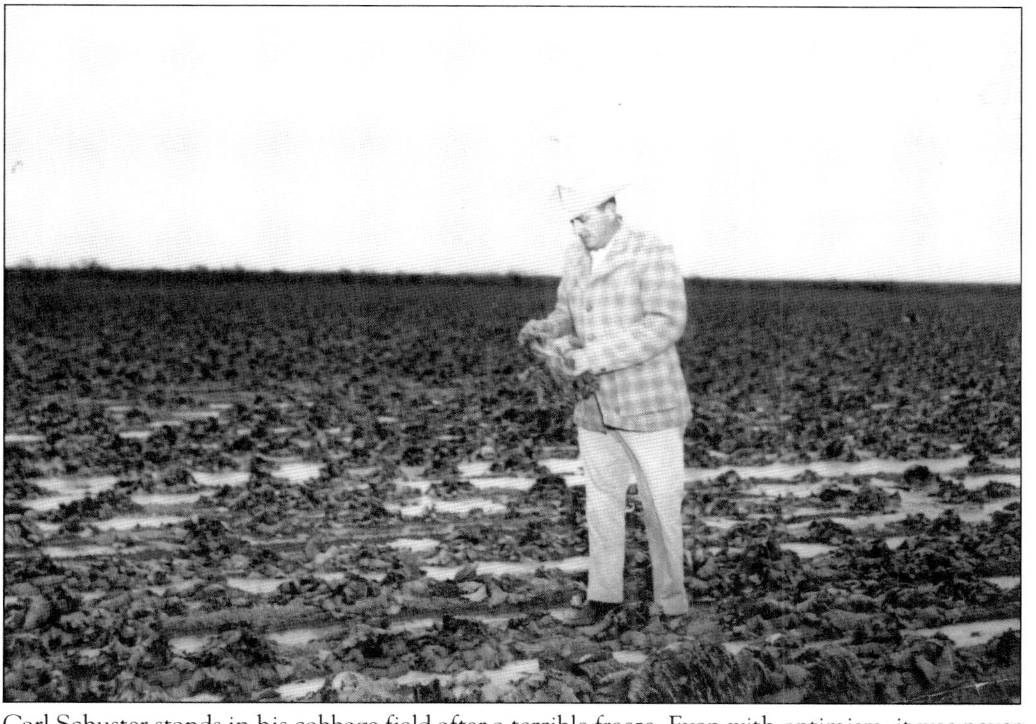

Carl Schuster stands in his cabbage field after a terrible freeze. Even with optimism, it was never easy to lose crops to a freeze. Valley farmers often battled the elements scrambling to save their crops. Several freezes occurred over the years; the last big one in the Rio Grande Valley was in 1983 when the picturesque valley lost the majority of its palm trees. (Courtesy of Schuster family.)

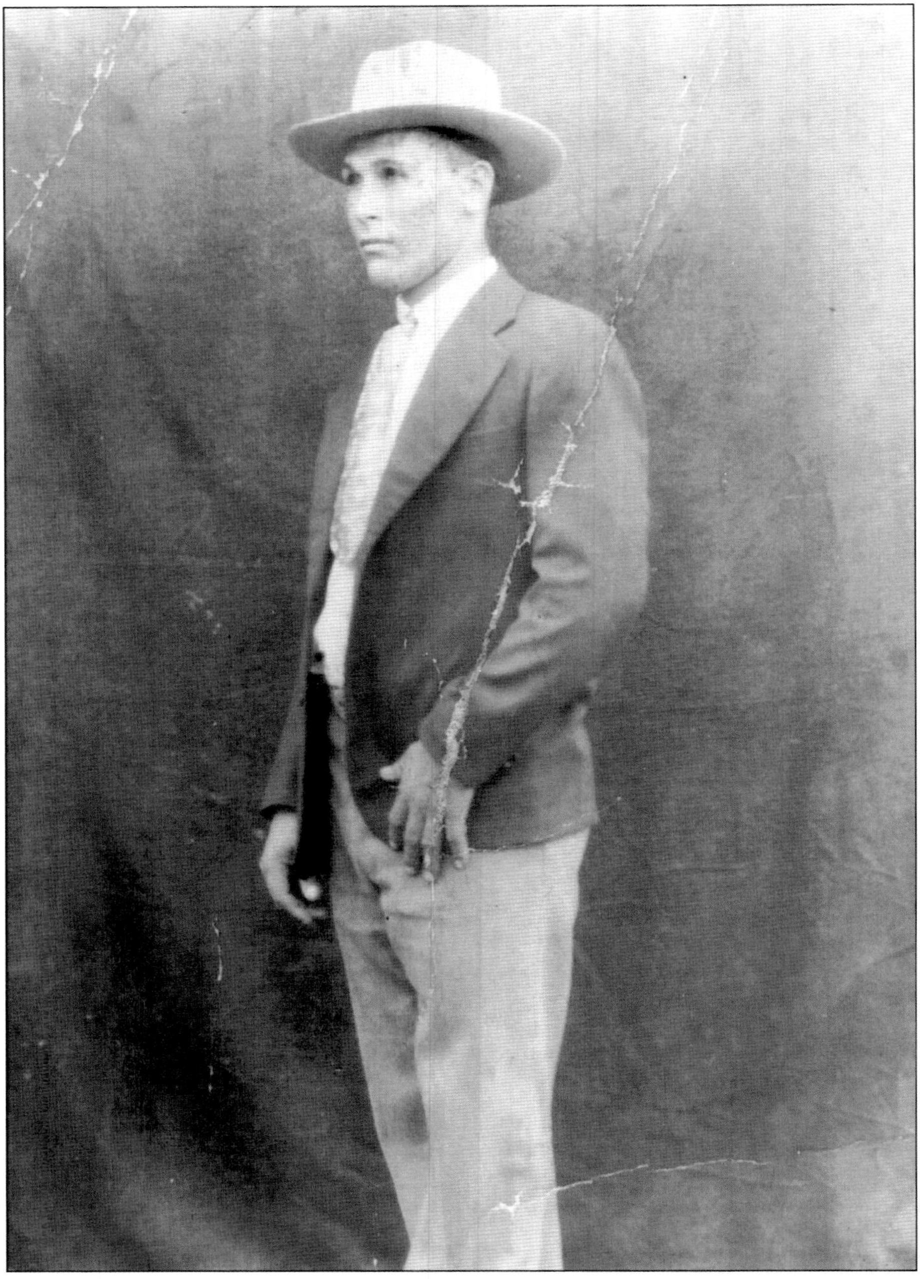

The handsome Julian Cantu poses at age 19 for a rare early photograph in 1927. He was the eldest son of Esteban and Piedad Tijerina Cantu. In 1912, the Cantus moved to San Juan from General Bravo, Mexico, to join other family members who already had settled in San Juan. They became seasonal migrant workers, annually traveling to and from Refugio, Texas. They purchased land in San Juan and raised crops such as carrots and cotton. At the request of the Catholic Church, Esteban Cantu sold some of his land in order to make way for the original shrine dedicated to the Virgin of San Juan de los Lagos in 1954. Julian Cantu was the oldest living member of the extended Cantu family. He died in 2005 at the age of 97. (Courtesy of Yolie Cantu Romero.)

Local farmers built row houses, such as those pictured here, to house their workers. (Courtesy of Estella Rojas.)

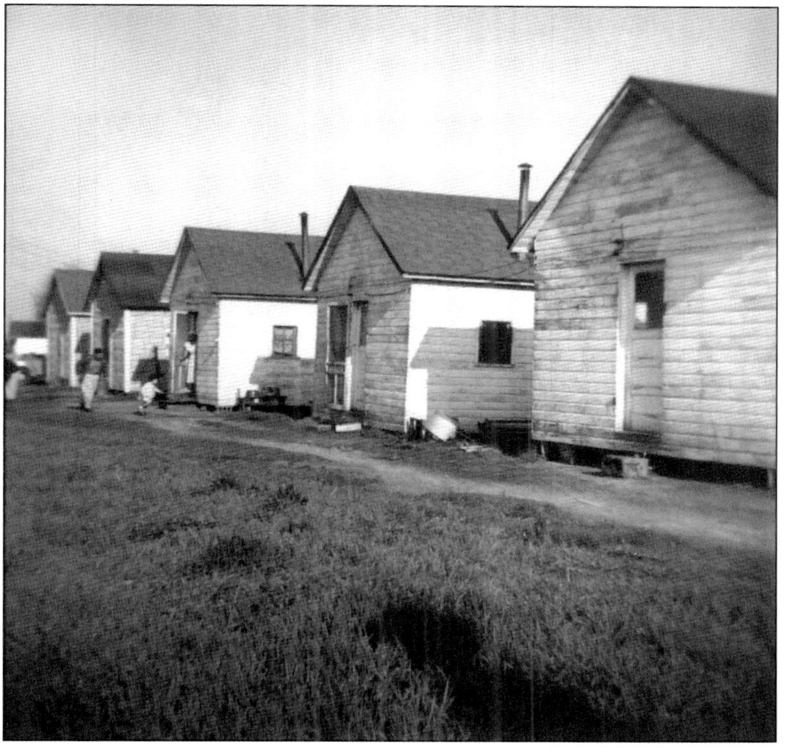

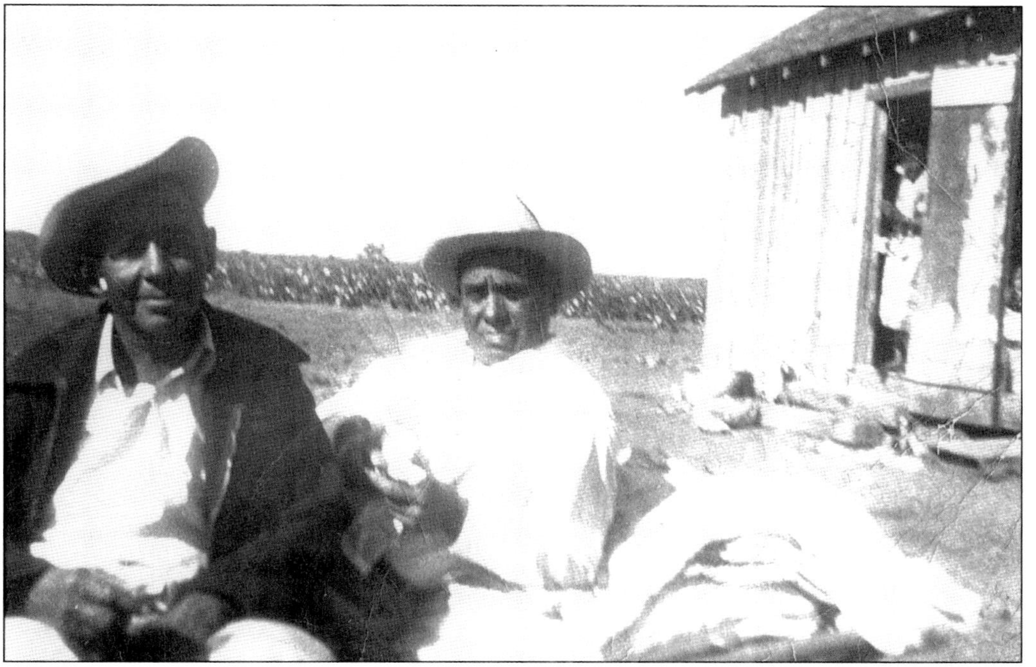

Eusebio Maldonado (left) is pictured with an unidentified friend around 1950 in the cotton fields near the labor camp houses as they enjoy a break from the rigors of work. The Maldonado family has lived on the northern banks of the Rio Grande for generations. (Courtesy of Estella Rojas.)

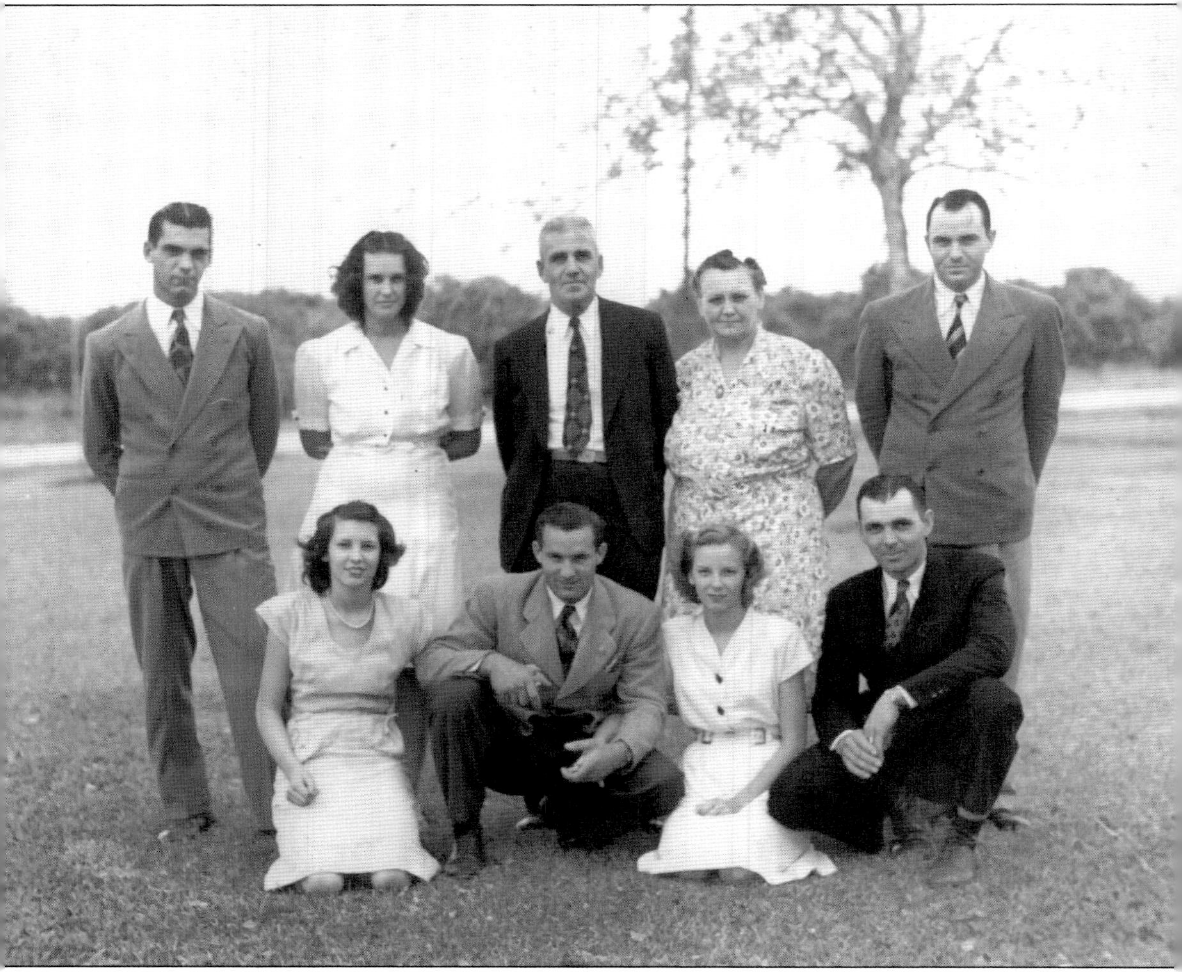

John G. C. Doedyns came to San Juan with his brothers, Arnold and Jim, in 1917. In addition to farming, these men were also carpenters and contractors. Jim Doedyns built the Peoples Covenant Church. The John G. C. Doedyns family in 1946, included, from left to right, (first row) Patsy, John Jr., Eny, and Arnold; (second row) Jim, Carolyn, John G. C., Olga Spicka, and Joe Doedyns. The Doedyns men have been known to serve the public interest. John G. C. Doedyns Jr. and Sr. both served on the Pharr-San Juan-Alamo School Board. Doedyns Elementary School in San Juan was named in their honor. Arnold served as city commissioner. Mike was also one of the members of the charter commission that prepared the San Juan City Charter approved by voters on April 5, 1975. (Courtesy of Mike Doedyns.)

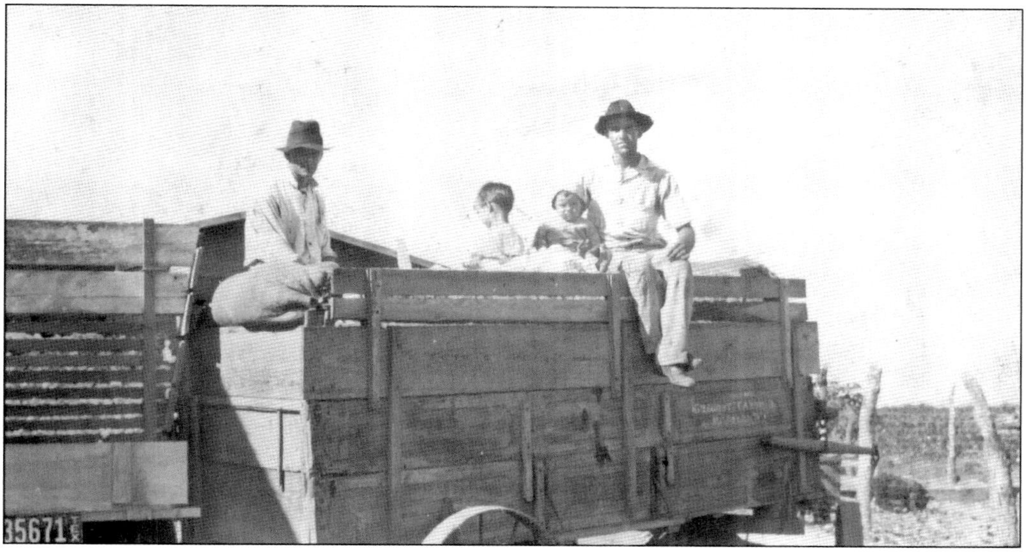

John G. C. Doedyns (far right), along with his sons Joe (second from right) and Arnold (center), sits with an unidentified man (left) on top of a trailer filled with bales of cotton in the 1930s. (Courtesy of Mike Doedyns.)

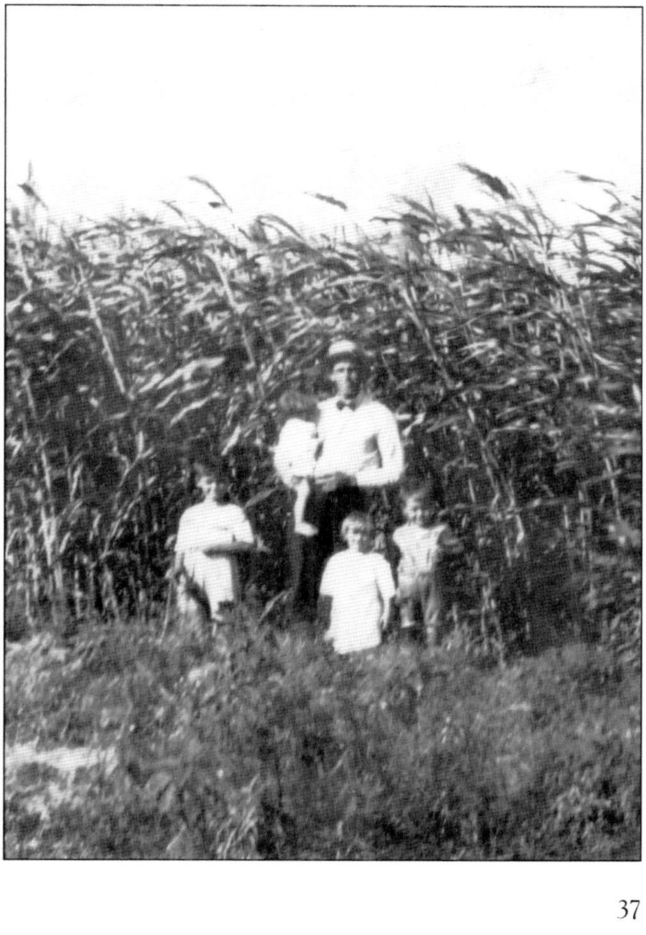

The Doedyns family built their homes in San Juan through the sales of their broomcorn, which can grow to be 10 feet high. Their first harvests were so successful that they enabled the family to pay for the majority of initial land purchases. Proudly standing in front of his crop in 1924 is John G. C. Doedyns holding son John Jr., with daughter Carolyn and sons Arnold (left) and Joe (right). (Courtesy of Mike Doedyns.)

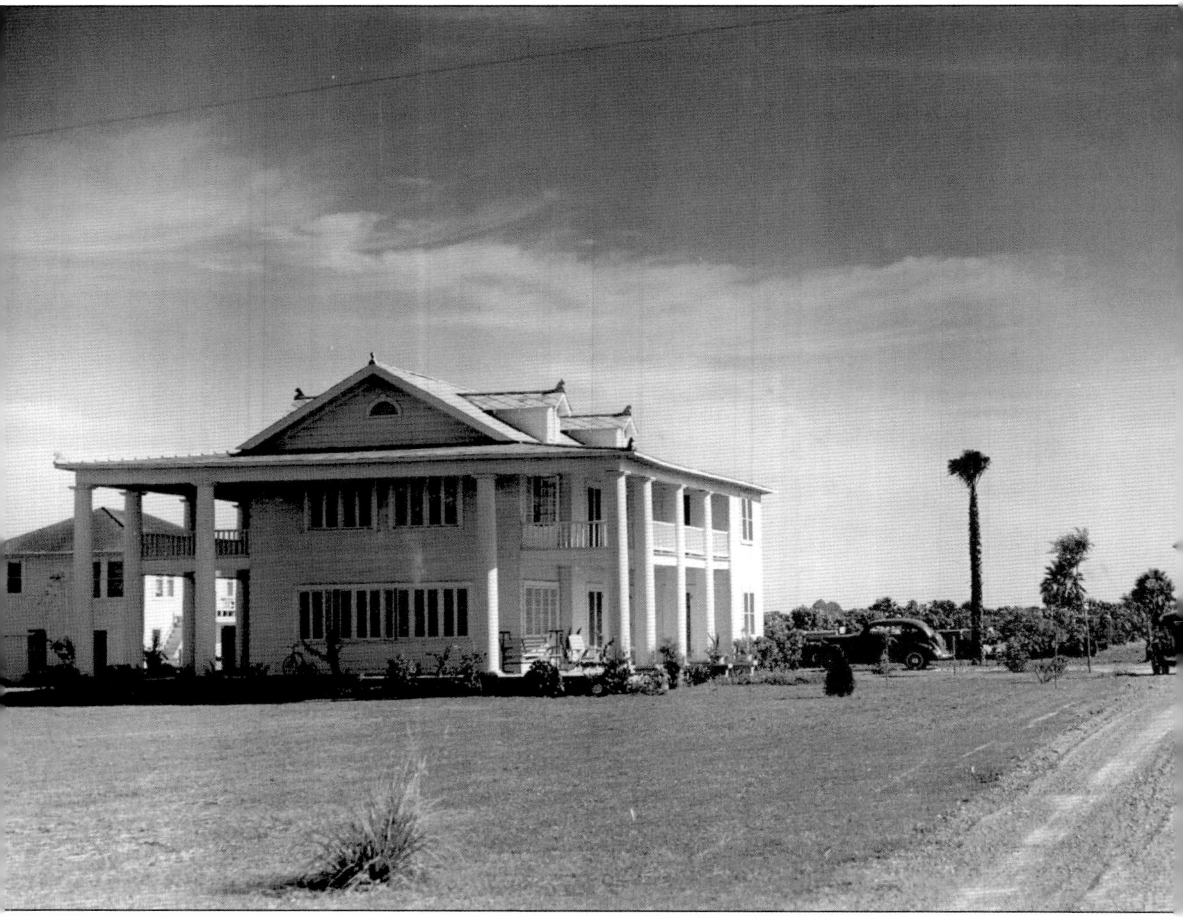

Clubhouses like the one here were often used to entertain prospective new land buyers and were typically modeled after southern mansions. Clark Mellenbruch purchased this plantation-style home in 1937. The house, which originally stood in Donna, Texas, was then moved to its current location in San Juan on the north side of U. S. Highway 83, just east of I Road. Adkins of Alamo moved the structure by collapsing the roof and removing the porches in the process. Since telephone lines at that time prevented clear passage along Highway 83, the house had to be moved a total of 21 miles north to Edinburg, then down I Road. Once it was moved to its new location on Mellenbruch's new 17-acre citrus farm, the roof and porches were restored to their original positions. (Courtesy of Jane Mellenbruch Hinkle.)

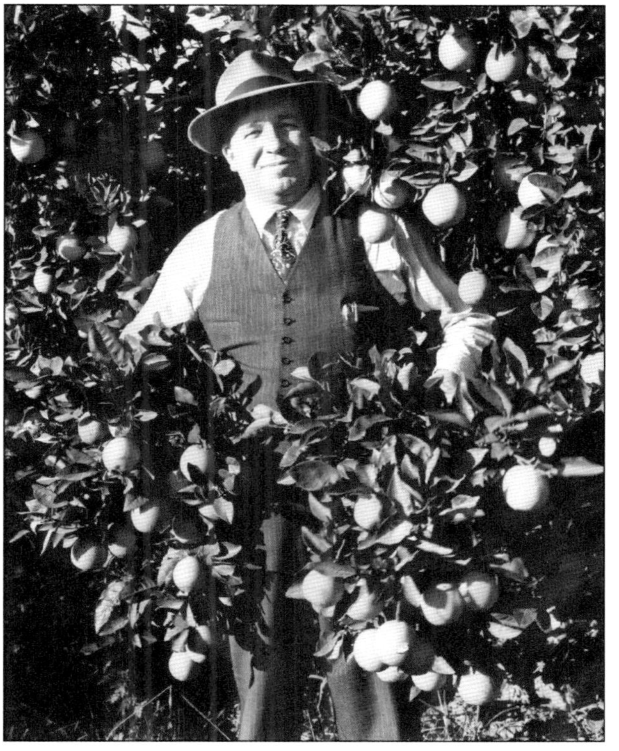

Coming from Kansas to San Juan in 1918, Clark Mellenbruch was known by many as a successful entrepreneur. Not only did he plant a 17-acre citrus grove, but he was involved with several other successful business endeavors. He shipped grapefruit and oranges and later built a lumberyard. He married Oleva Williams in 1926, and the couple had a beautiful daughter named Jane. (Courtesy of Jane Mellenbruch Hinkle.)

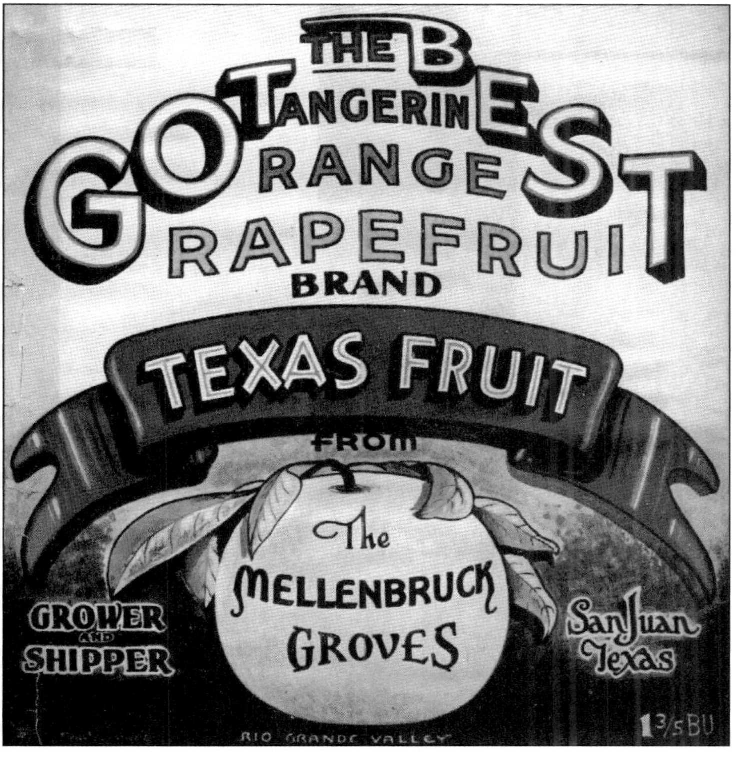

One of Clark Mellenbruch's many business ventures was the shipping of citrus fruit. Serving a dual purpose of promoting both his citrus groves and its fruit, he cleverly designed this packing label by using the starting and ending letters of the label's motto to incorporate the fruit for sale. (Courtesy of Jane Mellenbruch Hinkle.)

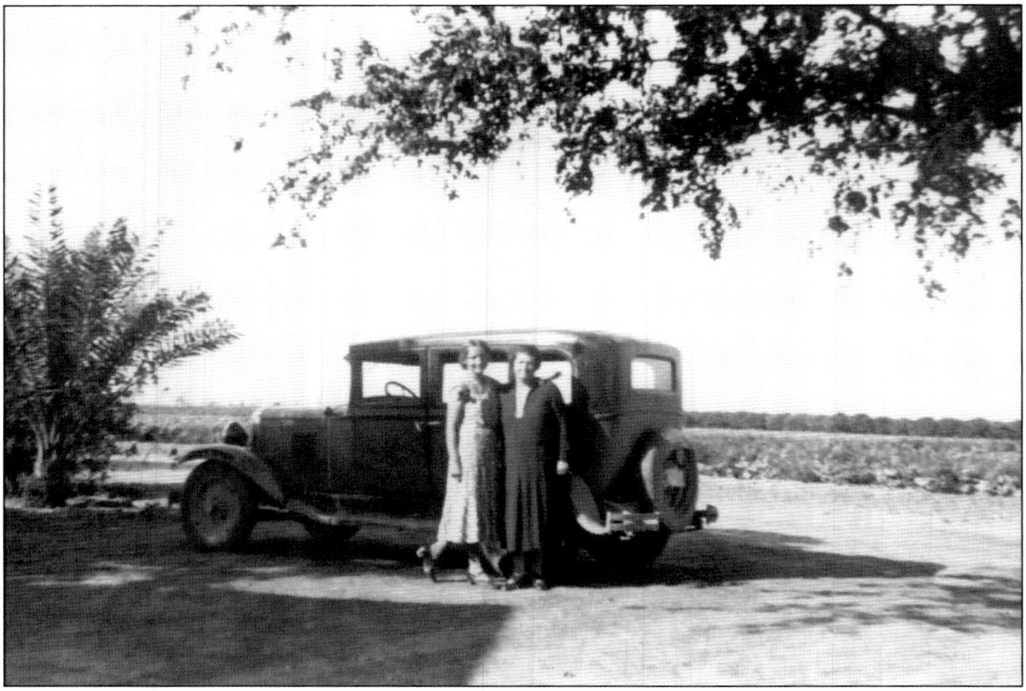

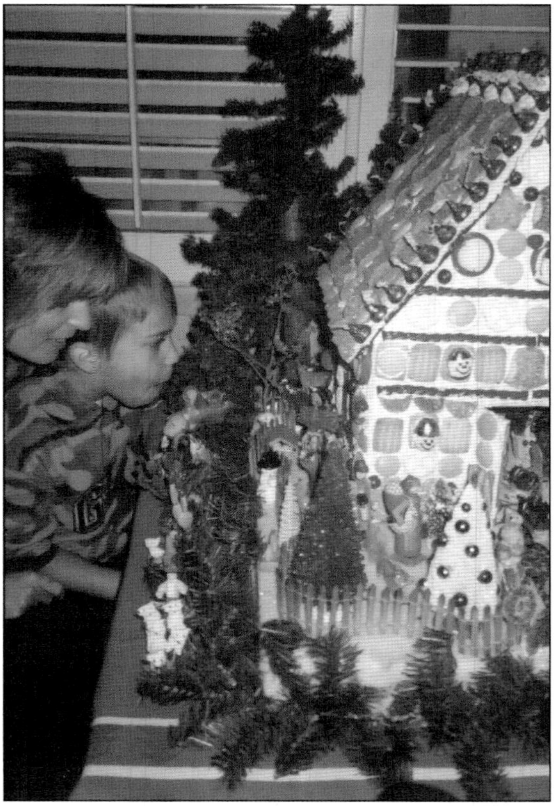

Fred Krenmueller's wife, Ilse, loved life in San Juan. She enjoyed the pioneer lifestyle with her husband out in the field busily cultivating his crops with his horses and mules. She often spoke about the beauty of her Austrian homeland. She played the guitar and sang Austrian folk songs in the evenings at home for entertainment. Privately she published a book called *Memories 1932–1952* for the enjoyment of her family. Pictured above are Ilse (left) and Stephanie Friedl around 1933. Carrying on their native Austrian traditions was very important to the Krenmueller family. As seen at left, Ilse Krenmueller made a holiday gingerbread house every year and displayed it for the enjoyment of family and friends. (Both courtesy of Trudy Forthuber.)

Three

Vital Local Enterprise

With the agricultural industry giving way to new trade, San Juan's commercial fabric grew rapidly. The main crossroads within the town were M Street (now known as Nebraska Street) and the main thoroughfare alongside the railroad (now known as U.S. Highway 83). Retail establishments peppered the corridor. The two main bank buildings not only housed banks but also contained a dry goods store, funeral home, the telephone company, and eventually the water district offices.

Moving east on Highway 83, other businesses emerged such as the La Fleur Café, a Studebaker garage, a drugstore called Leckie's, Nettleton's Dry Clean Shop, and George Marie's Curio Shop. There was Taylor Lumber Yard, the San Juan Hotel, a restaurant called the Sho-Side Inn, and the Rex Theater next door. The San Juan Variety Store opened later and so did Markowitz Grocery. One could also find Anderson's Café, a barbershop owned by Mr. Earhart, and Martin's Drug, located at the corner of Nebraska Street and Highway 83.

As many midwestern settlers relocated to San Juan, white settlers rapidly outnumbered the already established Mexican American families. A dividing line revealed itself along the railroad tracks that separated the two communities. Many other businesses emerged north of the tracks to cater to the Hispanic community. The San Juan Shoe Shop and the La Paz general Merchandise Store opened in the 1920s. Later several businesses opened up along Nebraska Street, such as S. Alanis and Sons General Merchandise Store, Jose Garza and Brother Grocery Store (known as La Gran Tienda Amarilla), Jose Rodriguez' Grocery, and Ben's Place Cantina. In the 1940s, Garza's Café, Cano's Grocery, and El Teatro Murillo added to the Hispanic business base.

By the 1950s, the downtown business district was the center of all celebration. Folks worked all week and half a day on Saturdays. They got paid after work on Saturday and spent their earnings in town, patronizing the local stores and greatly contributing to the local economy. Businesses were buzzing with customers, and San Juan was a picture of prosperity.

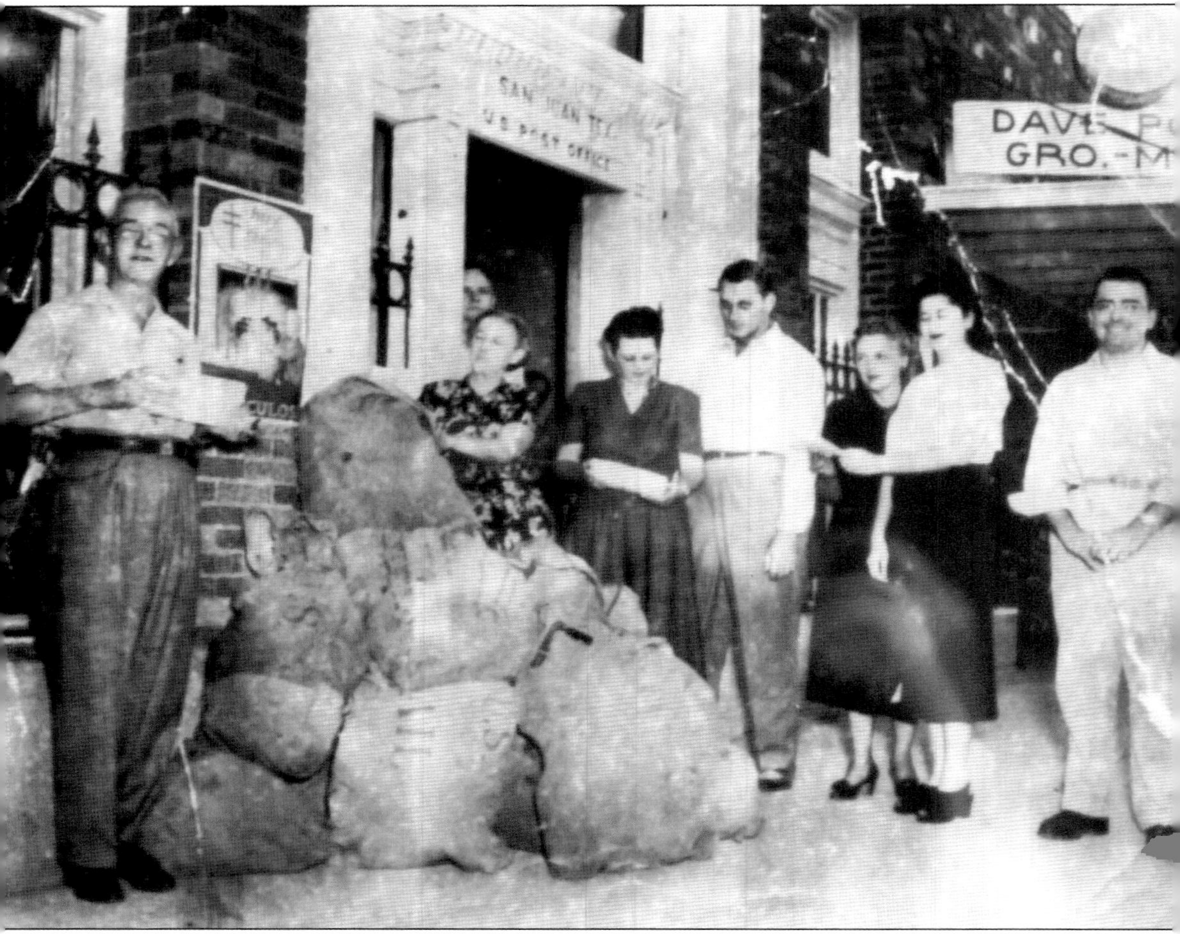

This photo from the *Valley Evening Monitor* shows F.C. Platt (left) as postmaster for the San Juan Post Office with his wife, Lura (second from left), who was the assistant postmaster. The shot was taken during a Christmas Seals drive in November of 1948. Also shown here are (in doorway behind Mrs. Platt and to the right) Howard Smith, Mrs. H.L. Murphey, Hal McKissick, Mrs. H.W. Riddle, Mrs. Mitchell Darby and William Ingram. (Courtesy of Edna Platt Walsh Estate.)

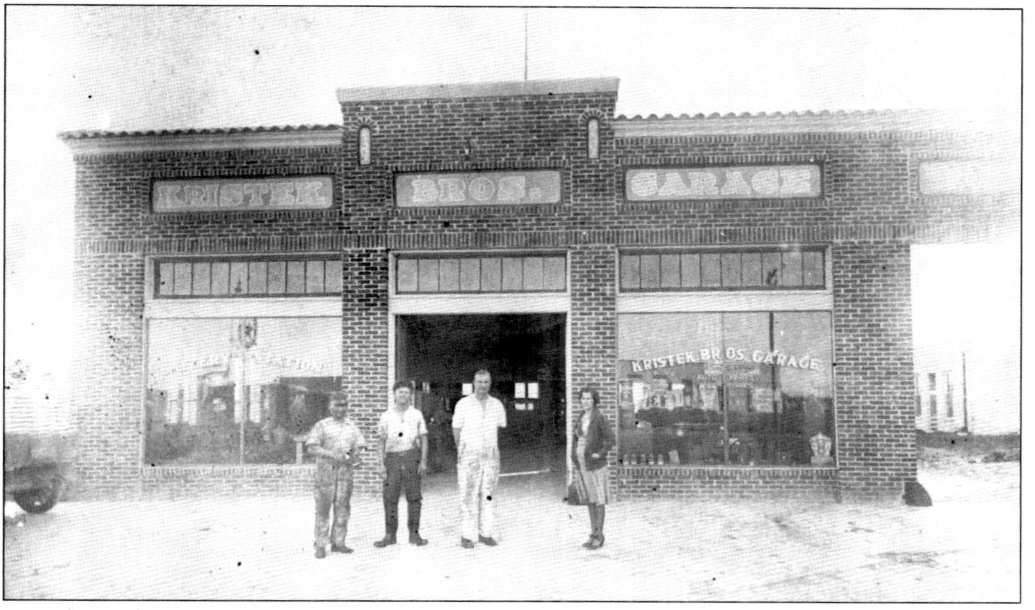

Kristek Brothers Garage provided service in a modern facility, pictured here in February 1930. Ed and Henry Kristek originally worked in the Temple Brothers Garage as mechanics when they first arrived in San Juan from California and eventually opened their own shop. This shop was located on the south side U.S. Highway 83, on the east side of Nebraska Street. Posing for this photograph from left to right are Isidro Robles, Cesar Cantu, Henry Kristek, and Beatrice Kristek. (Courtesy of Robert Kristek.)

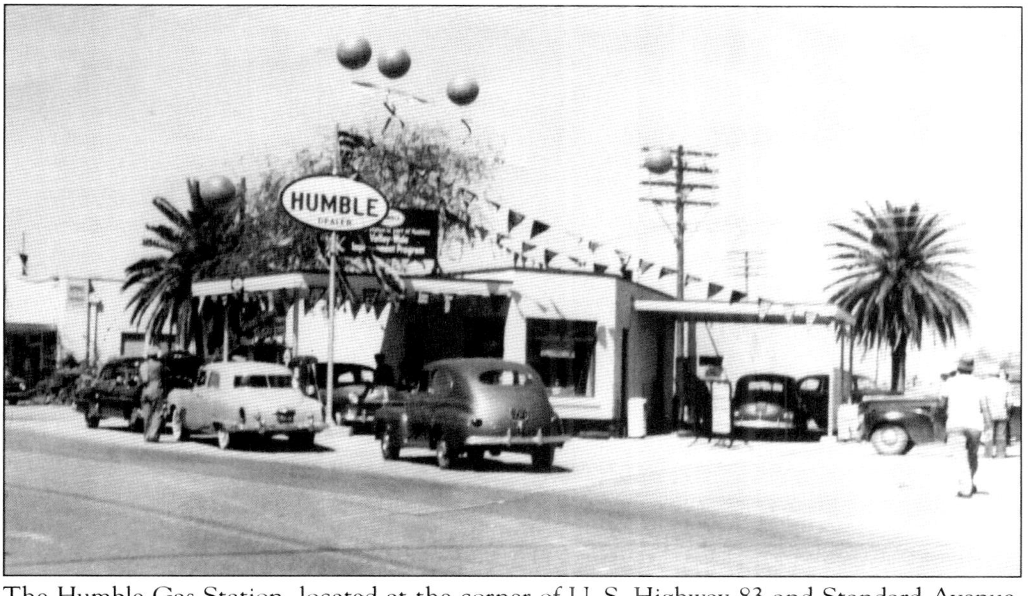

The Humble Gas Station, located at the corner of U. S. Highway 83 and Standard Avenue, beckoned customers after its remodeling in 1955, when gas cost just 2¢ per gallon. The station was owned by Carlos Salazar from 1951 to 1956 and was a popular meeting place. It was later owned by Rigo Pinon, Prajedes Garza, and Abelardo Garcia and was torn down in 1965. (Courtesy of Carlos Salazar.)

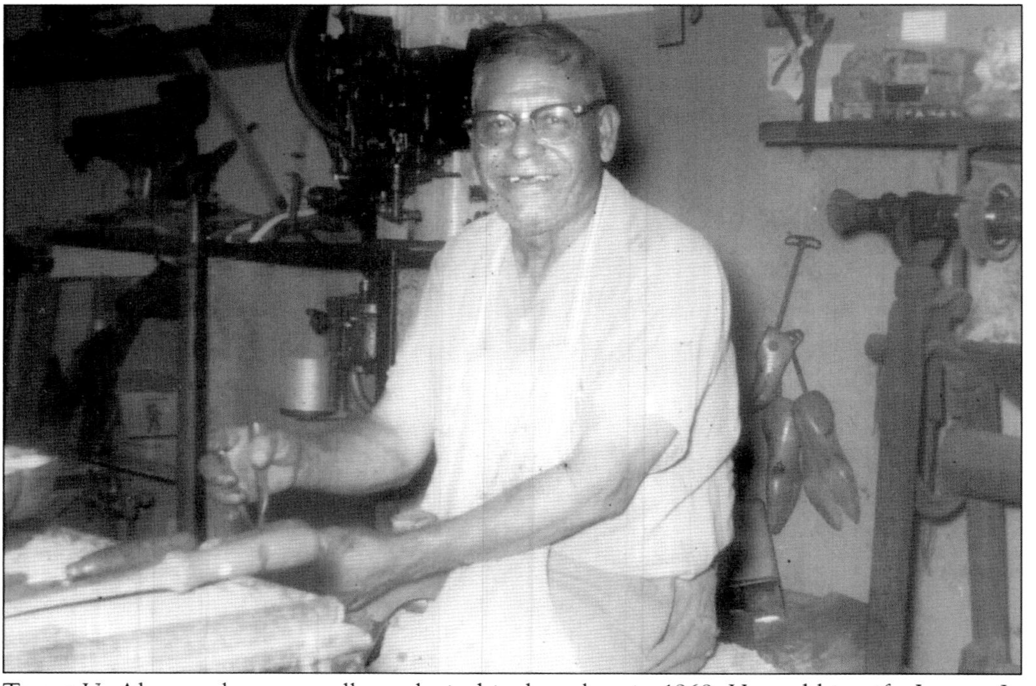

Tomas H. Alonzo, above, proudly works in his shoe shop in 1968. He and his wife, Leonor L. Lopez Alonzo, came to San Juan in 1919 from Matehuala, San Luis Potosi, Mexico. In 1927, he opened the San Juan Shoe Shop, and it is still in operation today. He worked in the shoe shop until 1975, when his son Steve Alonzo took over. Tomas Alonzo Jr. took over the shop in 1984 and is still running it today. Below, Tomas Alonzo Jr. and his sister Marina Alonzo pose in front of the shoe shop in 1968. Marin Alonzo died as a soldier in the U.S. Army during World War II. (Both courtesy of Tomas Alonzo Jr.)

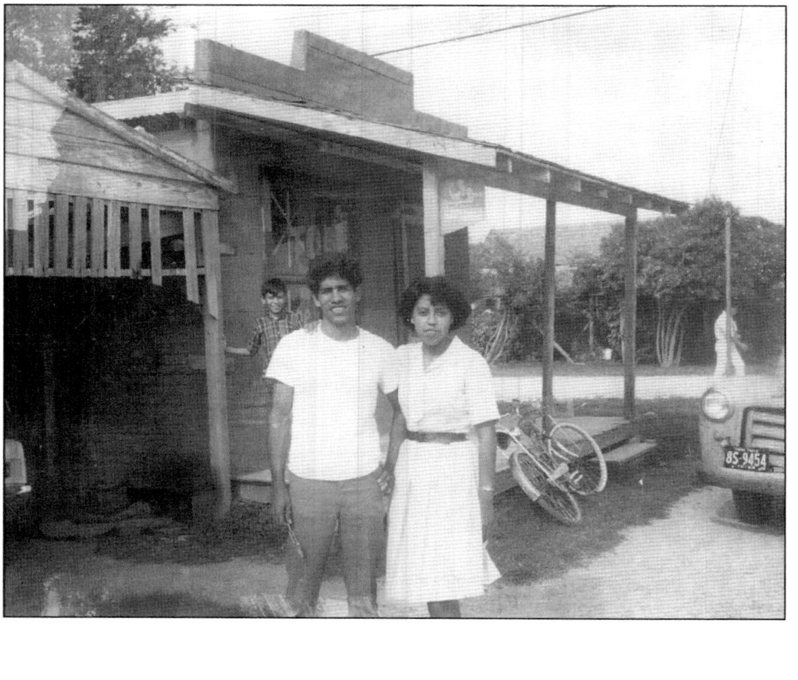

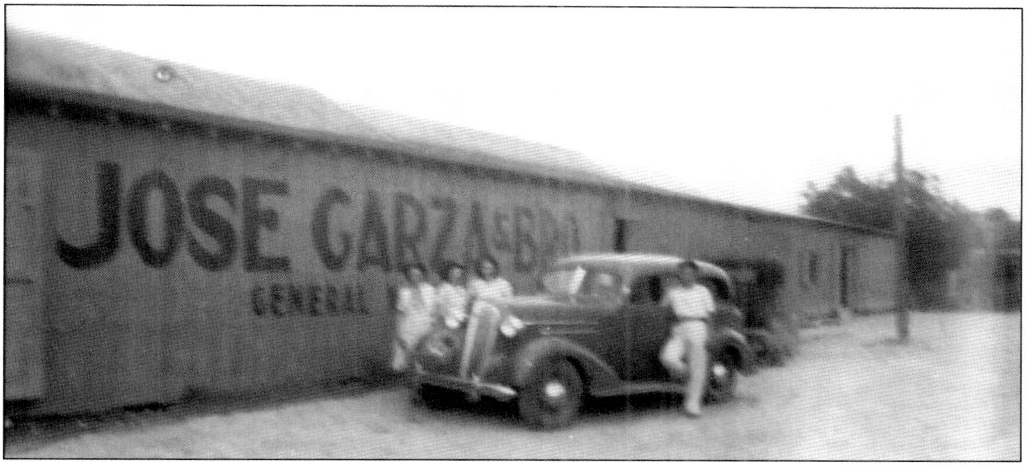

La Gran Tienda Amarilla (the big yellow store) is pictured above in 1939. Located at the northwest corner of Railroad and Nebraska Streets was the Garza Brothers Grocery, owned by Jose and Roque Garza. The store opened in the 1930s and was in business for 72 years. Many townspeople either worked at the store or shopped there. This wooden structure was eventually torn down and a brick building constructed. In the photograph above are a family nephew and girls employed as store clerks. Pictured below from left to right are Roque Garza, Nicasio Garza, and Jose Garza. Jose was the leader of the family and owned the store together with his brother Roque. Jose was taken from his home in Mexico as a young man and forced into the Mexican Revolution. The family originally came to San Juan to earn money and return to Mexico but instead permanently settled. (Both courtesy of Maruca Longoria.)

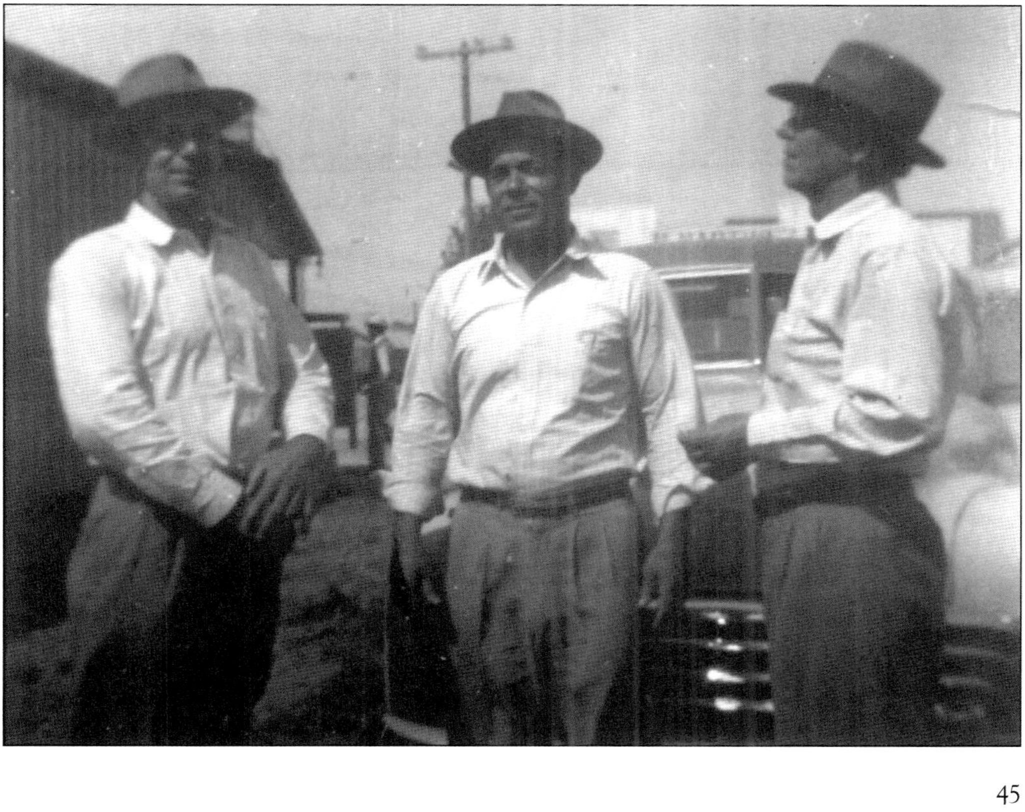

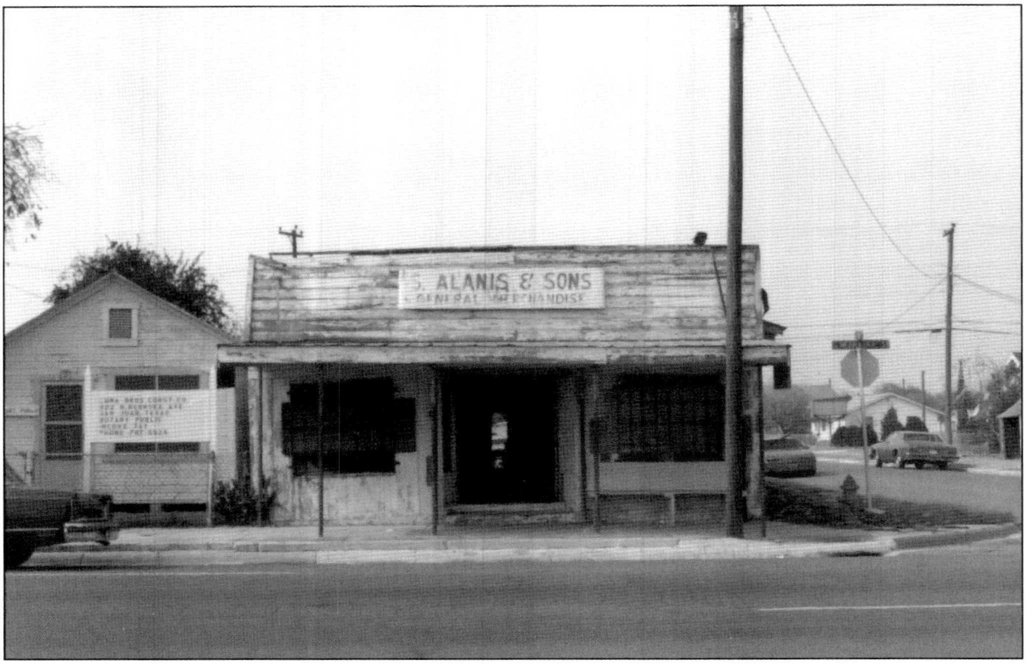

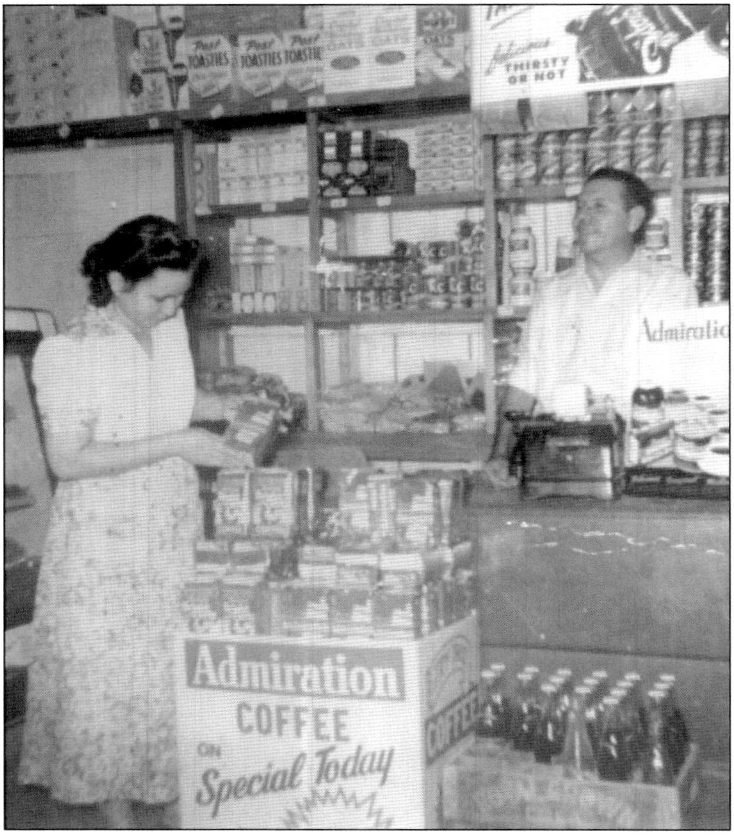

The S. Alanis and Sons General Merchandise Store was owned by Santiago and Manuela Treviño Alanis. It was opened one day before their wedding in 1936, and it was located on the corner of Fourth and Nebraska Streets. The Alanises ran a successful business there for 58 years, closing it in 1994. They even had a gasoline pump behind the store. Their son René remembers delivering groceries to the braceros (Mexican laborers) working on farms down by the river. At left are Santiago and Manuela busily working alongside each other in their store in 1950. (Both courtesy of René Alanis.)

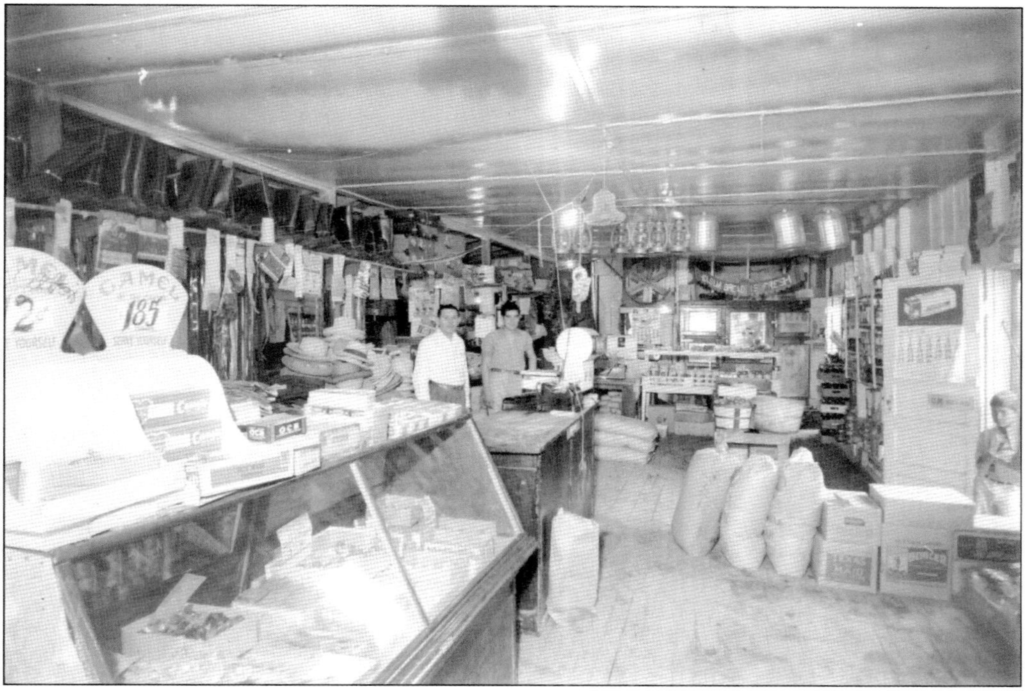

Leonel Treviño, nephew of Santiago and Manuela Alanis, is shown here (right) with his uncle (left) working inside the Alanis General Merchandise Store around 1940. He is also a recognized war hero who served as a soldier in the U.S. Army and was held as a prisoner of war in the Korean War. (Courtesy of René Alanis.)

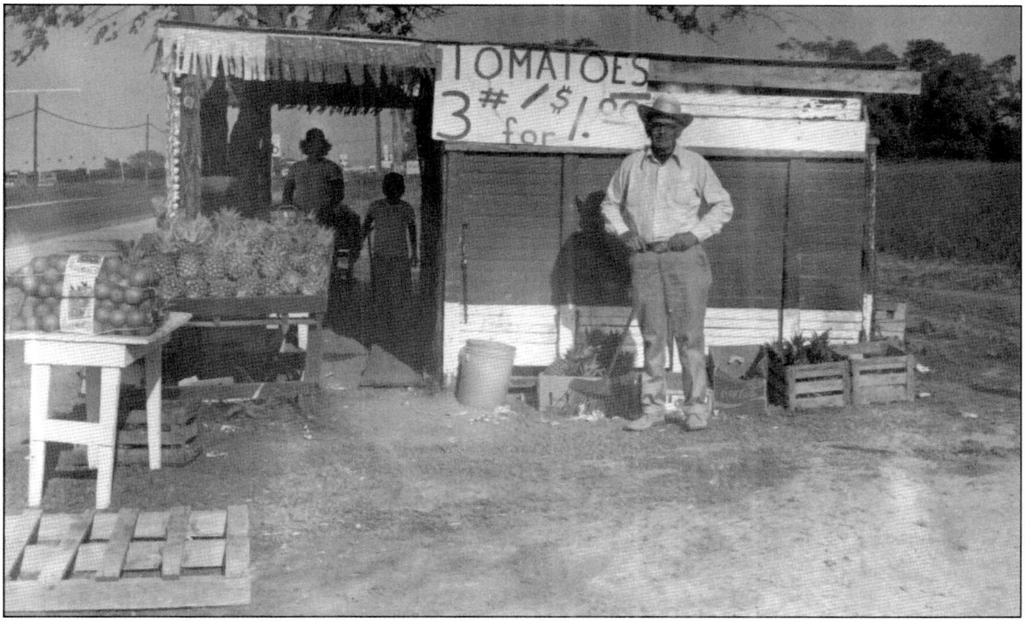

Natividad Alanis is pictured at a local roadside fruit stand located on Highway 83 alongside the canal. (Courtesy of Dr. Felipe Alanis.)

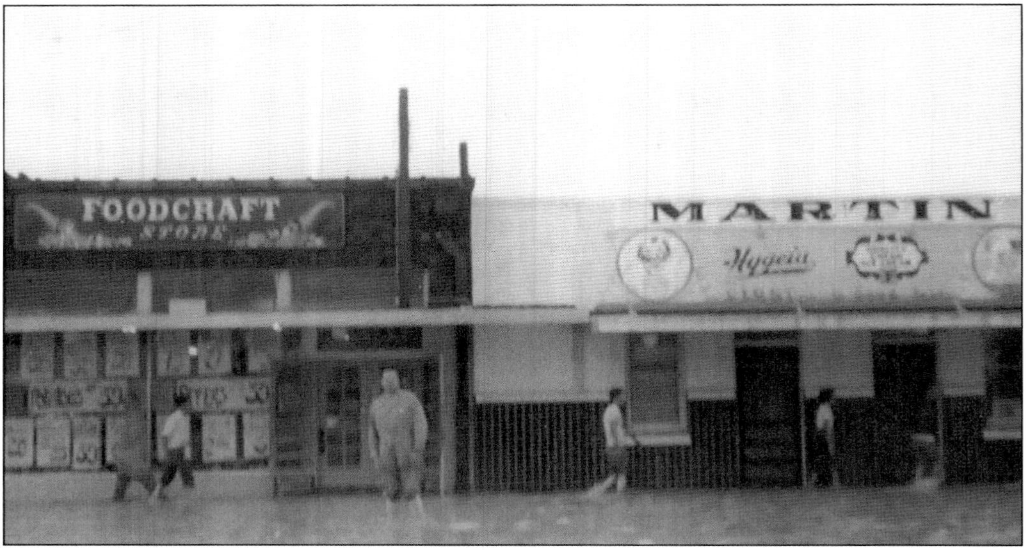

Floodwaters had townspeople rolling up their pants in front of Martin Drug located on the southwest corner of Highway 83 and Nebraska Street. A Foodcraft store was located directly south. Below, prescriptions of yesteryear fill the drugstore shelves. (Above, courtesy of Bill Lemen; below, Miguel Garza.)

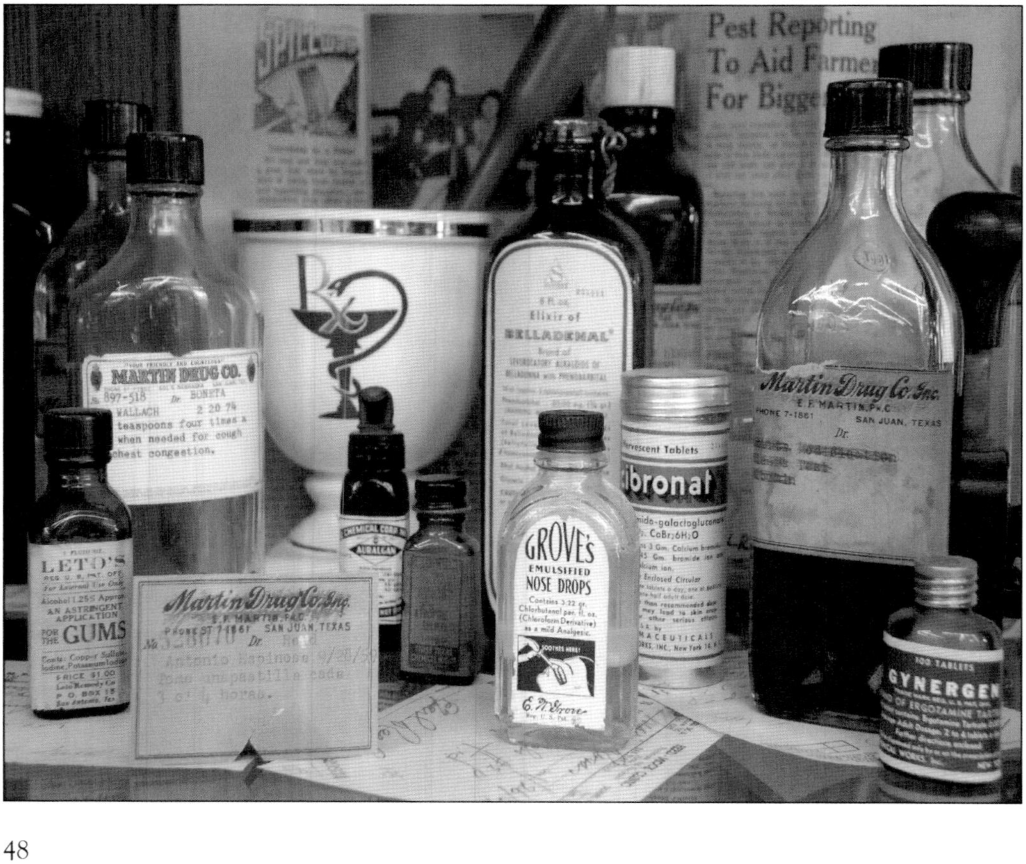

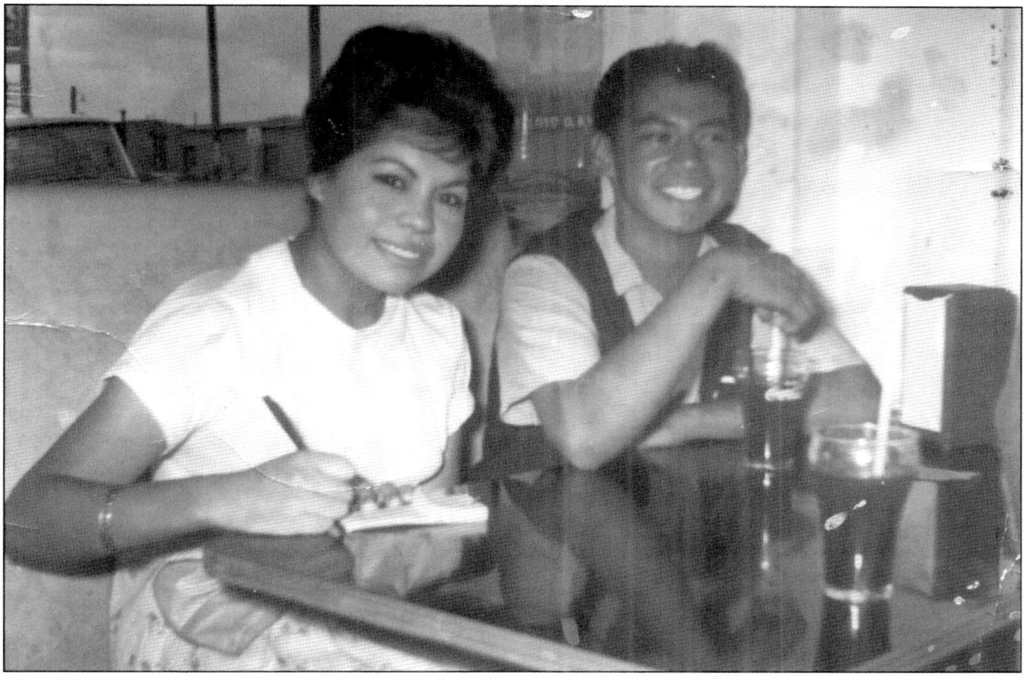

Cari Estrada served as a waitress at the soda fountain of Martin's Drug Store for four years and remembers many youngsters coming in to drink strawberry phosphates at the long counter. She also recalls Martin was strict about keeping the store clean. She is pictured here enjoying a break with her brother Mario in 1958. (Courtesy of Cari Estrada Murillo.)

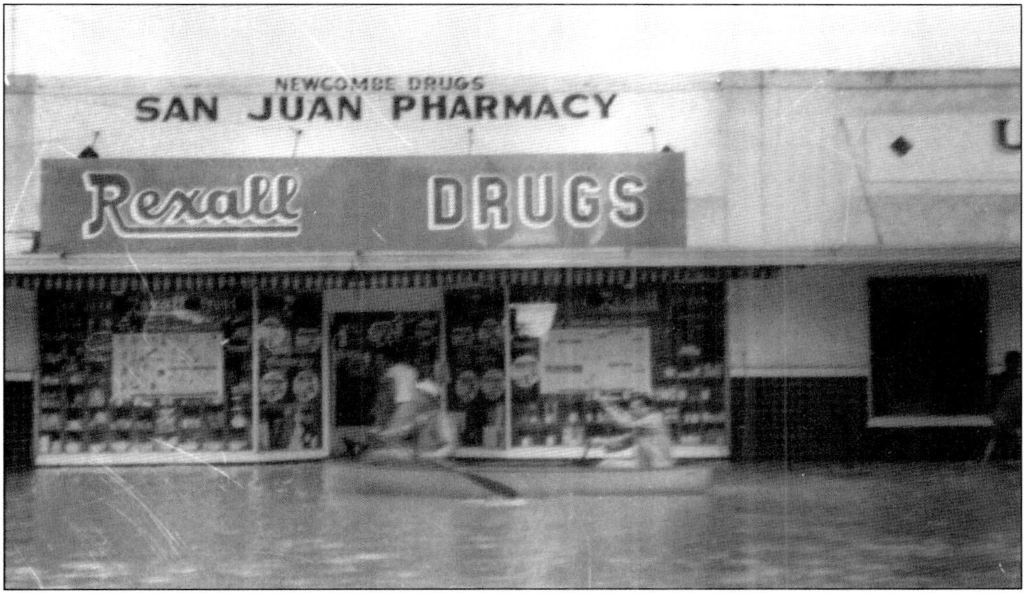

Floodwaters stand ominously in front of Newcombe's Drug Store in 1954. Local residents have fond memories of Newcombe's while they were growing up. The store was owned by Quentin Newcombe and featured a fountain with counter service and stools. A popular drink back then was the cherry coke for 5¢. (Courtesy of Robert Kristek.)

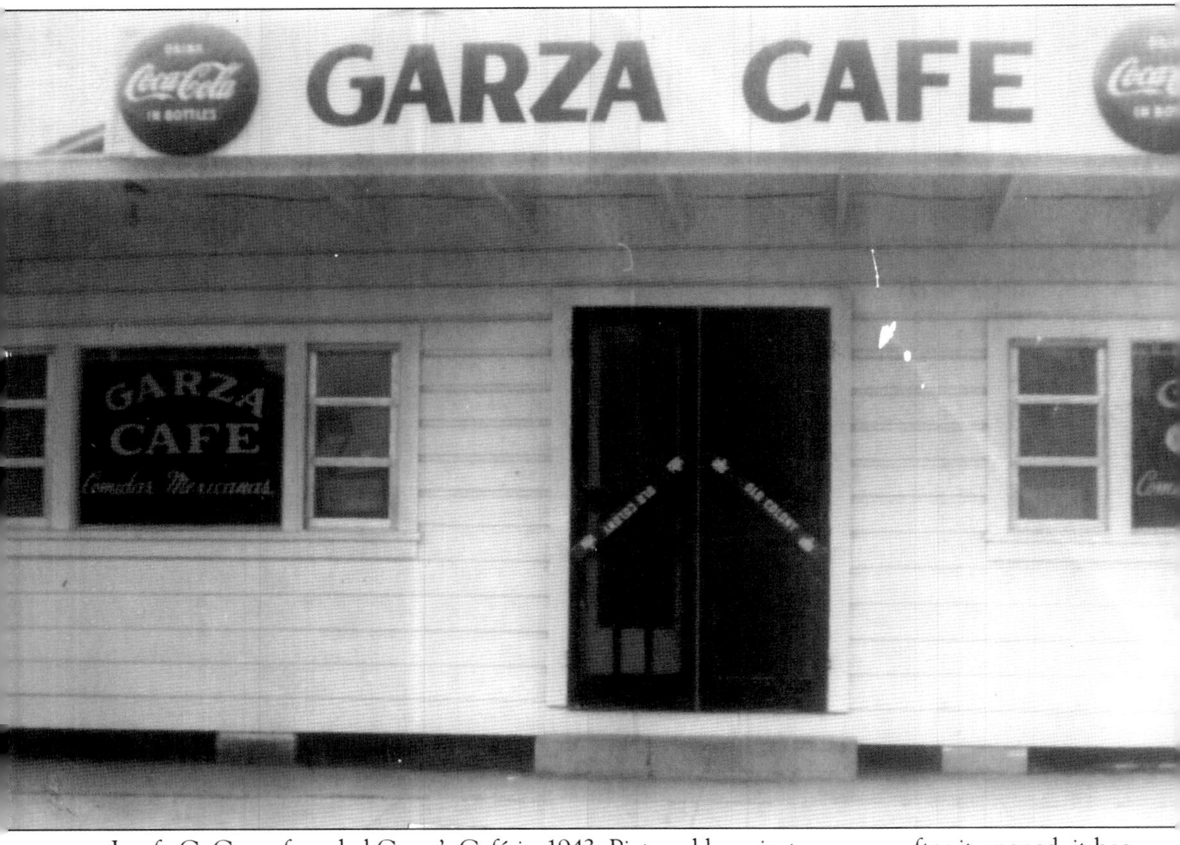

Josefa G. Garza founded Garza's Café in 1943. Pictured here just one year after it opened, it has since been remodeled three times and still stands in its original location on Nebraska Street. The café's ownership has remained in the Garza family, with Josefa's daughter Alicia G. Salinas as the present owner. They have consistently had good business throughout the years with local neighborhood customers as well as loyal winter Texans. One of the cooks has been an employee at Garza's since the day it opened over 60 years ago. (Courtesy of Alicia G. Salinas.)

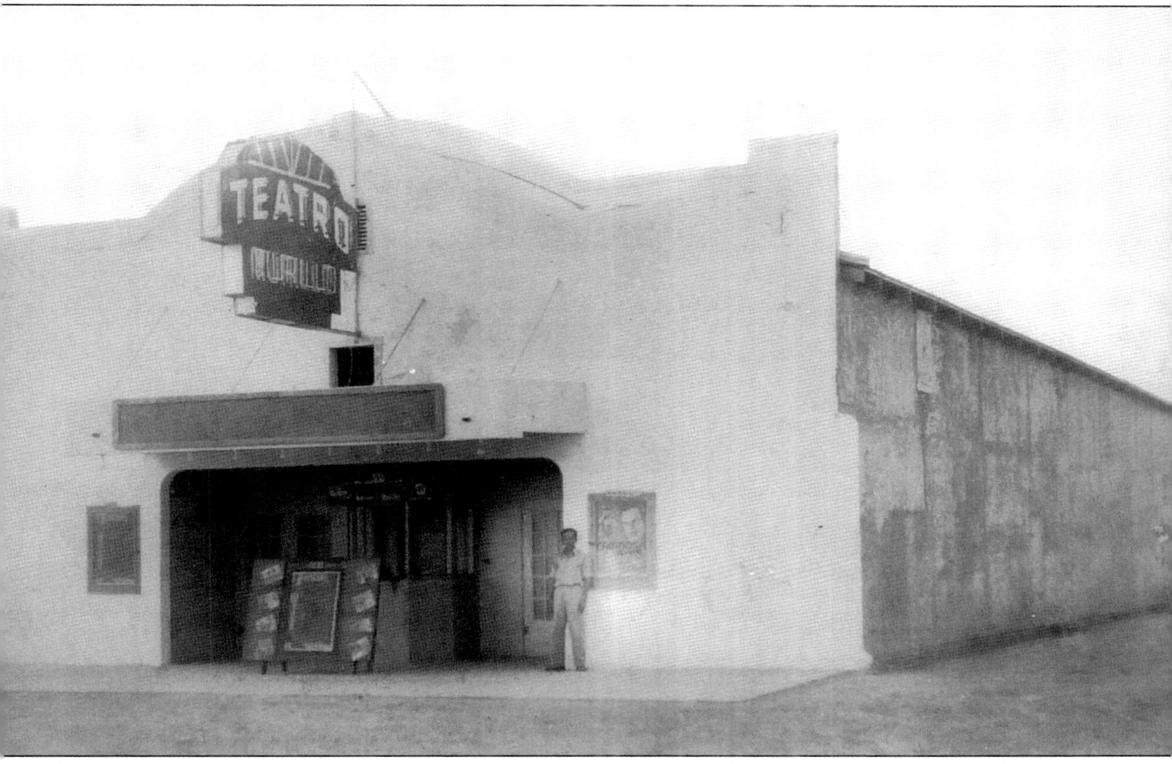

The Hispanic community enjoyed not only Mexican movies but also American movies at El Teatro Murillo. Amateur night, commonly known as "La Noche de los Aficionados" (also known as "La Noche de las Estrellas"), was held every Wednesday. Ruben Benavides, Pedro Suarez, and Pilo Trevino, radio announcers for local station KURV, sponsored music with "El Famosos" Benito Espinoza on the accordion and Chon Aceves on the guitar. Popular Valley *conjunto* musicians such as Pedro Ayala played at El Murillo along with other famous Mexican singers such as Luis Aguilar and Pedro Infante. Lupita Trevino and Ofelia Barrera were mambo dancers who entertained the audience. "El Baile de la Papa" was a popular contest with the younger crowd where couples would dance while holding a potato between their foreheads. Although El Teatro Murillo is now in San Juan's distant past, it remains a fond memory in the hearts of many people who are still living today. (Courtesy of Raquel Murillo Torteya.)

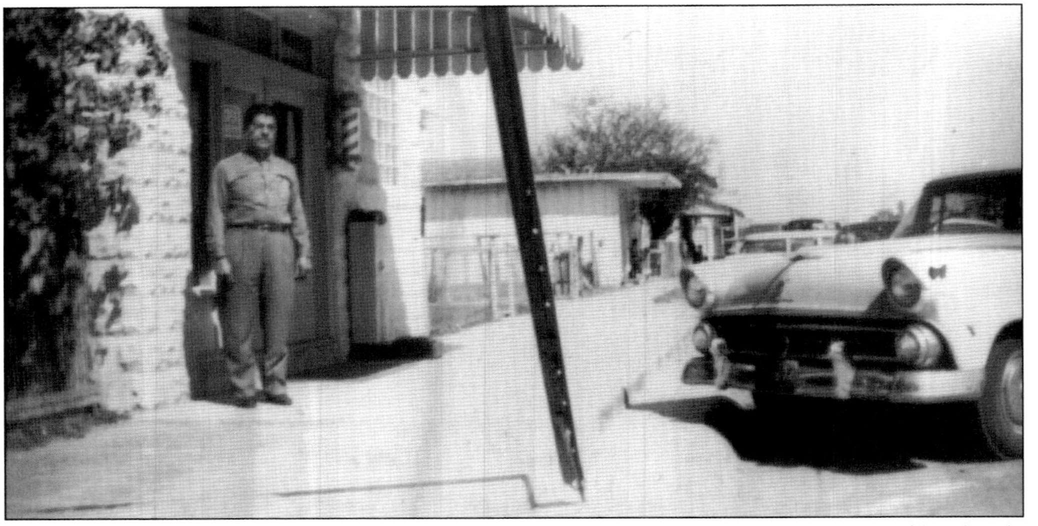

Marcelino Solis poses in front of his barbershop on Nebraska Street in 1960. Solis and his family came to San Juan from San Luis Potosi, Mexico, in order to escape the Mexican Revolution. He started working as a barber for Chico Reyna in a small pink brick building. In 1945, he built his own barbershop, which is still standing today. (Courtesy of Jesus Solis.)

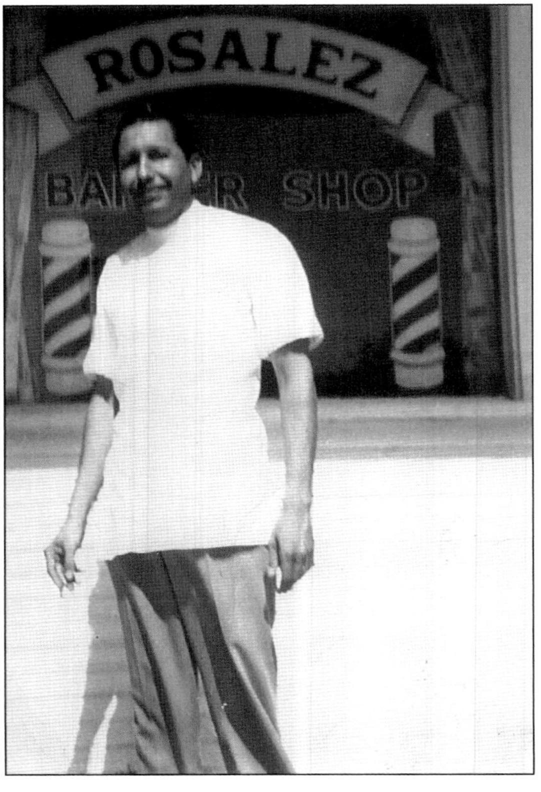

Agapito V. Rosalez, known as El Maestro (the Master) served as a barber in San Juan for 44 years. Rosalez was an active member of the Lions Club and Woodmen of the World. He was appointed to serve on the military draft board during President Johnson's term. (Courtesy of Juanita Flores.)

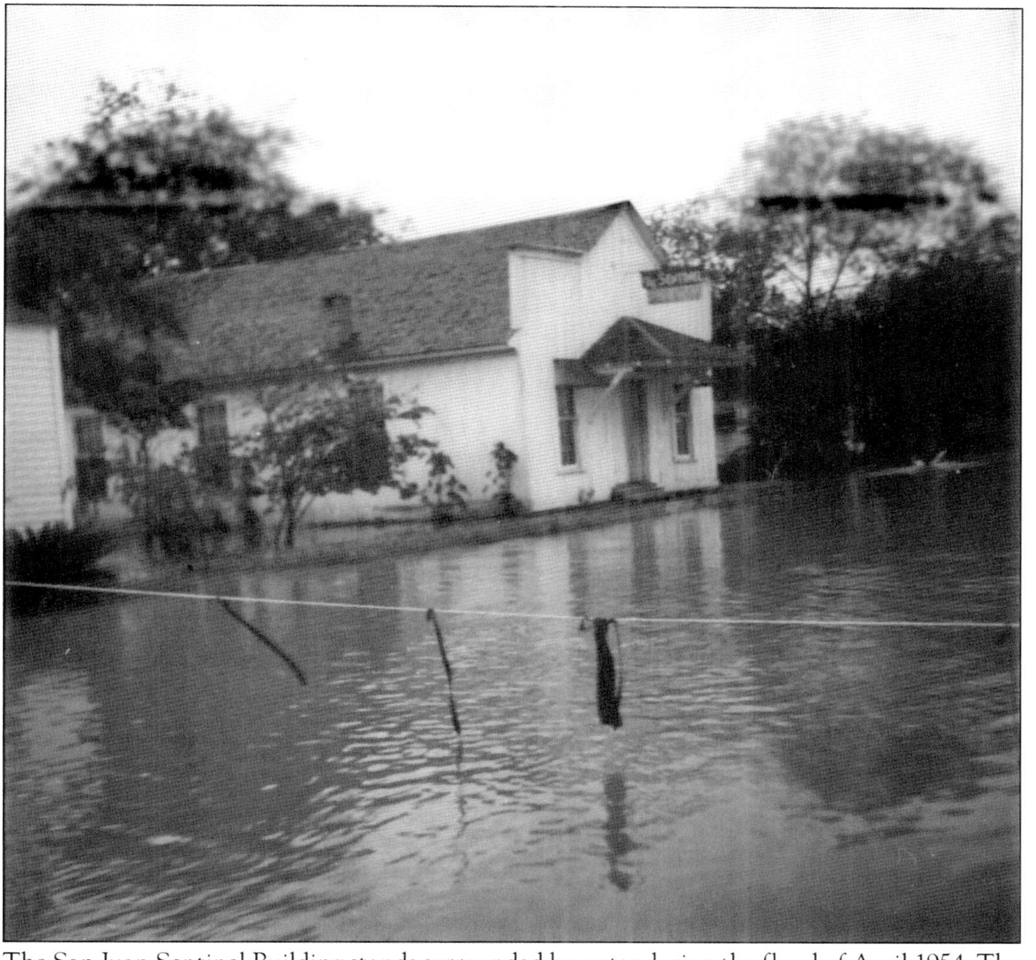

The San Juan Sentinel Building stands surrounded by water during the flood of April 1954. The *San Juan Sentinel* was the local newspaper that started in 1922 and continued into the 1960s. During the 1930s, T. E. Thompson was the editor and publisher, with Nancy Thompson as associate editor and Vivian Bigger as reporter. A three-month subscription at that time cost 75¢. The San Juan Sentinel Building was located on Nebraska Street south of Highway 83 near the city hall building but no longer exists. (Courtesy of Robert Kristek.)

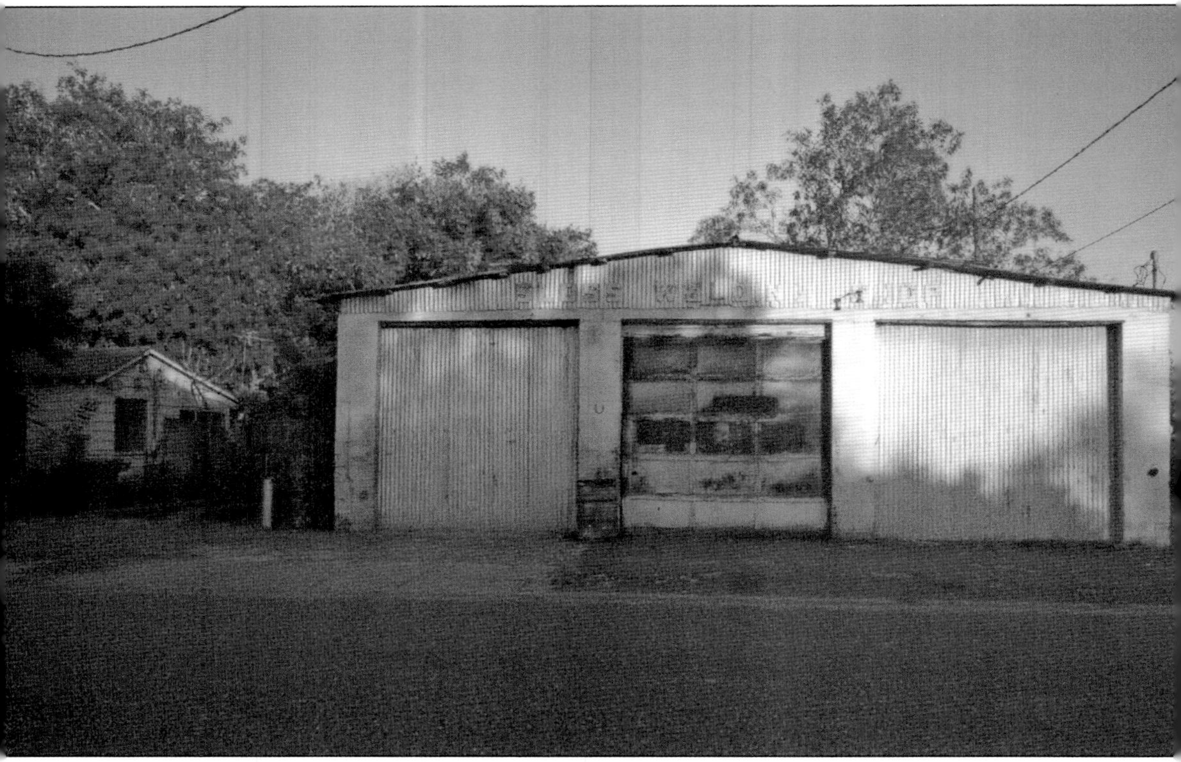

The Sloss Brothers Welding Shop, opened in 1933, was originally located at Nebraska and Fourth Streets and was managed by Manuel and Jose Sloss. In addition to producing and installing mufflers for commercial or passenger vehicles, the Sloss brothers also had a blacksmith business where they worked on farm equipment. The business prospered for 55 years and closed its doors in 2008 after serving San Juan for two generations. (Courtesy of Manuel J. Sloss.)

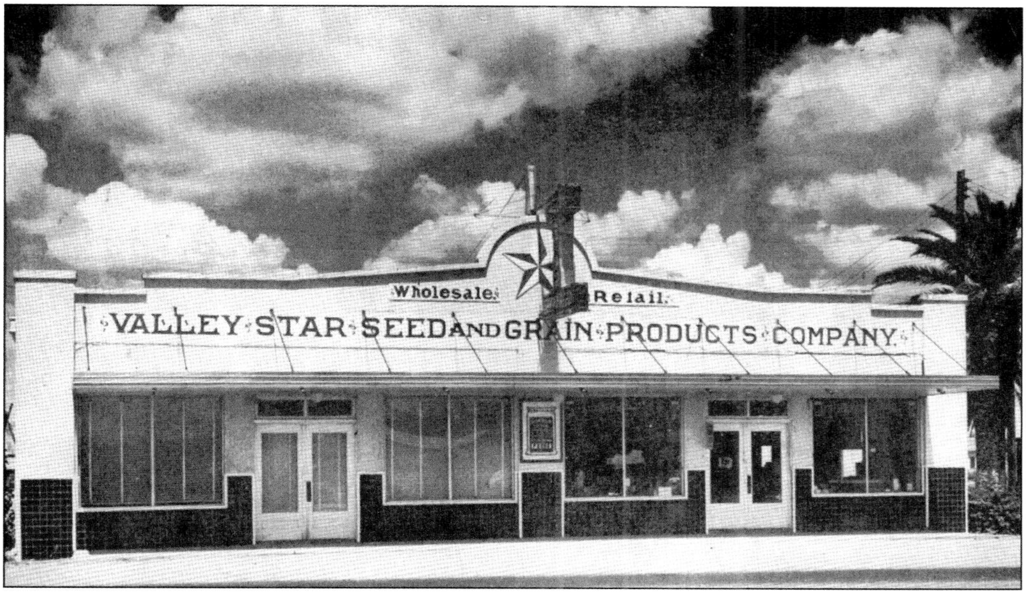

Valley Star Seed and Grain Products Company, shown here in 1977, provided a much-needed commodity to local farmers. Former city commissioner Louis Briedenbach originally founded the store in the 1920s. In 1939, Henry Kristek bought his brother Ed's portion of Kristek Brother's Garage so he could take ownership of the seed and grain business for his father-in-law. (Courtesy of Robert Kristek.)

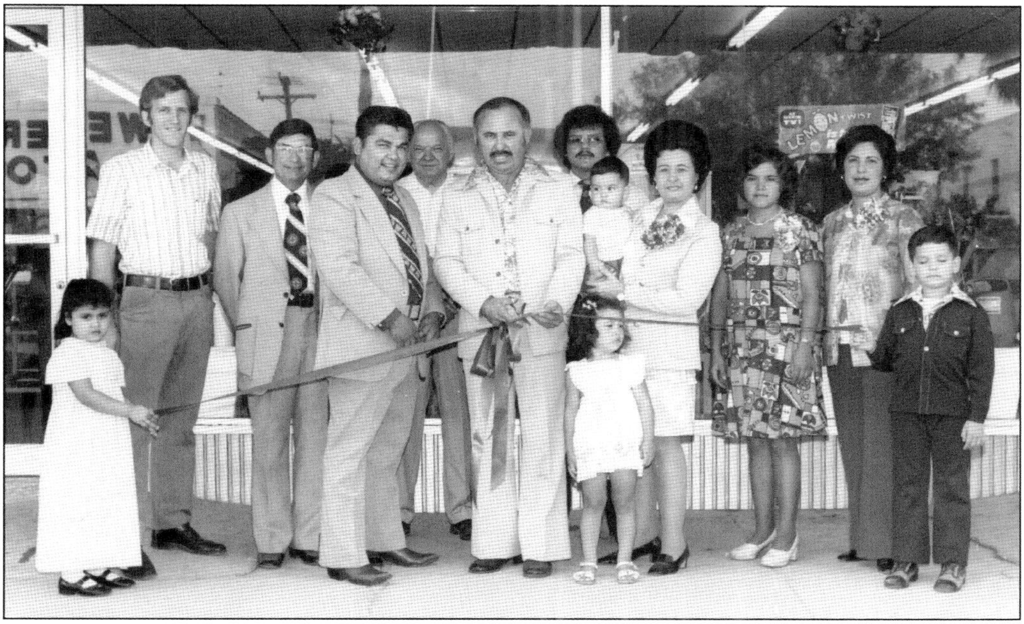

The ribbon cutting for the opening of Mark's Five and Ten in April 1976 was heavily anticipated. Pictured here from left to right are L. Sondra Alaniz, Fr. Bob Wright OMI, Bill Lemen, Mario Alaniz, Bill Bormann, Lalo Arcaute, Hector Hernandez, Lisa Alaniz, Oralia Alaniz (holding Mark Alaniz, for whom the store is named), Imelda Garza, Aida Aguilar, and Mario Alaniz II. (Courtesy of Mario Alaniz.)

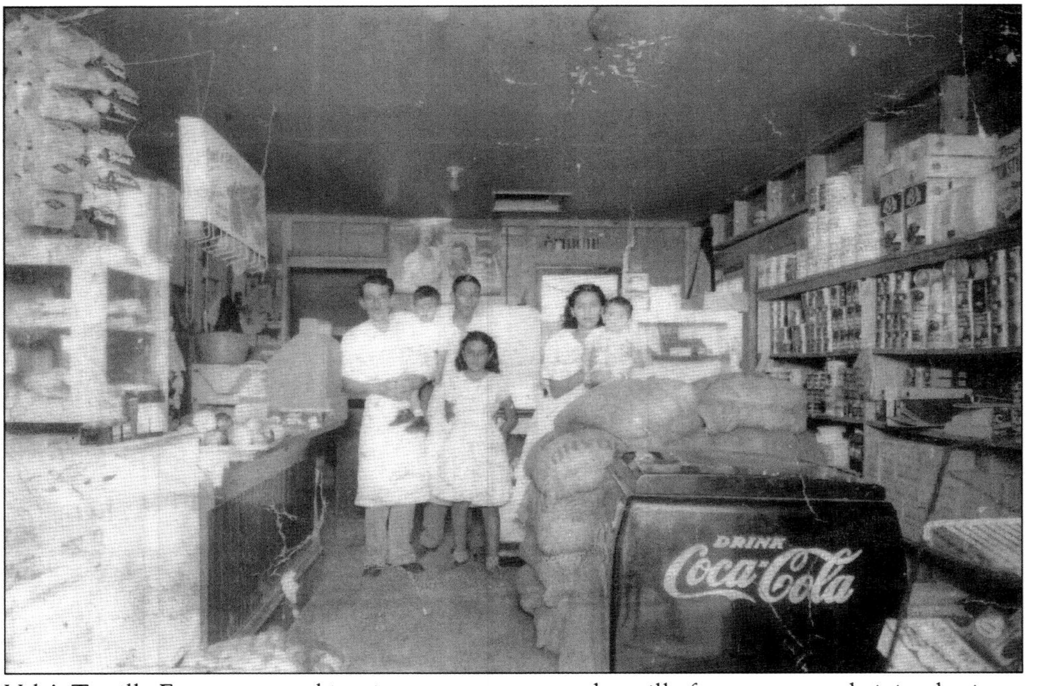

Vela's Tortilla Factory, a combination grocery store and tortilla factory, was a thriving business as seen in this January 1950 photograph. The store opened in 1948, and after an unfortunate accident forced its closure in 1954, it never reopened. In this photograph from left to right are Manuel Vela Sr. holding son Manuel Jr., Porfirio Trevino, Eva De Los Santos, and Cipriana M. Vela holding Juanita Vela. (Courtesy of Manuel Vela Jr.)

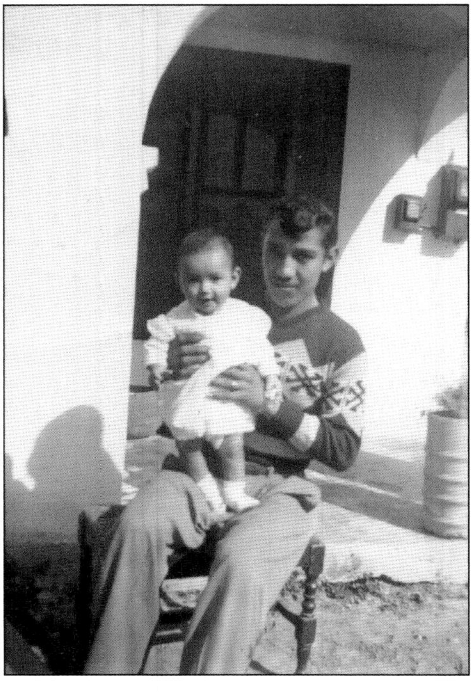

Gilbert Garcia, local neighborhood barber, is shown here with his baby sister Estela Garcia Salazar sitting on his lap in 1951. Garcia had his barbershop on West Railroad Street for over 25 years. Known as quite a prankster, he was always fun to be around and always had a joke to tell. (Courtesy of Estela Salazar.)

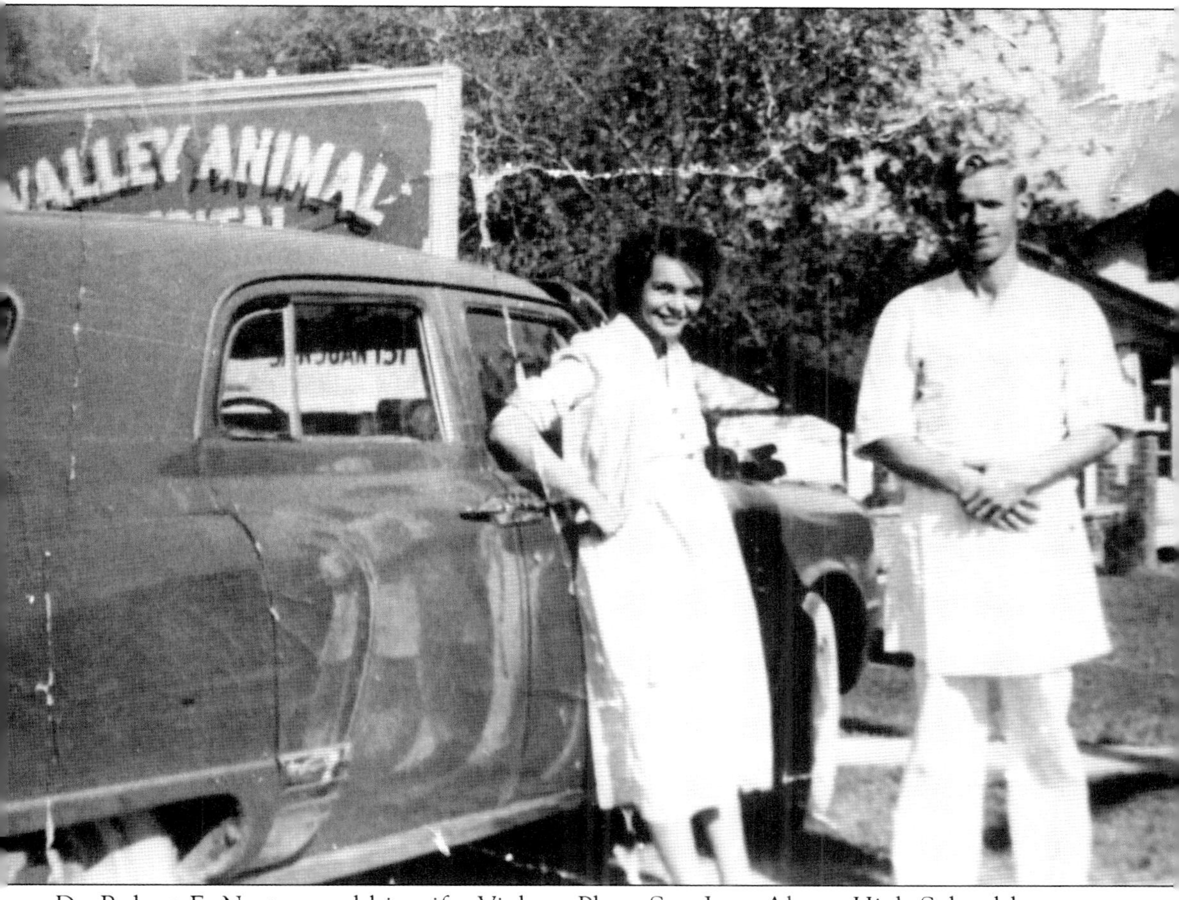

Dr. Robert E. Norton and his wife, Viola, a Pharr-San Juan-Alamo High School home economics teacher, pose in front of the Valley Animal Hospital in 1949. Dr. Norton held his veterinarian business on Railroad Street in San Juan for four years before moving it to Pharr in 1950. Dr. Norton arrived in San Juan in 1946 from Iowa and recalls a very welcome reception by the locals upon his arrival. Residents were anxious to have veterinarian services available to them, and he immediately developed a long list of customers. Dr. Norton has been a loyal member of the San Juan Lions Club for many years, boasting a perfect attendance record. He has been a valued Hidalgo County historian and was instrumental in the preservation of the Hidalgo Pumphouse. (Courtesy of Dr. Robert E. Norton.)

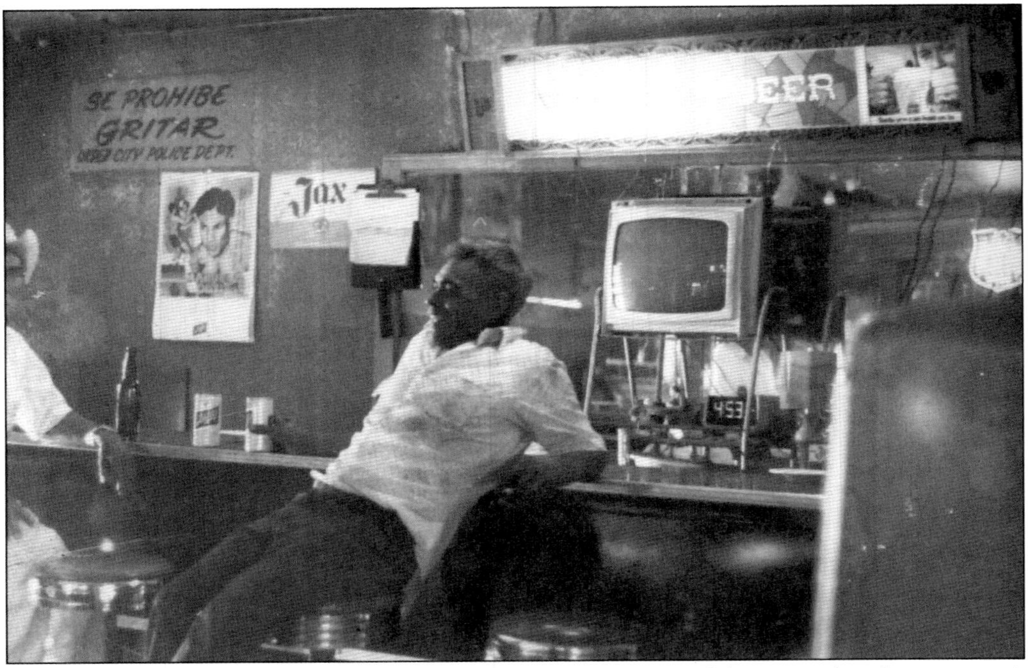

Trevino's Lounge on Nebraska Street, shown here in 1976, served for many decades as a man's watering hole. Today the recently refurbished Trevino's features plenty of great rock and blues music alongside whatever is on tap for both the young and the young at heart. Early in San Juan's history, it was called Ben's Place, and it was the first cantina in town. (Courtesy of Dr. Felipe Alanis.)

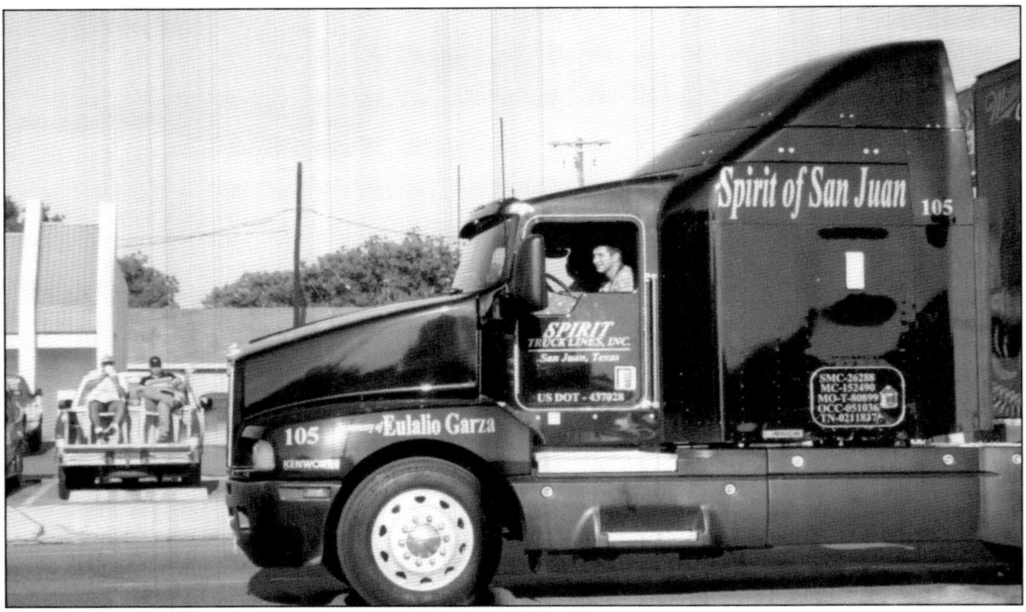

Spirit Trucking, a major logistics company located on Earling Road in San Juan, travels the highways throughout the entire United States. Initially started by the oldest Garza brother, Raul, the company expanded to include his brothers Leonel, David, Johnny, and Ramiro Garza, who share duties in its operation. (Courtesy of Spirit Trucking.)

Four

Education and Religion

Education and religious enlightenment have historically been pillars upon which communities have been built. Early San Juan boasted fine schools and wonderful places of worship. San Juan Plantation built a small church called St. John the Baptist down by the river. It also had a schoolhouse where local children were educated. As the town blossomed, so did its amenities.

The People's Covenant Church, for example, held its first service on the steps of the original wood frame structure of the San Juan Hotel in 1911. Missionaries from the Lutheran church began serving the Mexican community as early as 1919, while the Methodist church was established in 1923 and the Baptist church in 1938. Inspired by San Juan Plantation's earlier church, the Oblates of Mary Immaculate dedicated the second St. John the Baptist Catholic Church, a small wooden chapel located on the northeast corner of Second and Nebraska Streets. Opened with much fanfare in 1954, the third St. John the Baptist Catholic Church suffered a fiery plane crash in 1970, making way for the existing Basilica of Our Lady of San Juan del Valle National Shrine, completed in 1980.

Along with the religious community came the need for educational institutions. As more settlers came, a local resident named Mr. Stevens became the town's teacher. Children were also educated within local residents' homes. On the north side of town, Amanda Garza Peña and Santiago Alanis taught classes at the Mexican school on the southwest corner of Second and Nebraska Streets. On Third and Lincoln Streets, Lilia Vasquez rented a small wooden home as a school for the African American children in town. Later the public Sorensen School emerged on the south side of town and the Vida N. Clover School on the north side.

Built in 1915, the Pharr-San Juan High School graduated nine students in its 1917 first class. Alamo was included in the district in 1919 to form the current PSJA School District. Dr. Felipe Alanis made his native San Juan proud when he became Texas commissioner of education.

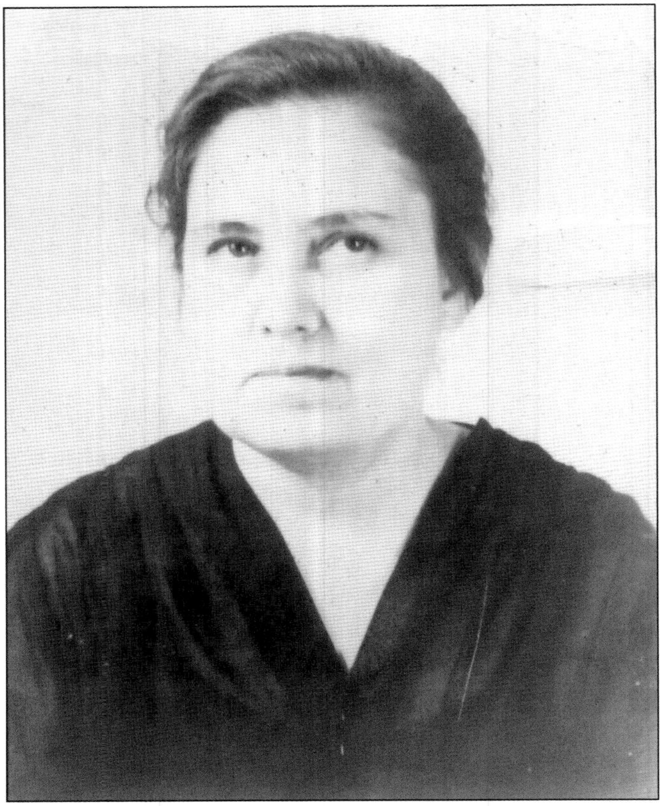

Amanda Garza Peña and her family were early Valley pioneers, arriving in San Juan from Chihuahua, Mexico, in 1920. Coming from a family of merchants and educators, she opened a private one-room, one-teacher school and conducted classes in Spanish for over 40 years, covering all subjects from mathematics to geography. The Amanda Garza Peña Elementary School in San Juan was named in her honor. (Courtesy of Alicia Salinas.)

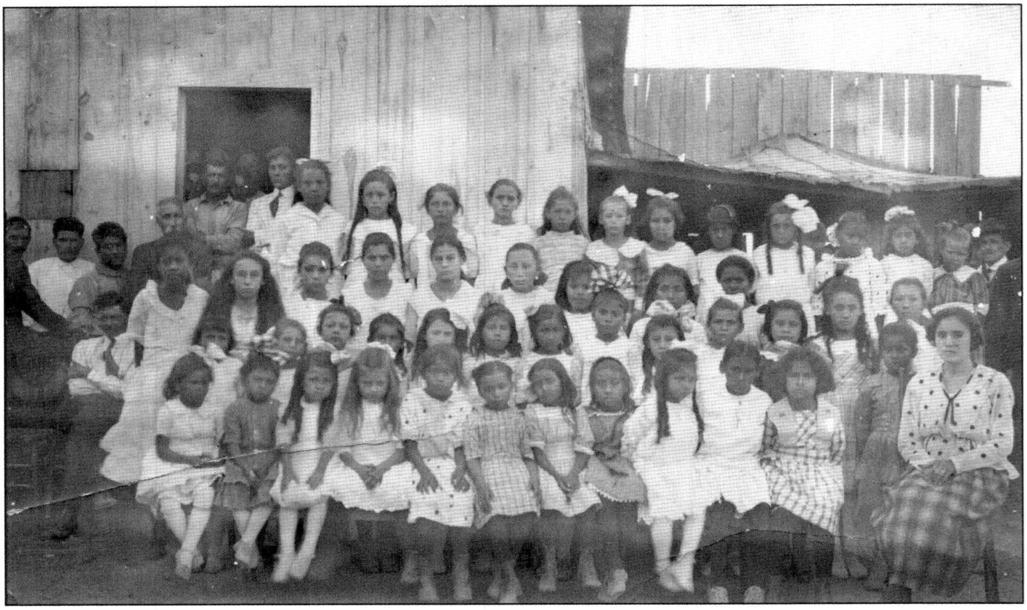

Teacher Amanda Garza-Pena (front right) played a major role in the education of San Juan children. This photograph shows her class of girls from the Mexican School in 1918. (Courtesy of Manuela T. Alanis.)

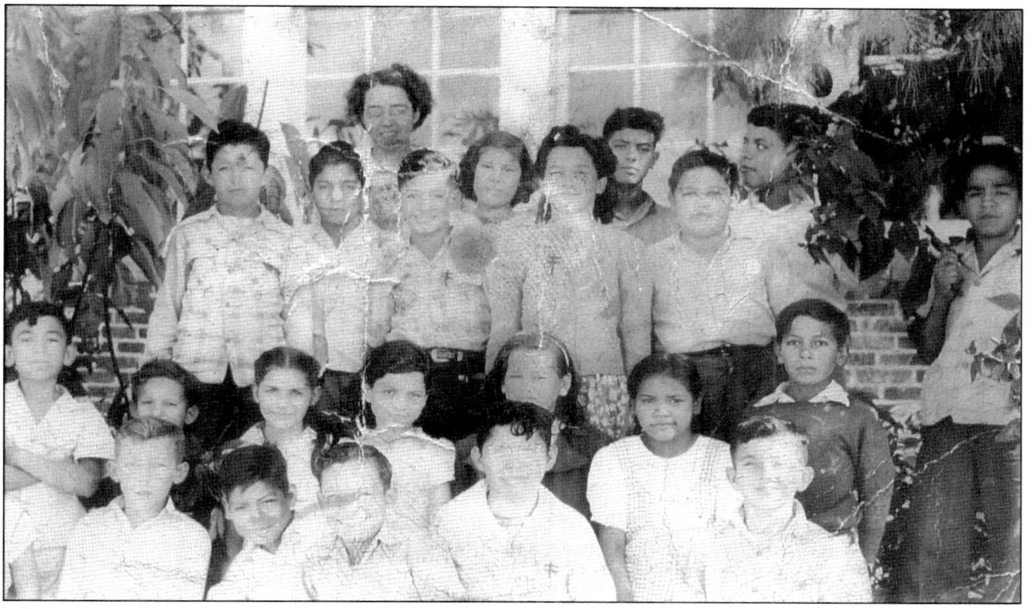

This is Mary Ester Mahaffay and her class from the North San Juan School. From left to right they are (first row) Humberto Gonzalez, Gavino Castillo, Henry Guzman, Chuy Garza, and unidentified; (second row) Leonardo ?, unidentified, Elia Jackson, Hilda Paz, Florencia Garza, Maria Espinosa, and Porfirio Trevino; (third row) Chabelo Quintanilla, Fidencio Martinez, Miss Mahaffay, Ruben Morin, Anita Bravo, Candicia Aguilar, Placido Leija, Naftaly ?, Marcelino Solis, and Ismael Guerra. (Courtesy of Estella Rojas.)

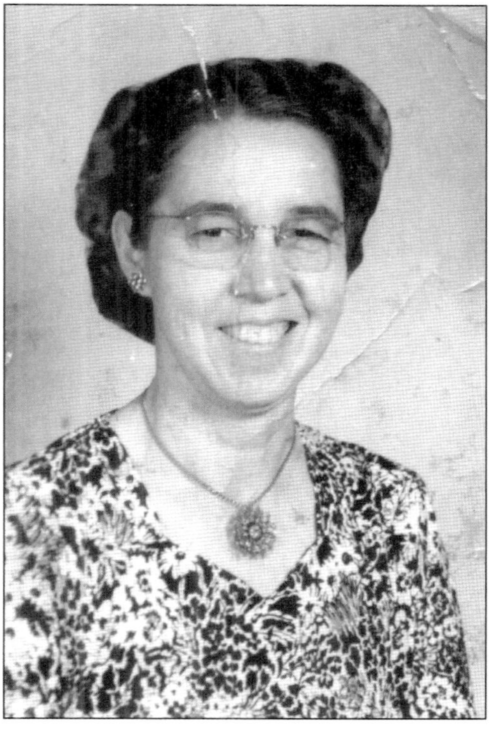

Mary Ester Mahaffay was a teacher at the Vida N. Clover School. She was the niece of Dr. Ira Mahaffay, an osteopathic physician who came to San Juan in 1907. She taught in the Pharr-San Juan-Alamo Independent School District for 36 years. (Courtesy of Agustin and Elodia Treviño.)

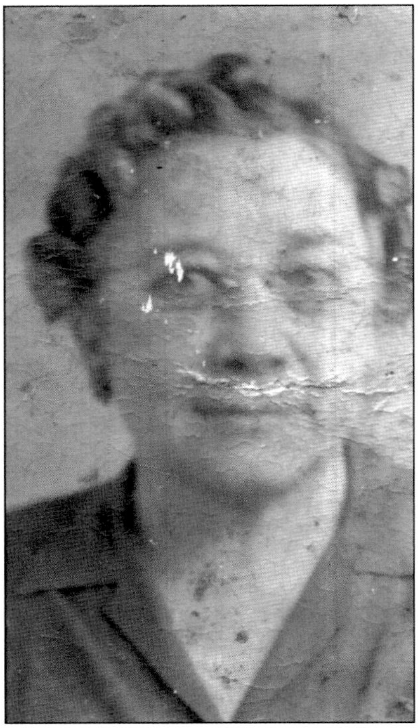

Vida N. Clover moved from Nebraska to Texas in 1916 and taught in a school in Peñitas. Then she worked for the Pharr-San Juan-Alamo School District for 33 years as a teacher and a principal. In 1927, she became principal at the North San Juan School, and in 1950 the same school was named in her honor. (Courtesy of Agustin and Elodia Treviño.)

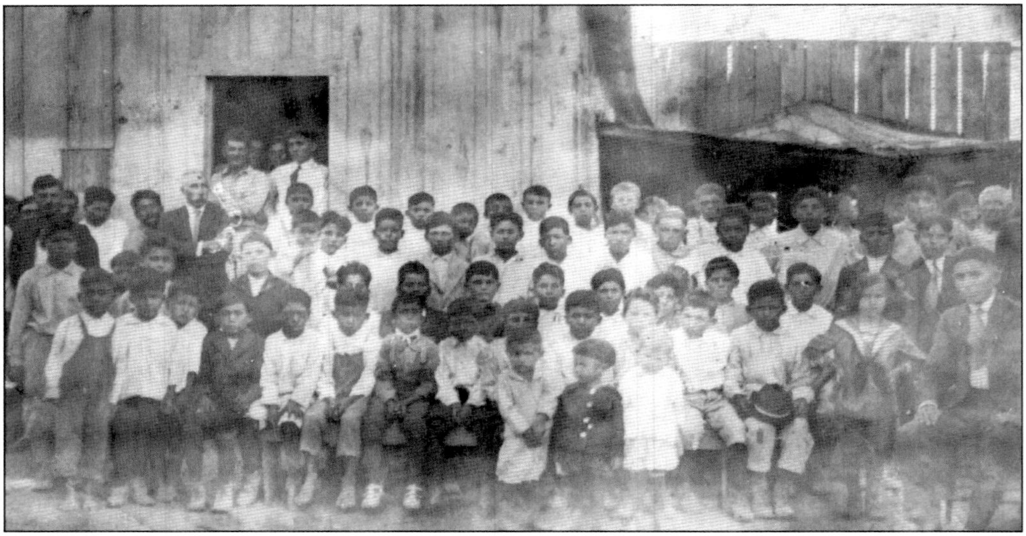

Santiago Alanis served as a teacher of the boys at the Mexican School. He emigrated from Mexico to San Juan as a young teenager in 1917. Although he had a limited education himself, his appetite for knowledge was very strong. He believed that the way to a better life was through education and instilled those values in his family and other members of the community. (Courtesy of Dr. Felipe Alanis.)

Pharr-San Juan's first high school class of 1917 graduated nine students, pictured here with the superintendent. From left to right they are (first row) Lou Piper, Lillian Thompson (Rowson), superintendent R. B. Fore, Nellie Shulze (Gunther), and J. Floyd Hetrick; (second row) Arthur Reichert, Vera Martin, Earl Hancock, Maybelle Hancock (Hetrick), and Roy Allen. (Courtesy of Joe Hetrick.)

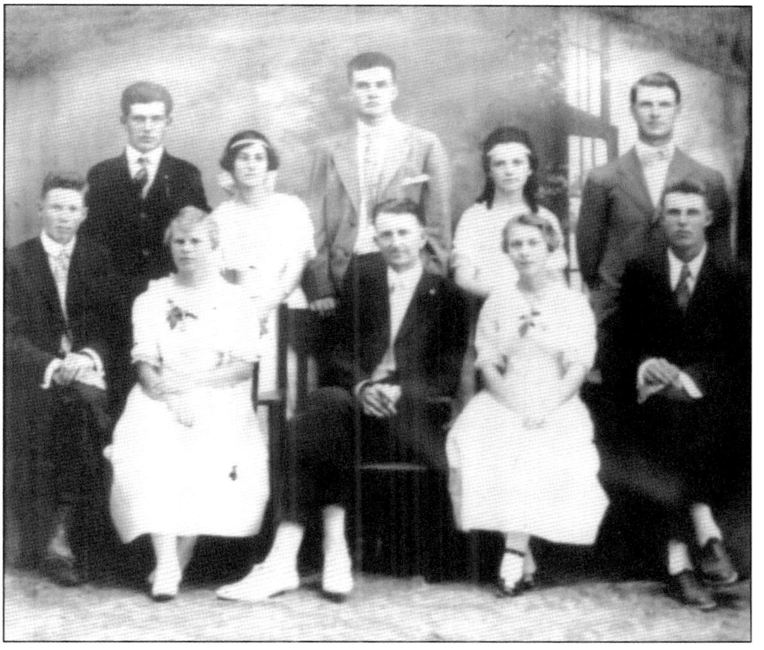

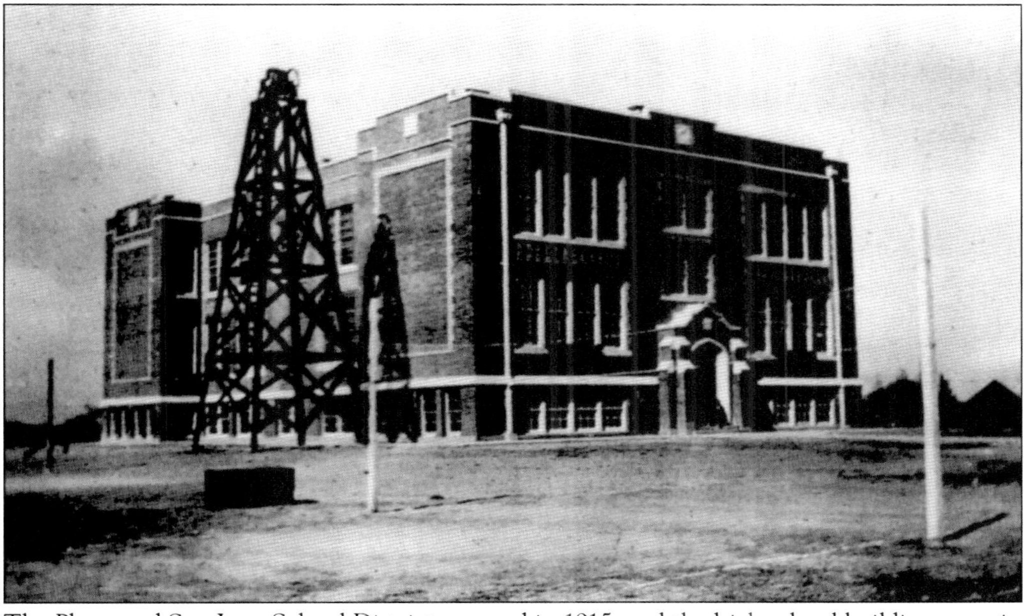

The Pharr and San Juan School Districts merged in 1915, and the high school building, seen in this photograph, was completed in 1915 at a cost of $40,000. Considered very modern for its time, it had domestic art and science laboratories as well as physics and chemistry laboratories. The doors to this school opened in the fall of 1916 with 143 children enrolled. (Courtesy of Hidalgo County Historical Commission.)

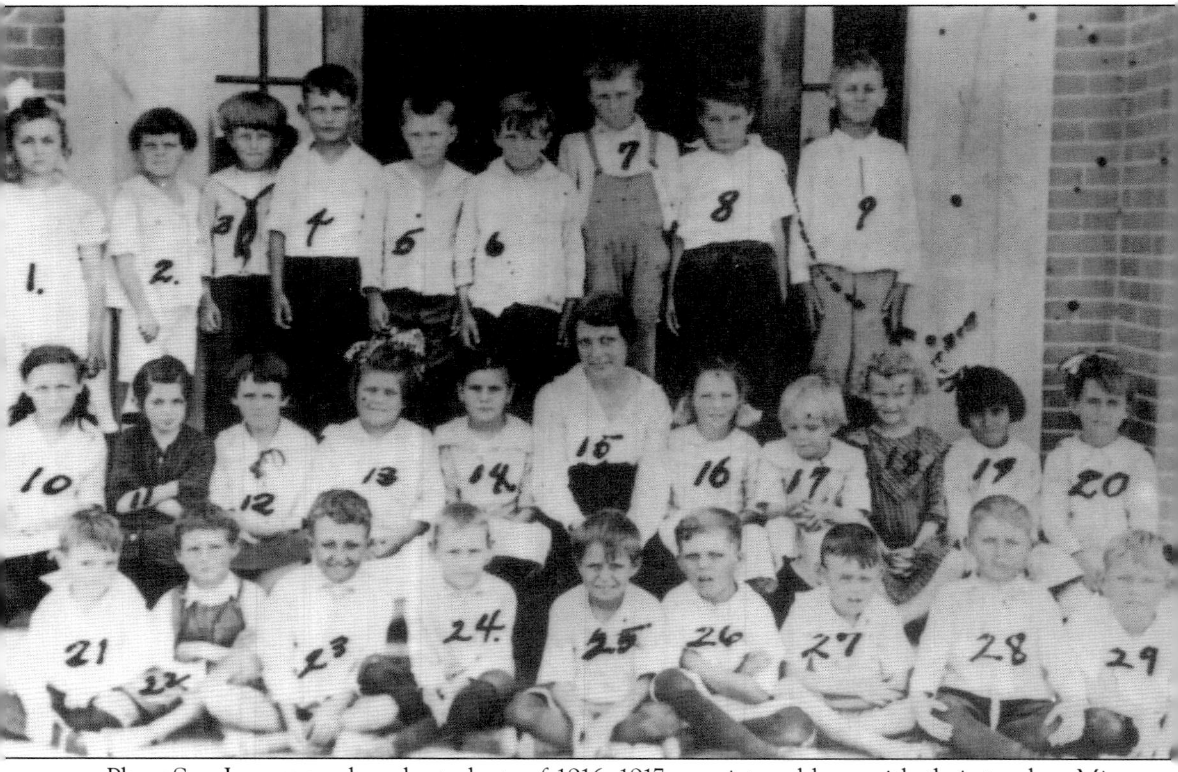

Pharr-San Juan second grade students of 1916–1917 are pictured here with their teacher, Miss Osborn. From left to right they are (first row) Carl Evans, Billy Pew, James Forsythe, Forrest Smith, Jack Piper, Maurice Boyer, Harold Schafroth, Morris Kelso, and Sam Hamilton; (second row) Helen Boss, Florence Griffith, Fern Fox, Doris Hecox, Hazel Lovett, Miss Ester Osborn, Alice Clark, Mary Ellen Savage, Maggie Bellamy, and the Norris sisters; (third row) Helen Cooper, Edwin Hancock, Rollin Swiebert, Arthur Glow, Eugene Thomas, unknown, George Slayton, Alex Voss, and Lyle Bellemy. (Courtesy of Robert D. Schafroth.)

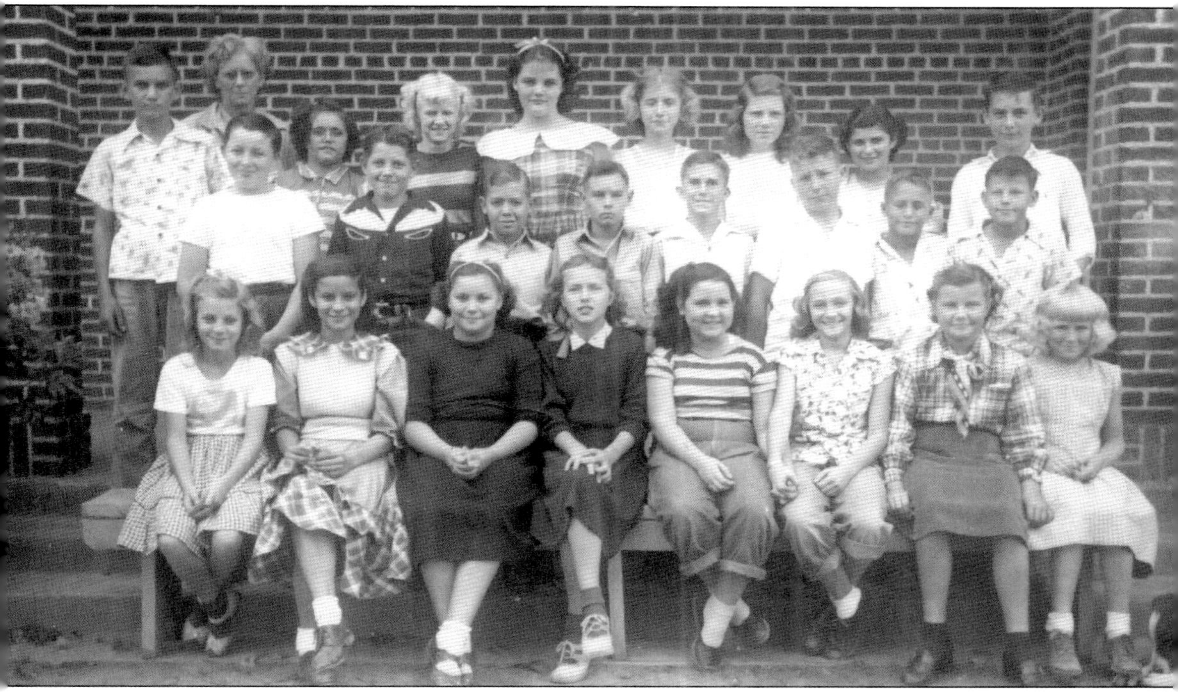

Members of the sixth-grade class of Sorensen School in 1949, are, from left to right, (first row) Annie Hickman, Carolyn Southerland, Patsy Edgermon, Delores Bartley, Maxine Prine, Elizabeth Borman, Barbara Leeper, and Sue Davis; (second row) Bobby Chaney, unidentified, ? Wilcox, Phillip ?, Robert Deal, Bobby Hill, David Vessels, and Charles Brasfield; (third row) Royal Millen, unknown, Gay Davis, Karen Davies, Judy DeMange, Edna Wisdom, Wanda Edgermon, and John Ward; (fourth row) class teacher Mrs. Woodruff. (Courtesy of Sue Stevenson.)

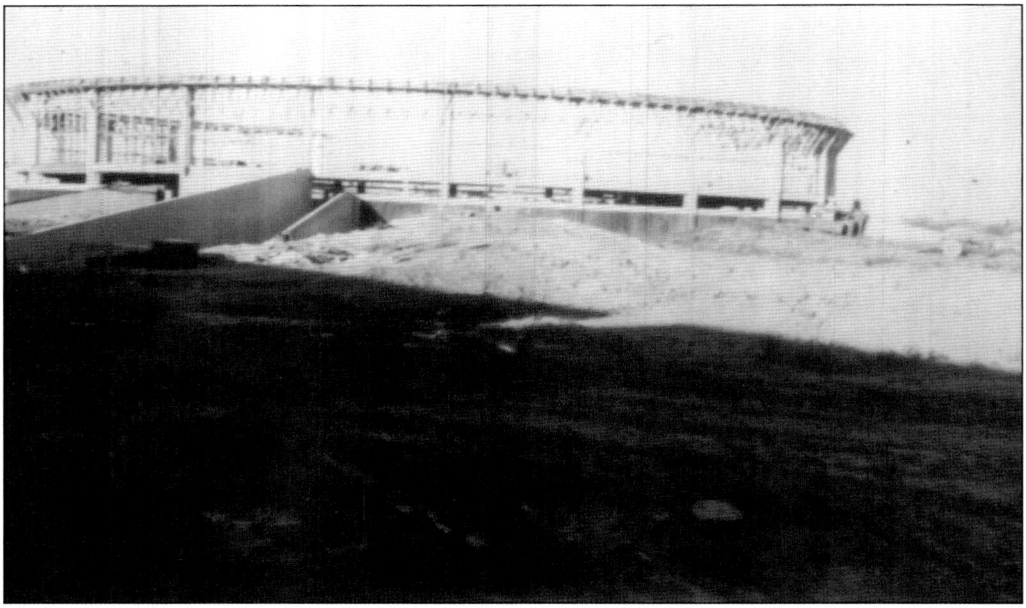

The Pharr-San Juan-Alamo Independent School District built a new high school on South I Road in 1960. These two photographs show the ground-breaking ceremony below and the construction stage of the new gymnasium above. The new campus was designed to include an auditorium, a gymnasium, agriculture shops, a music building and a power plant building. The *San Juan Sentinel* reported on April 14, 1960, that this new high school would be built for a cost of $1.2 million. Pictured below are Wayne Muir, kneeling, and then standing in front from left to right Verne Carlson, superintendent Newell O'Dell, Marvin Kautsch, Paul Kruse, and Gene Darby Jr. (Both courtesy Dr. Robert E. Norton.)

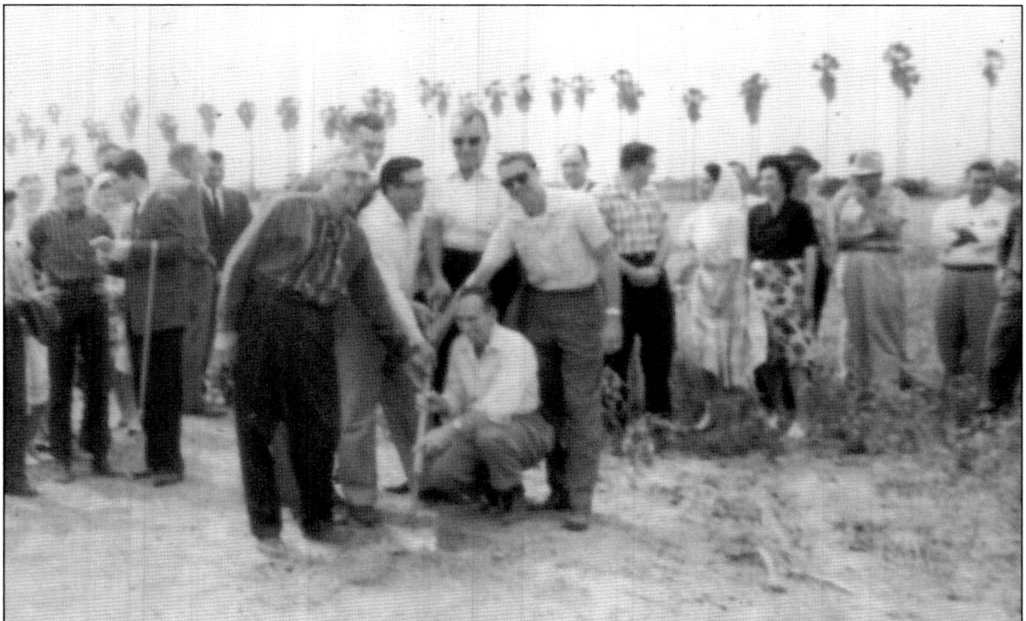

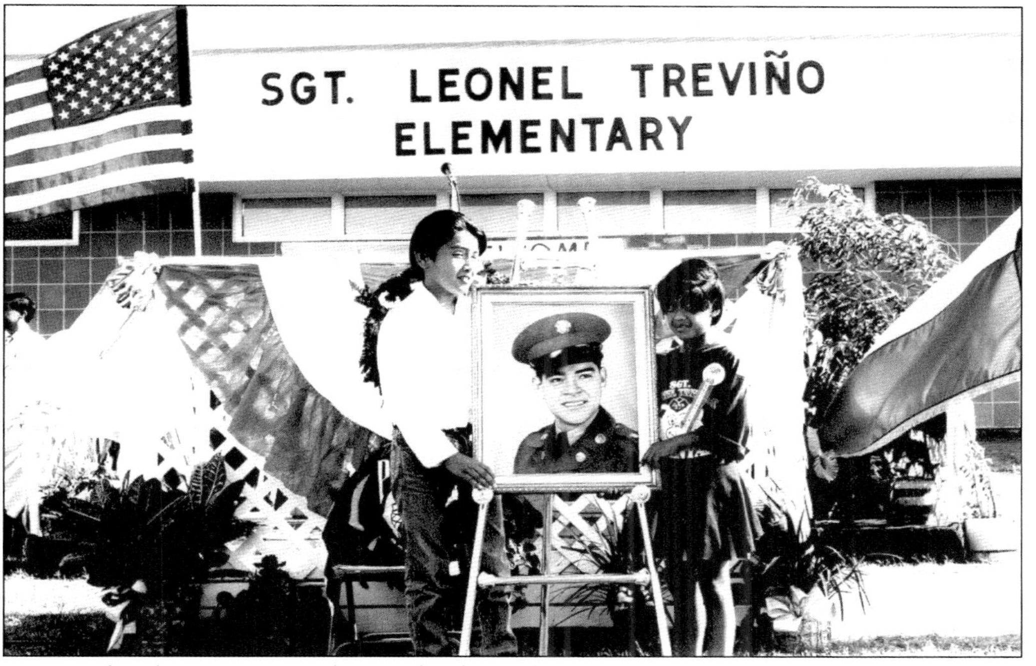

In 1994, the Pharr-San Juan-Alamo School Board paid tribute to Sgt. Leonel Treviño, a former Korean War prisoner of war, by naming an elementary school after him. (Courtesy of Agustin and Elodia Treviño.)

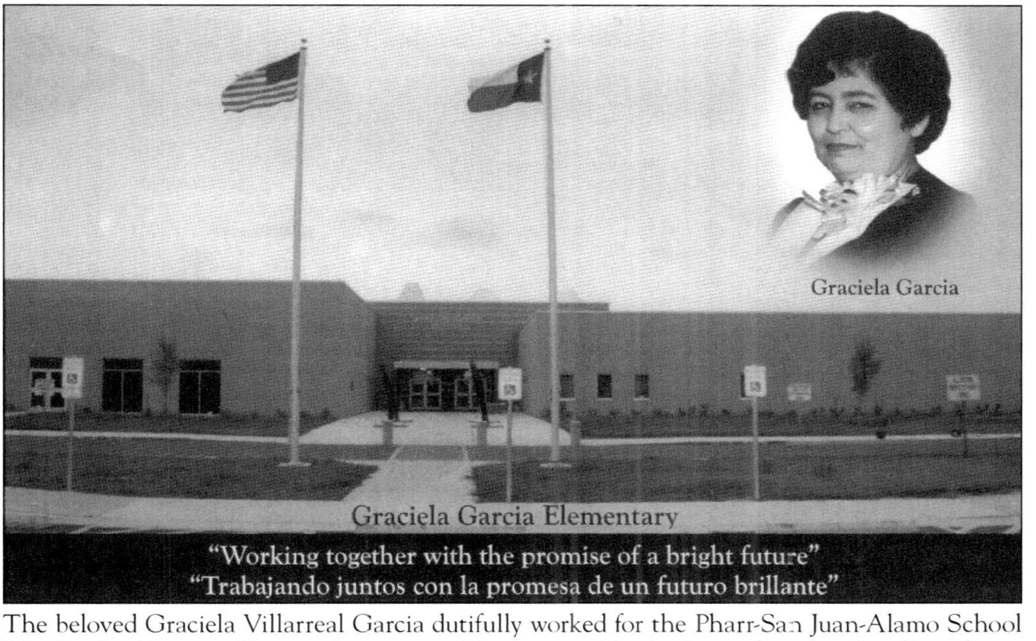

The beloved Graciela Villarreal Garcia dutifully worked for the Pharr-San Juan-Alamo School District for 40 years. Her passion was working to provide the best education for all students, including indigent ones, as a high school Spanish teacher and as the district Title I programs director. After her death in 2001, the school district named a school in her honor in Las Milpas. (Courtesy of Sylvia Prado Sandoval.)

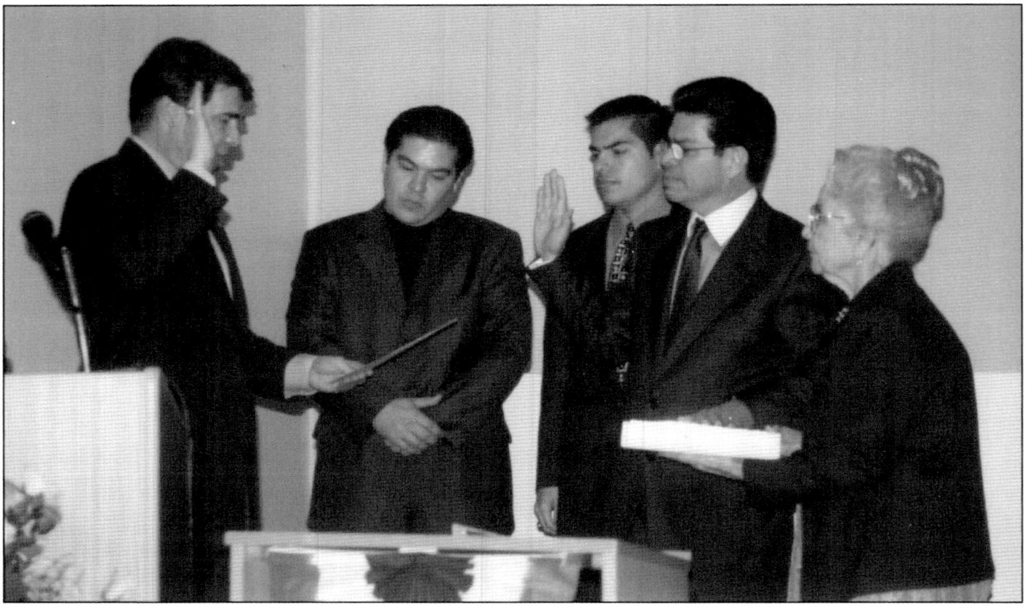

On March 26, 2002, San Juan native Dr. Felipe Alanis was sworn in as the commissioner of education for the state of Texas. Gov. Rick Perry performs the ceremony while Dr. Alanis's mother, Manuela T. Alanis, holds the bible. Dr. Alanis has vowed to make sure South Texas schools achieve excellence in education. Also pictured here are Felipe E. (Philip) Alanis (second from left) and Marco Alanis. (Courtesy of Manuela T. Alanis.)

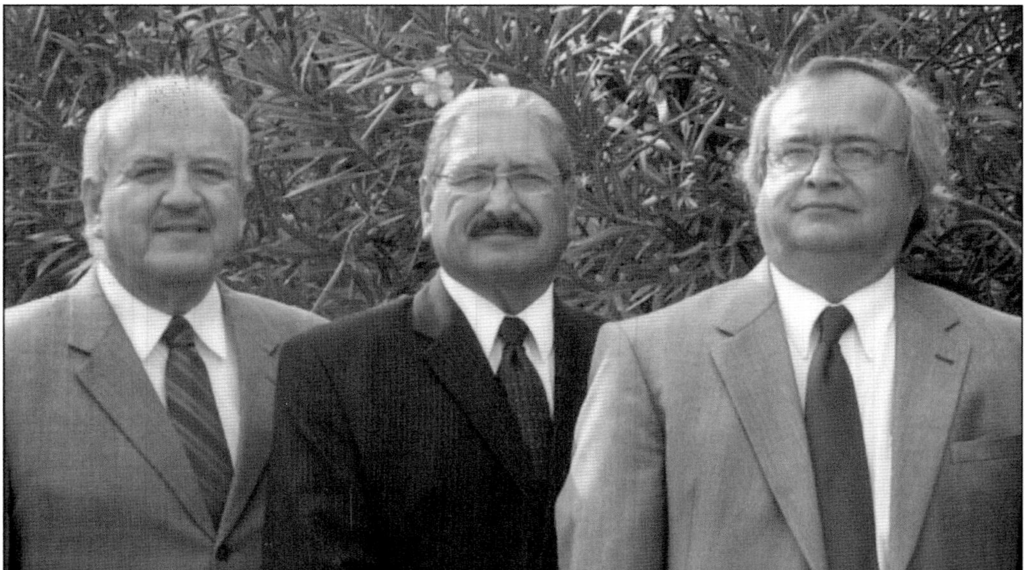

San Juan natives serving as superintendents of area school districts include, from left to right, Roberto Loredo (former San Juan mayor and current Donna School superintendent), Arturo Guajardo (former San Juan mayor and Pharr-San Juan-Alamo School District superintendent), and Dr. Fernando Castillo (former Pharr-San Juan-Alamo School Board member and current Progresso School District superintendent). (Courtesy of Dr. Fernando Castillo.)

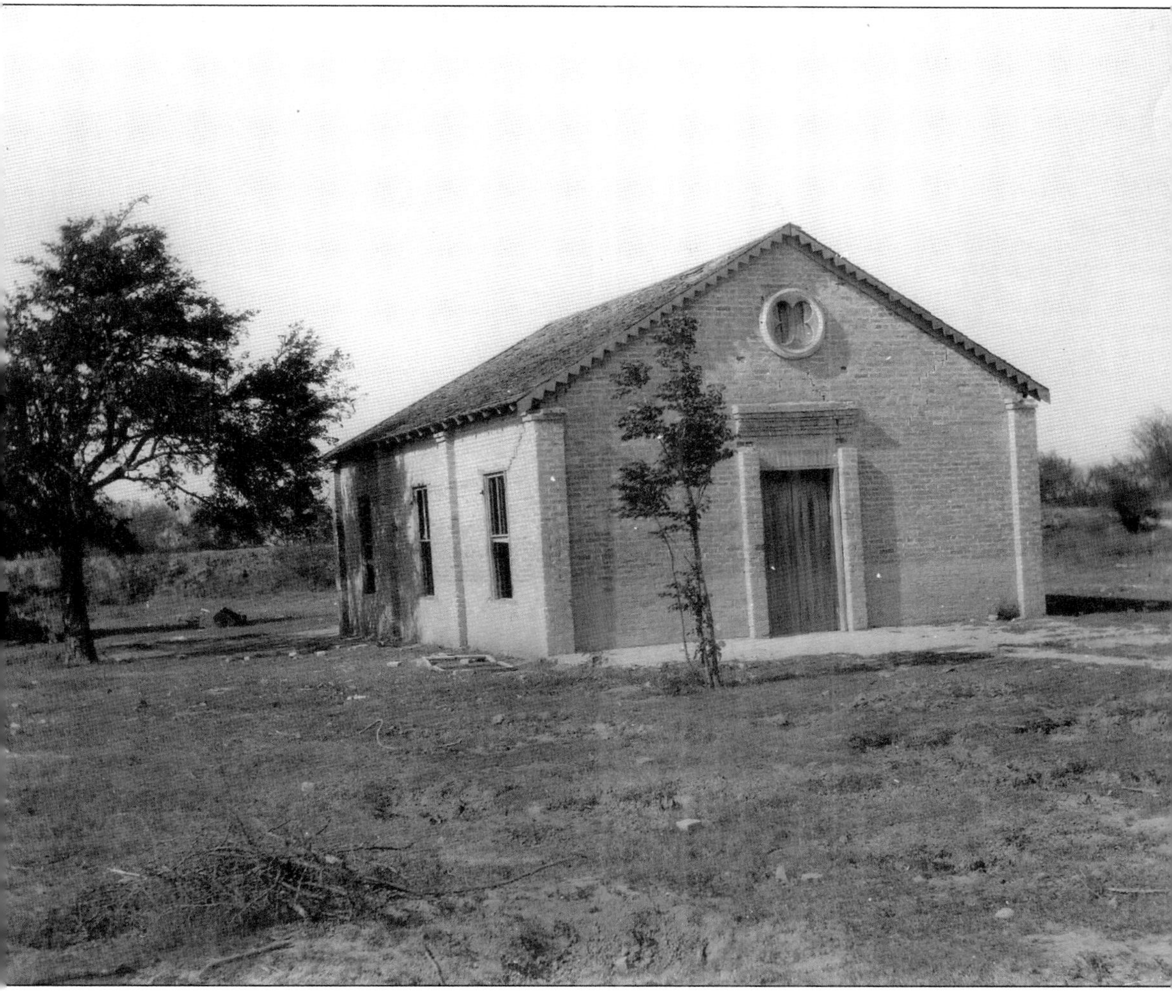

In 1908, John Closner built a small wooden chapel close to the river on the grounds of his San Juan Plantation. The Oblates of Mary Immaculate (OMI) priests dedicated it to St. John the Baptist. The chapel no longer stands today and can only be identified by a small corner of the building left in the brush. The OMI priests and brothers who were stationed in Brownsville at the time traveled throughout the Rio Grande Valley along the Oblate Trail (now called Military Highway) and established churches and missions along the way. This chapel photograph was taken in 1928. (Courtesy of Southwestern Oblate Historical Archives, San Antonio, Texas.)

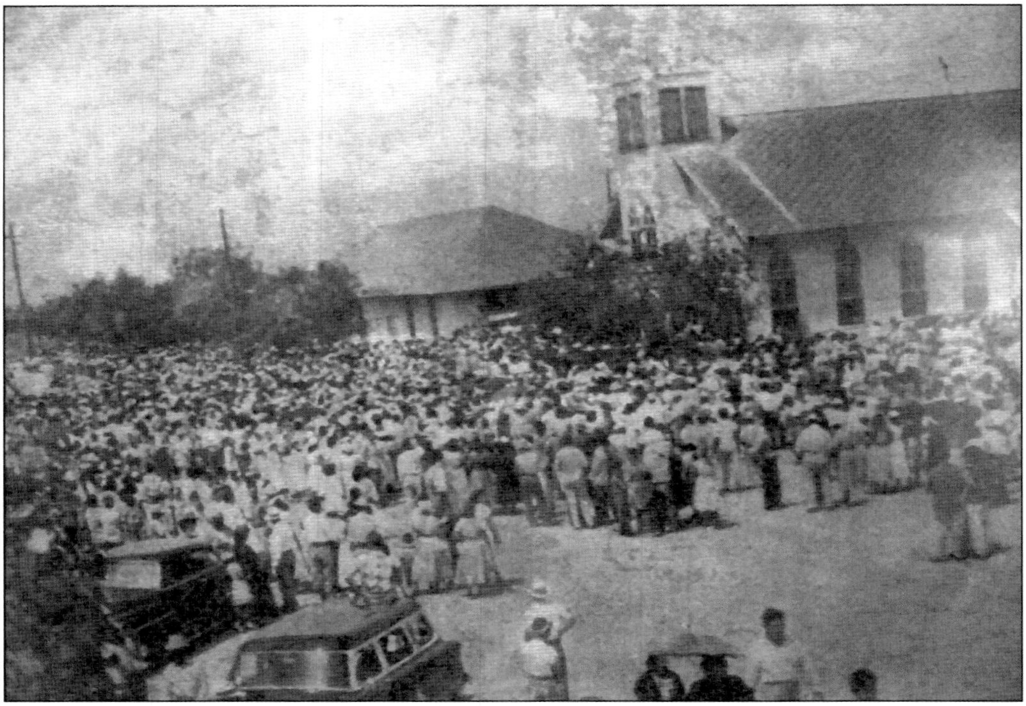

A new wooden chapel was built within the new town site of San Juan in 1925 as a re-creation of the San Juan Plantation chapel. Also named St. John the Baptist, this small structure stood on the corner of Second and Nebraska Streets. This chapel now stands in Lopezville. (Courtesy of Basilica of Our Lady of San Juan Del Valle National Shrine Archives.)

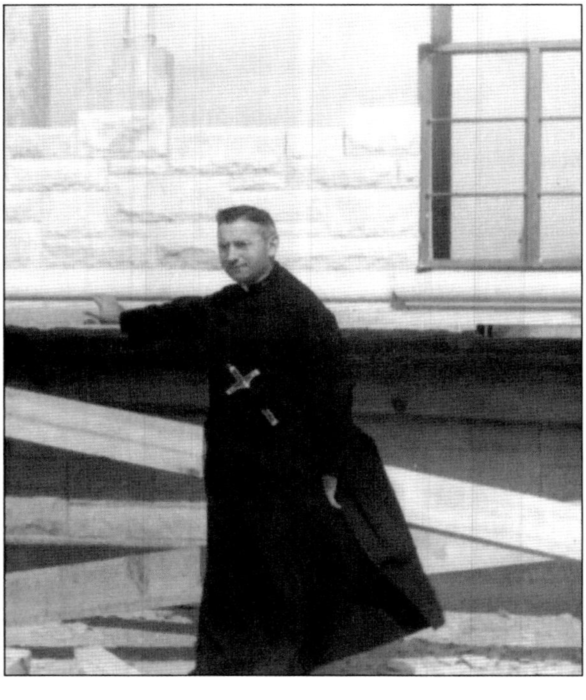

In 1948, Fr. Jose Azpiazu traveled to San Juan de los Lagos in Mexico with two members of the church choir to find a statue of Our Lady of San Juan to bring back to his congregation. The statue was officially blessed and placed inside the San Juan Chapel in December 1948 for the adoration of parishioners. (Courtesy Our Lady of San Juan Del Valle National Shrine Archives.)

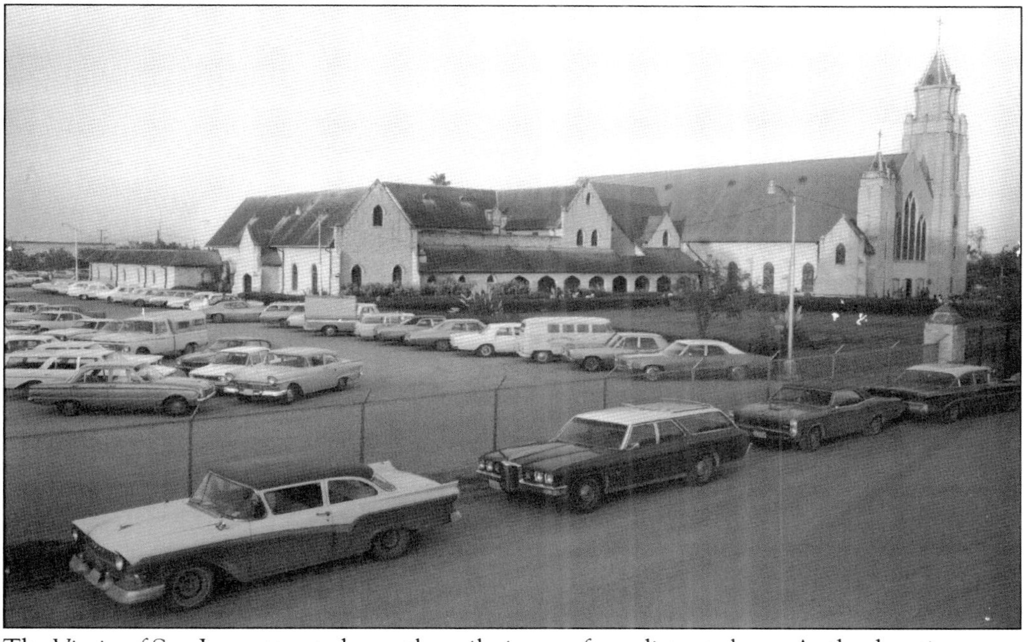

The Virgin of San Juan attracted countless pilgrimages from distant places. As the devotion grew, Fr. Jose Azpiazu was inspired to build a beautiful new shrine a few blocks north of the chapel, which would be dedicated to the Virgin of San Juan. On May 2, 1954, some 60,000 pilgrims turned out to witness the dedication of their new shrine, shown in the photograph above. Tragically a local pilot deliberately flew his plane into the shrine on October 23, 1970, destroying all but the tower that still stands today as seen in the photograph below. Miraculously no one inside the church was hurt and the statue of the Virgin of San Juan was unharmed. Plans for a new shrine began as pilgrims continued their travels to visit the shrine. The statue was placed in the parish cafeteria until the new shrine was built. (Both courtesy of Basilica of Our Lady of San Juan Del Valle National Shrine Archives.)

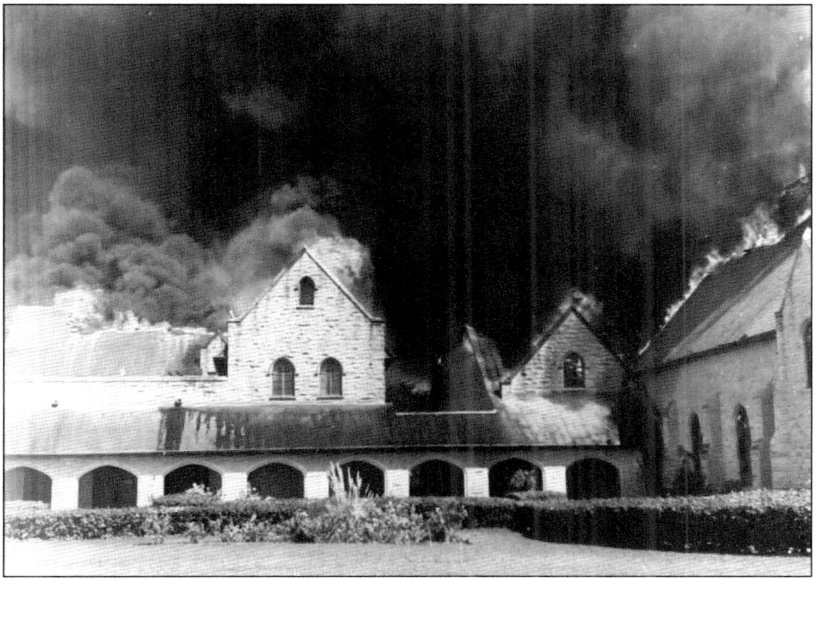

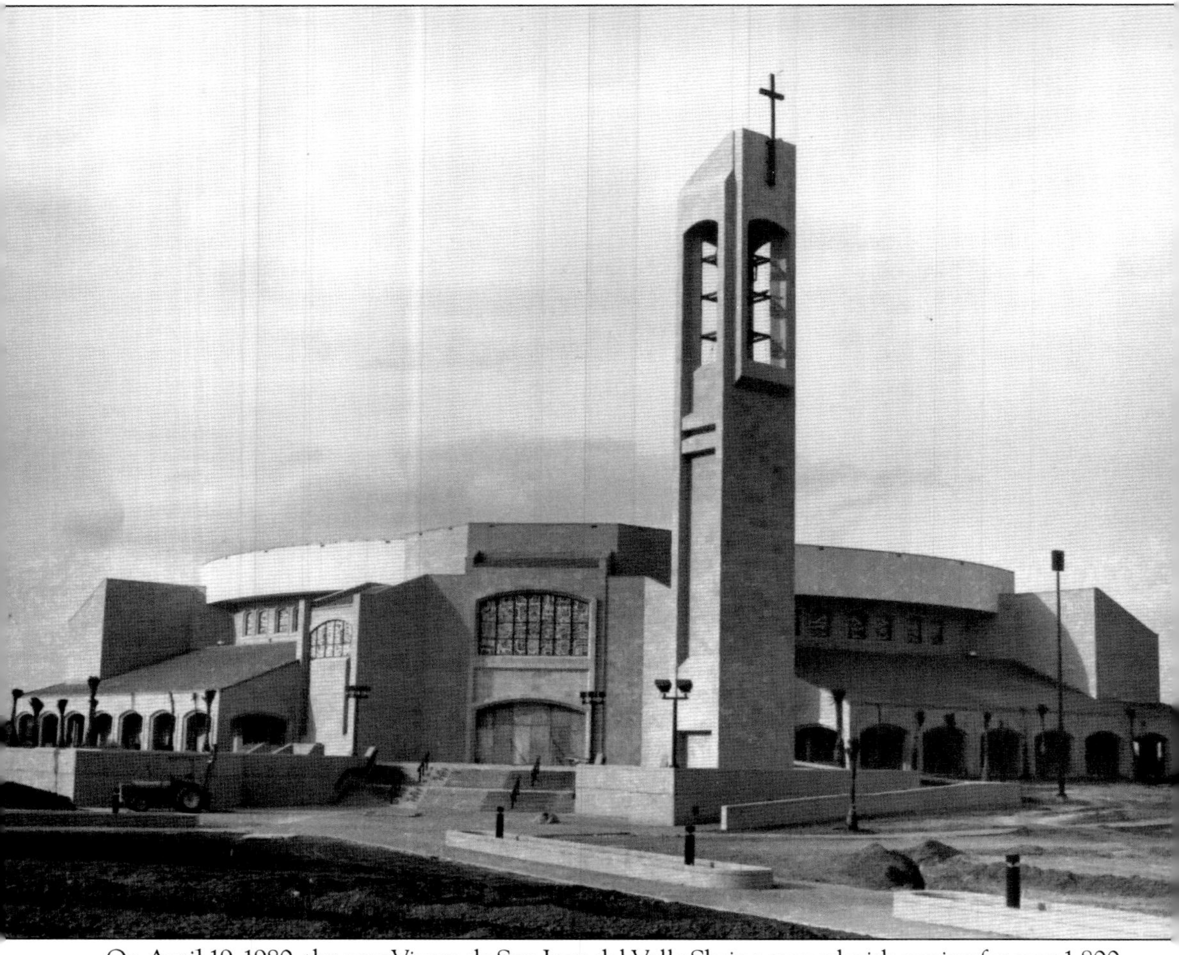

On April 19, 1980, the new Virgen de San Juan del Valle Shrine opened with seating for over 1,800. In 1998, it was designated as a national shine, and in 1999 it was honored as a basilica. Officially it is now called Basilica of Our Lady of San Juan Del Valle—National Shrine. Each weekend, the basilica welcomes over 25,000 visitors who come to adore the Virgin and to participate in religious services. Distinctive as one of three basilicas in the state of Texas, this complex is also one of three national shrines located in Texas as well. Worshipers can also enjoy a 3/4-mile path around the basilica grounds that includes beautiful, life-size bronze statues representing the Stations of the Cross. (Courtesy of Basilica of Our Lady of San Juan Del Valle National Shrine Archives.)

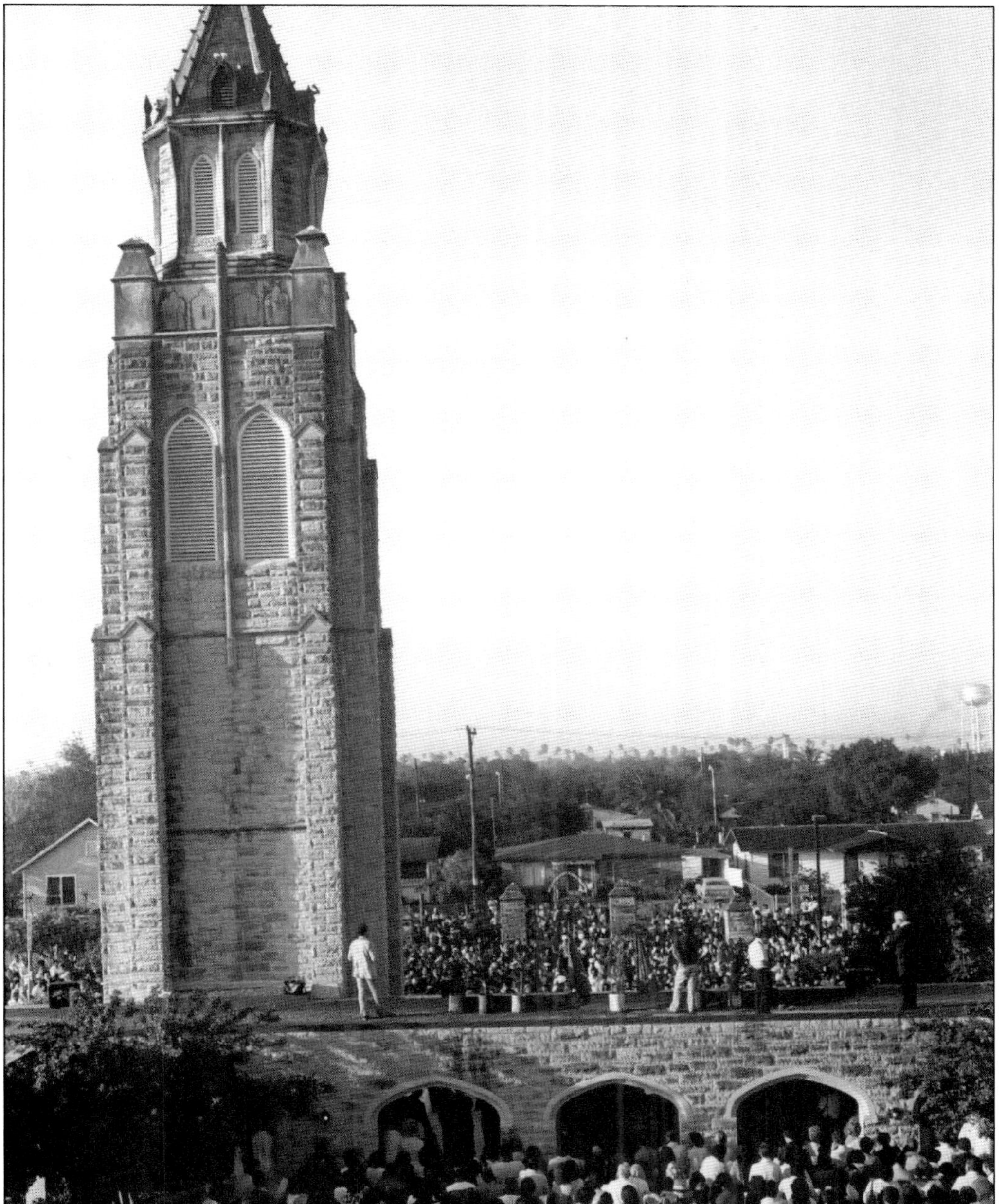

As a symbol of strength and fortitude, the tower of the original shrine built in 1954 still stands high in the courtyard just south of the basilica. In April 1980, thousands of devoted worshipers filled the courtyard in order to be present to witness the opening of the Virgen de San Juan del Valle Shrine. Proud San Juan residents and community leaders stood alongside many others from all over the world who came to share in the overwhelming experience of adoration and joy. (Courtesy of Basilica of Our Lady of San Juan Del Valle National Shrine Archives.)

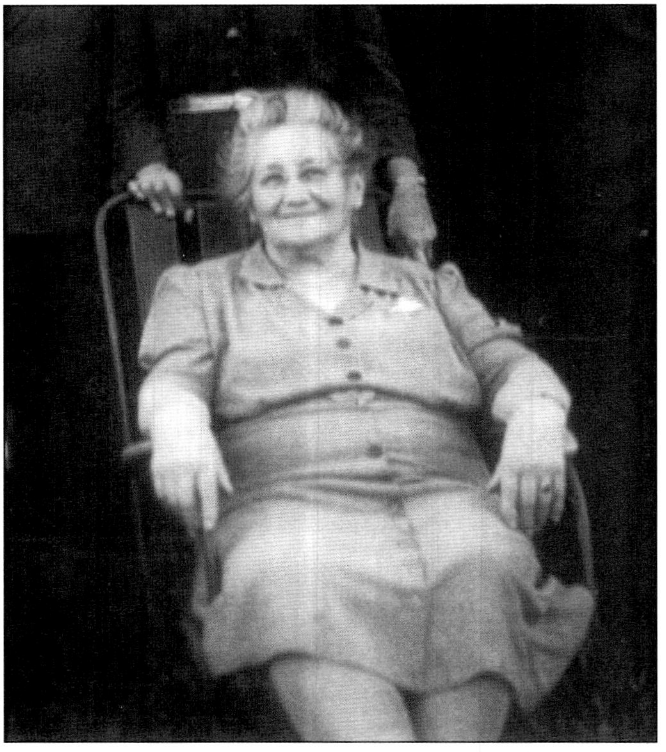

Laura Mellenbruch began her mission work with the Mexican population in San Juan in 1919. She held Sunday school classes on her porch while one of the children would translate. She would knock on doors in the community, spreading her ministry and inspiring neighborhood families to the Lutheran church to worship. (Courtesy of Jane Mellenbruch Hinkle.)

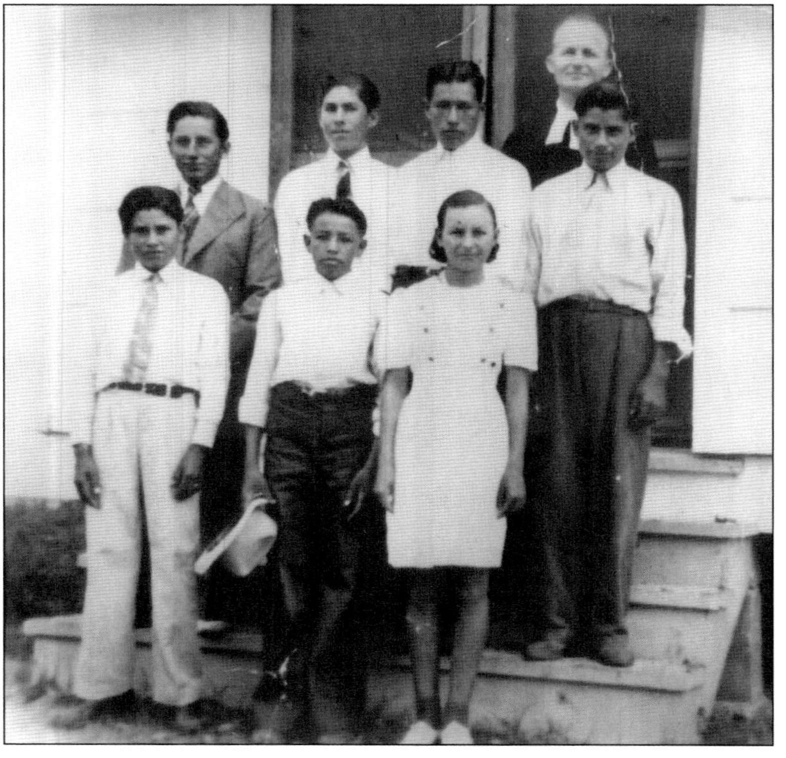

Reverend Koehler was one of the ministers sent to study religion, to teach the laypeople, and to serve the growing congregation of St. John Lutheran Church. He is pictured here with the following members of his Sunday school class, from left to right, (first row) Lupito Bravo, Pancho Vasquez, and Esefana Garza; (second row) Joe Bravo, Erasmo Bravo, Jose Vasquez, and Amador Bravo. (Courtesy of Erasmo Bravo family.)

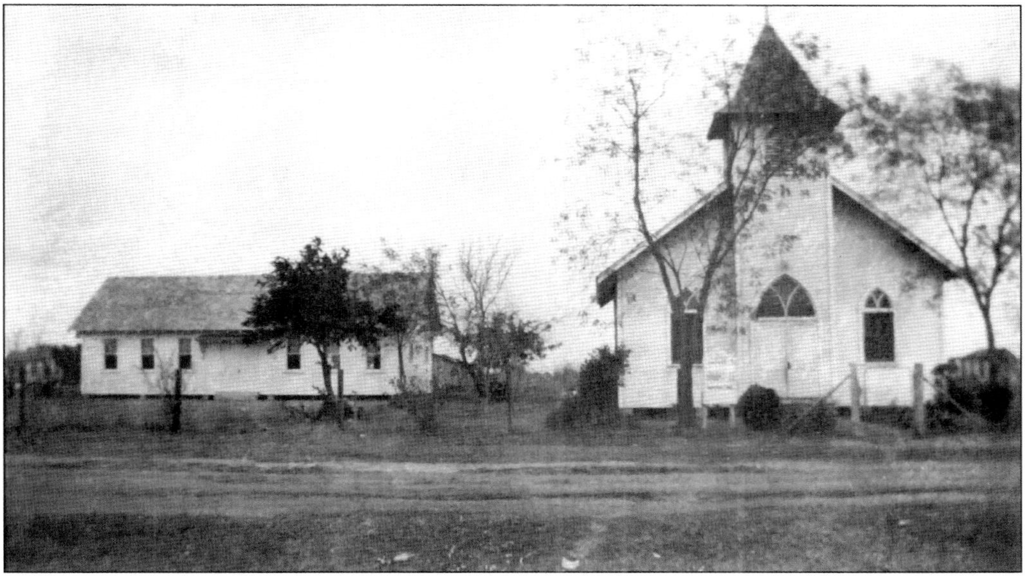

The St. John Lutheran Church was officially founded as a congregation in 1924 but dates back as early as 1919. Originally located on Fourth and Nebraska Streets, the church had a ceremony of confirmation on November 16, 1924, to commemorate its new beginning. Shown above are the original church and the parsonage buildings. Now located in a new building further north on Nebraska Street, the new church thrives with members who represent a blend of cultures who graciously serve the local community and beyond. Pastor Sylvia de la Garza stands below at the altar of the church ready to serve her congregation. (Above, courtesy of Manuel T. Alanis; below, Sylvia de la Garza.)

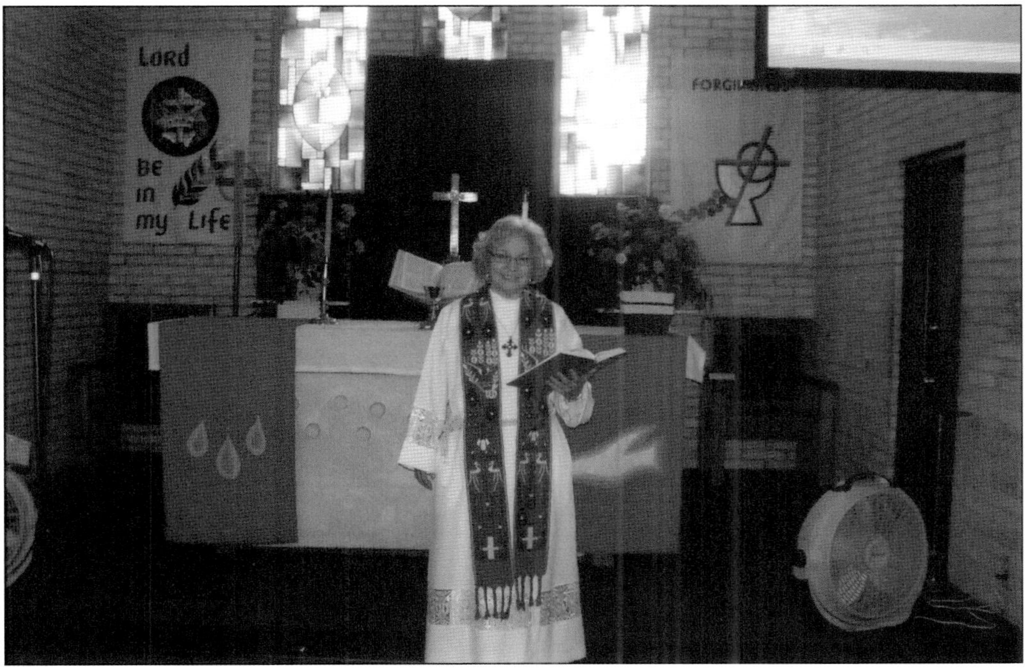

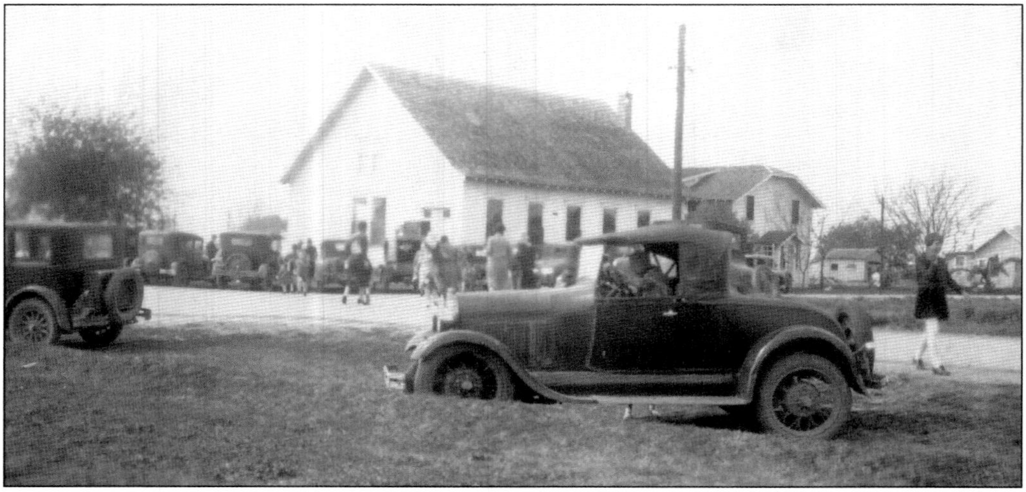

Local churchgoers flock to the original People's Covenant Church building in the 1930s. The parsonage building to the rear still stands today, but the original church building was destroyed by a hurricane in 1933. Minister Leon M. Thompson started the church in 1911 on the porch of the original San Juan Hotel, and it was officially founded in 1912. (Courtesy of Michael Doedyns.)

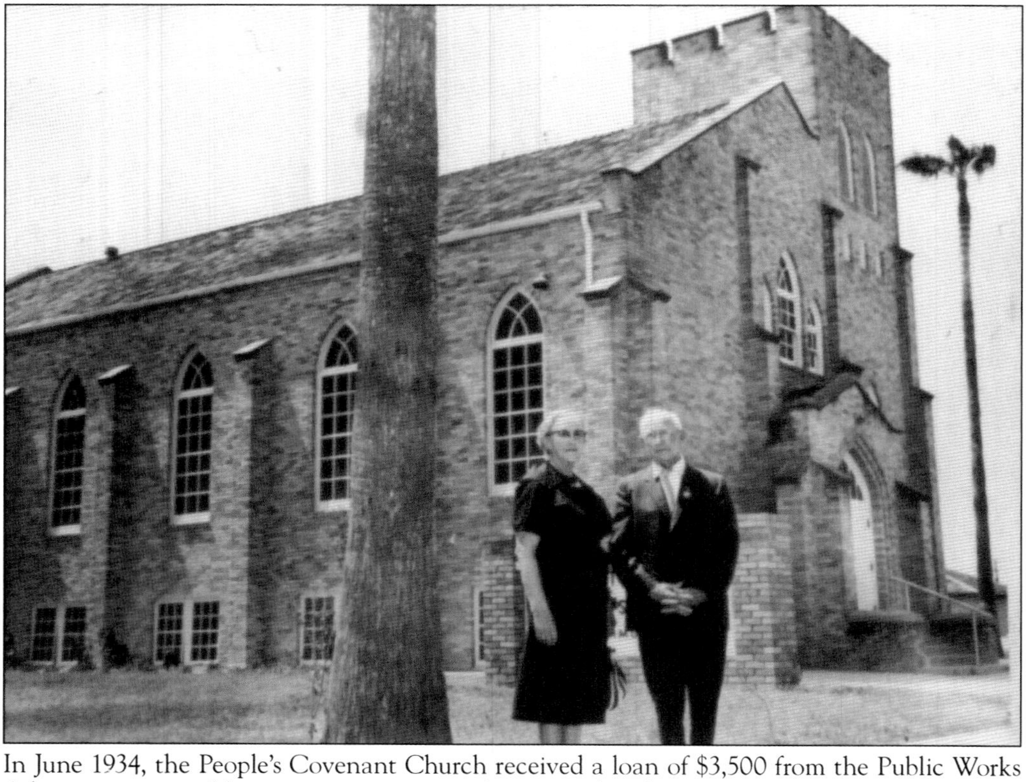

In June 1934, the People's Covenant Church received a loan of $3,500 from the Public Works Administration and began construction on their new church in January 1935. Creative church members were active participants in raising money to help pay for additional expenses. This photograph shows F. C. and Lura Platt on their 50th wedding anniversary around 1960. (Courtesy of Edna Platt Walsh estate.)

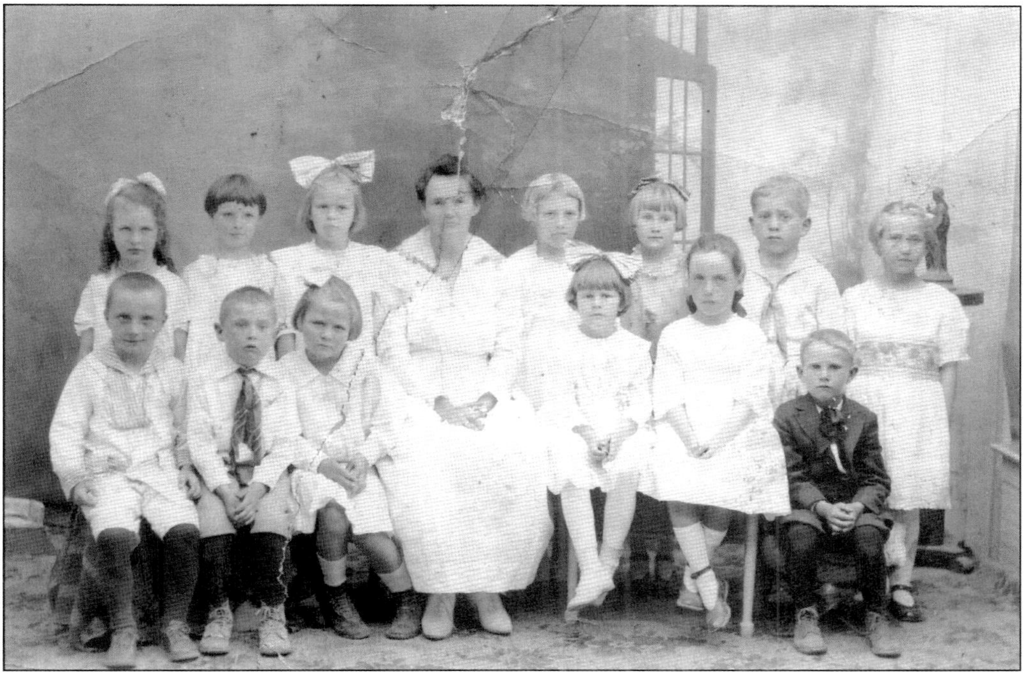

Very active in the church community, Elsie Schafroth is featured here with her Little Sunbeams Sunday school class in August 1919. (Courtesy of Ronald and Dorothy Beamsley.)

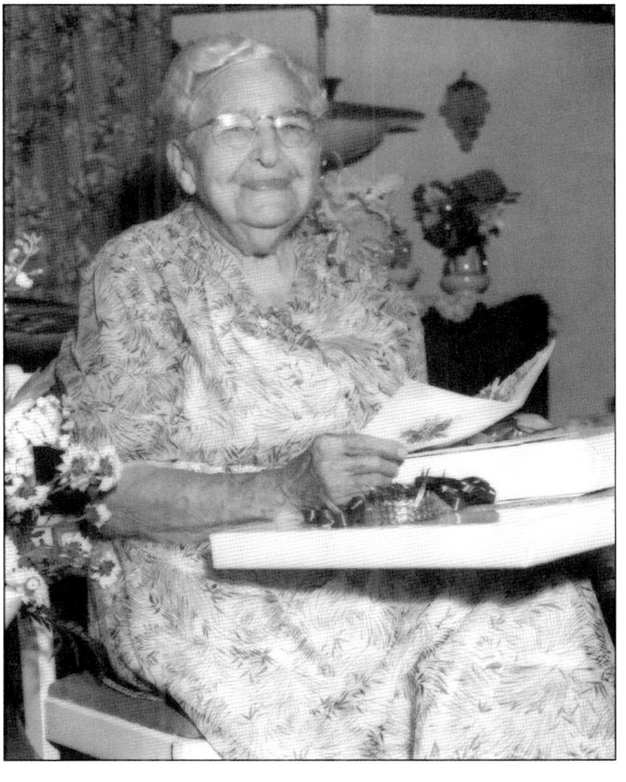

Pictured here in June 1961, Mrs. I. F. Mahaffay, also known as Aunt Allie, was one of San Juan's most beloved citizens. She was a Sunday school teacher for the People's Covenant Church. Although her husband, Dr. Ira Mahaffay, originally purchased land in San Juan in 1907, he did not officially settle in the area until he returned with his wife in 1922. (Courtesy of Mary Stotler.)

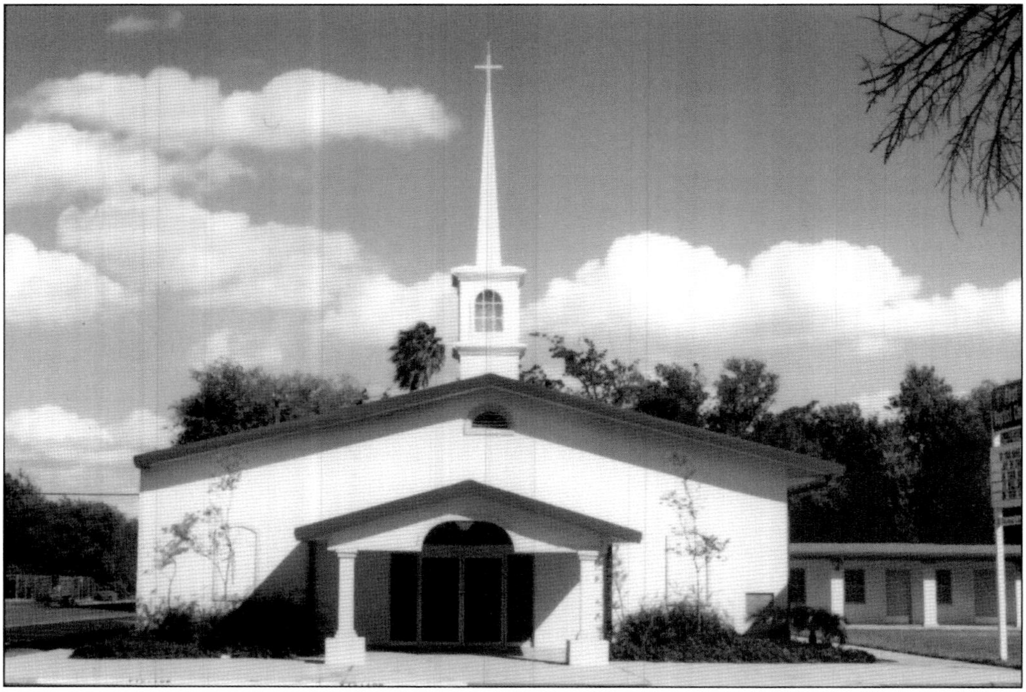

The First Baptist Church of San Juan was organized on February 6, 1938. The congregation met there for about a year before moving to their church on Seventh and Lincoln Streets. (Courtesy of Sue Stevenson.)

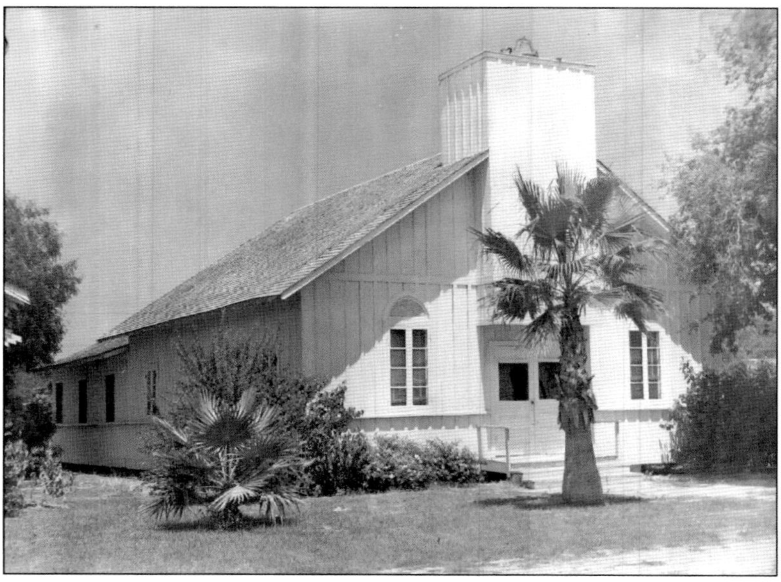

The San Juan United Methodist Church was first opened as a Missionary Sunday School in February 1923 with 13 charter members. By February 1951, they had 232 members and had built a new church building, shown here. Today this church is located on South Nebraska Street. (Courtesy of San Juan United Methodist Church.)

Five

Leadership and Heroism

Over the past 100 years, many men and women have led the community with creativity, compassion, and fortitude. Initial town leaders such as R. L. Savage, F. C. Platt, and Franklin Ewers started businesses and helped establish the town. By 1917, San Juan had instituted R. L. Savage as its first mayor, and he helped to implement the commission form of government. San Juan was also home to legendary Texas Ranger Tom Mayfield, symbolic of a typical Wild West cowboy, who was revered and feared by local residents. He was an officer of the law known to administer "sidewalk style justice."

Politics is not the only measurement of leadership. Residents gained the trust and respect of their friends and neighbors through community service. Leadership was found in those who were not afraid to stand up for their beliefs and their right to be heard, and those committed citizens, who led by example, inspired others. In the 1970s, both boisterous and unassuming Hispanic leaders pushed the majority Mexican American citizenry to the forefront as the change of guard occurred in San Juan governmental leadership.

Many of San Juan's sons and daughters have dutifully served in all branches of the armed forces, in particular World War II, the Korean War, the Vietnam War, and the wars in Iraq and Afghanistan. Throughout the years, the city has honored military servicemen and women. In 1944, the San Juan Lions Club prominently and proudly displayed an honor roll listing all San Juan World War II military servicemen. Donated by local businessman James Shawn, Liberty Park was created to memorialize local veterans. The city recently paid tribute to military heroes who paid the ultimate sacrifice with a beautiful memorial dedicated on June 14, 2009.

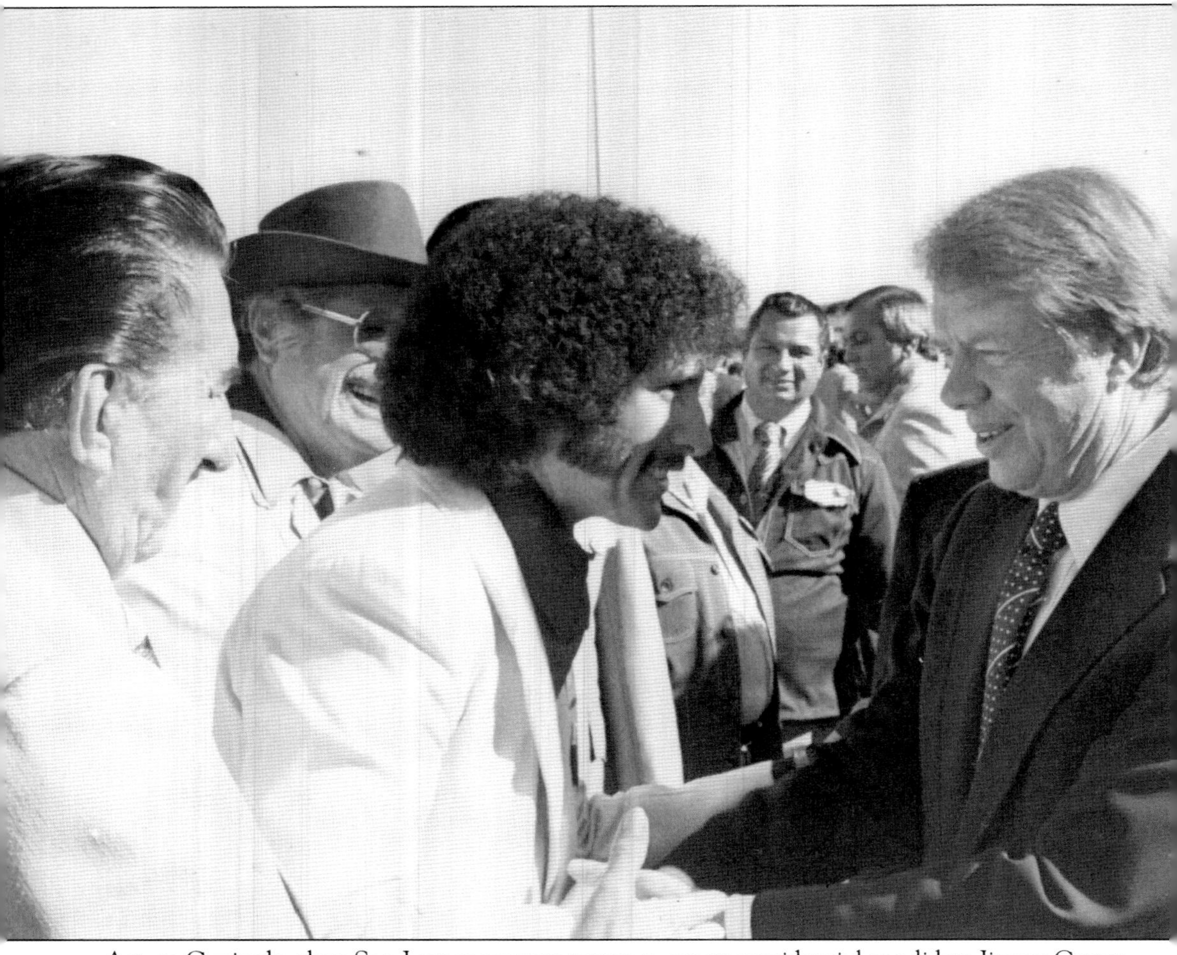

Arturo Guajardo, then San Juan mayor pro tempore, greets presidential candidate Jimmy Carter in 1976. Guajardo credits Carter's administration for providing funds for San Juan's improvement of its water and sewer systems as well as the paving of streets on the north side of town. Guajardo was among the first in Texas to get a master's degree in bilingual education. As superintendent of the Pharr-San Juan-Alamo Independent School District, he went on to incorporate bilingual education into the curriculum at the high school level. (Courtesy of Arturo Guajardo.)

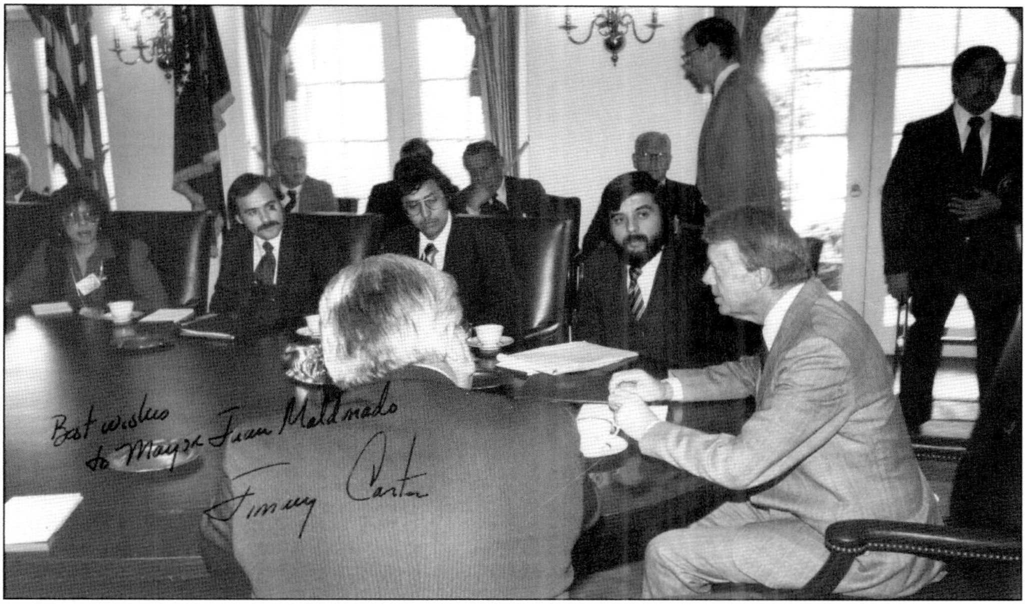

In 1979, Mayor Juan Maldonado was invited to a leadership conference in Washington, D.C. Maldonado, seated second from the left, listens as Pres. Jimmy Carter addresses the group at the White House. Forever recorded in the daily diary log of President Carter is a notation on November 15, 1980, that he spoke to Juan Maldonado at 3:58 p.m. and at 4:17 p.m. (Courtesy of Juan Maldonado.)

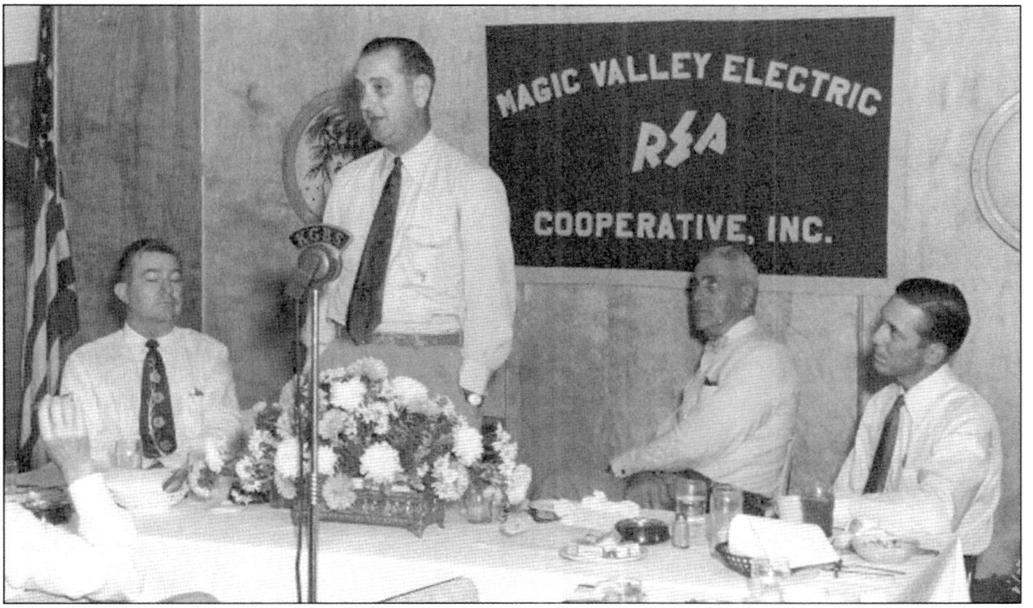

John G. C. Doedyns Sr., third from the left, attends the 15th anniversary celebration of the Magic Valley Electric Cooperative in 1952. Then U.S. Senator Lyndon B. Johnson, standing, and U.S. Congressman Lloyd Bentsen, far right, addressed the group. Doedyns served on the board of directors of the MVEC as president. Also present in the photograph is J. E. Wilder to the far left. (Courtesy of Mike Doedyns.)

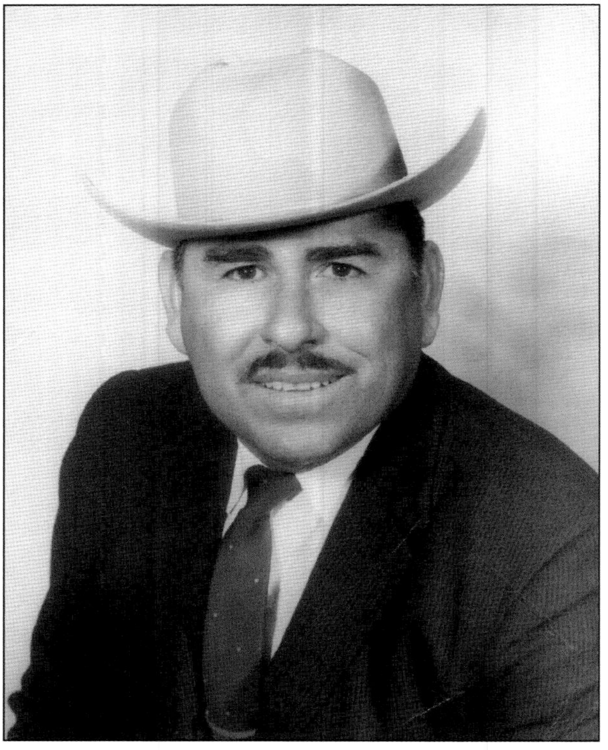

Erasmo C. Bravo became San Juan's first Hispanic patrolman in 1962. Shown here in 1968, he also became the first Hispanic constable in San Juan in the same year. A devoted husband and father, he and his wife, Virginia, raised four sons who followed their father's footsteps into law enforcement. He was very committed to his work with the citizens of San Juan. (Courtesy of Erasmo Bravo family.)

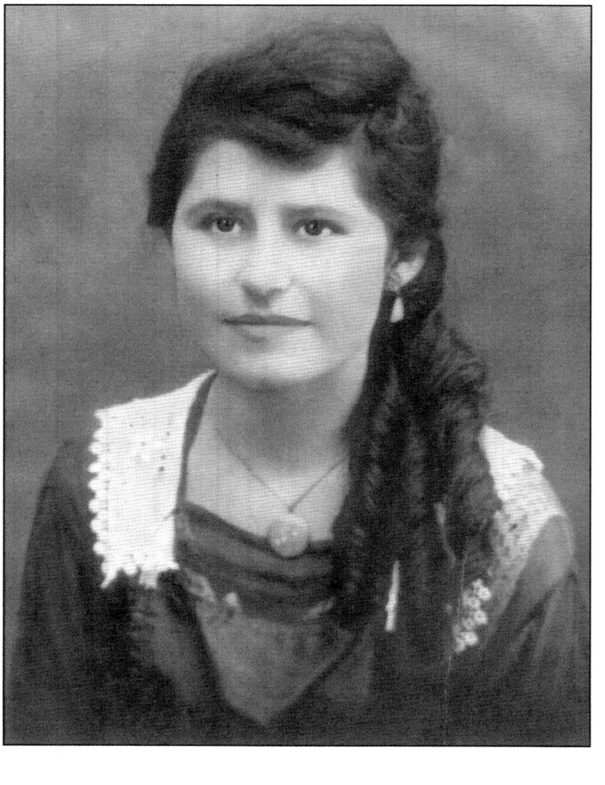

Matron officer for the Hidalgo County Jail in Edinburg for many years, Adela Sloss Vento and her husband guarded prisoners and illegal aliens caught by the border patrol brought in for custody. She was also considered one of the first female civil rights activists in the valley. In 1977, she authored a biography entitled *Alonso S. Perales: His Struggle for the Rights of Mexican-Americans.* (Courtesy of Estela Salazar.)

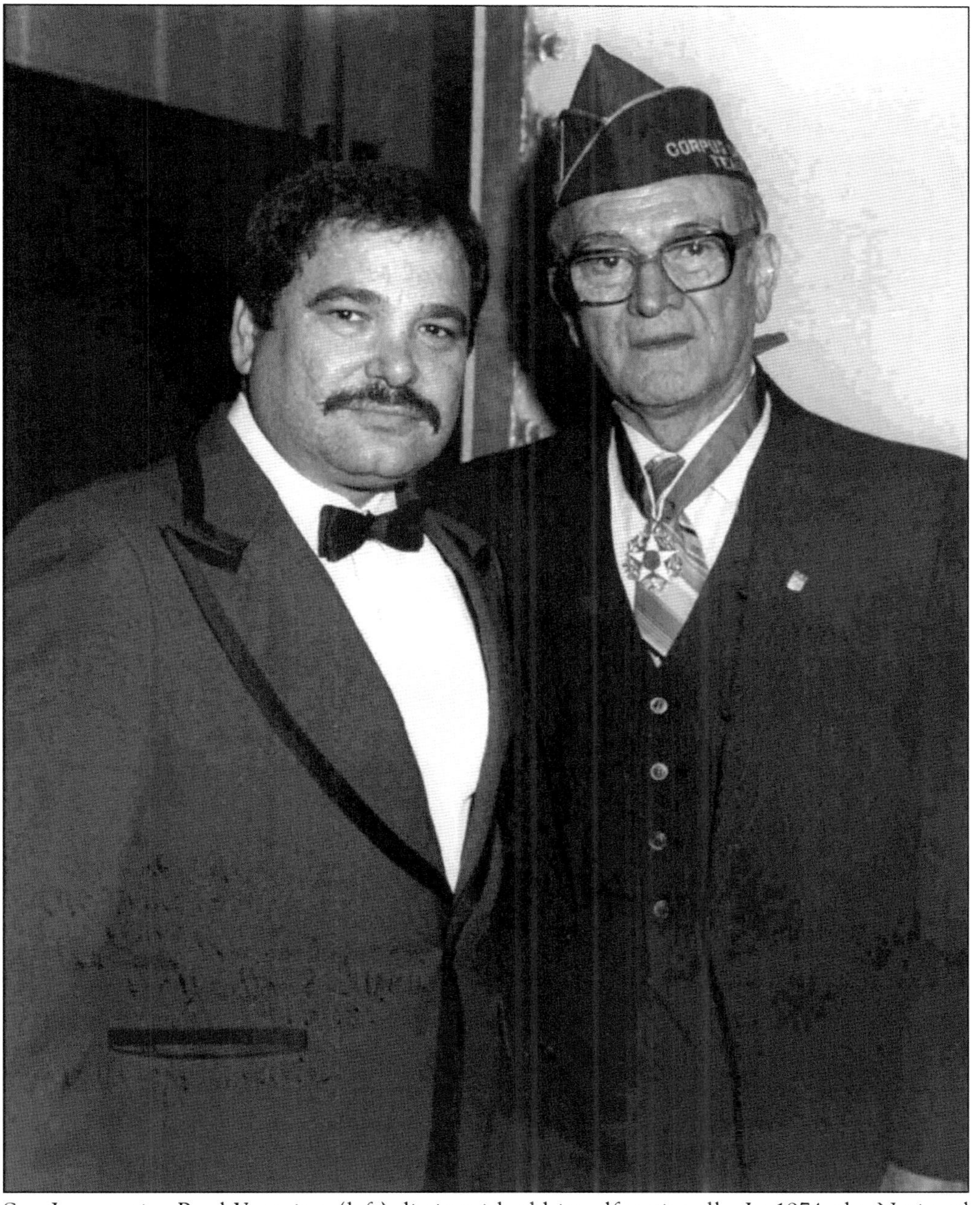

San Juan native Raul Yzaguirre (left) distinguished himself nationally. In 1974, the National Council of La Raza named him as their executive director. He served the Hispanic rights organization as president and CEO until 2004. The NCLR's national headquarters in Washington, D.C., is named in his honor. Yzaguirre is quoted as being "very proud of the leadership that San Juan has nurtured, the wonderful people that pioneered the city including my grandfather and grandmother, Gavino and Elisa Morin, and the many young people who went to foreign lands to defend our country." He is shown here with his mentor and founder of the American G.I. Forum, Dr. Hector P. Garcia. (Courtesy of Raul Yzaguirre.)

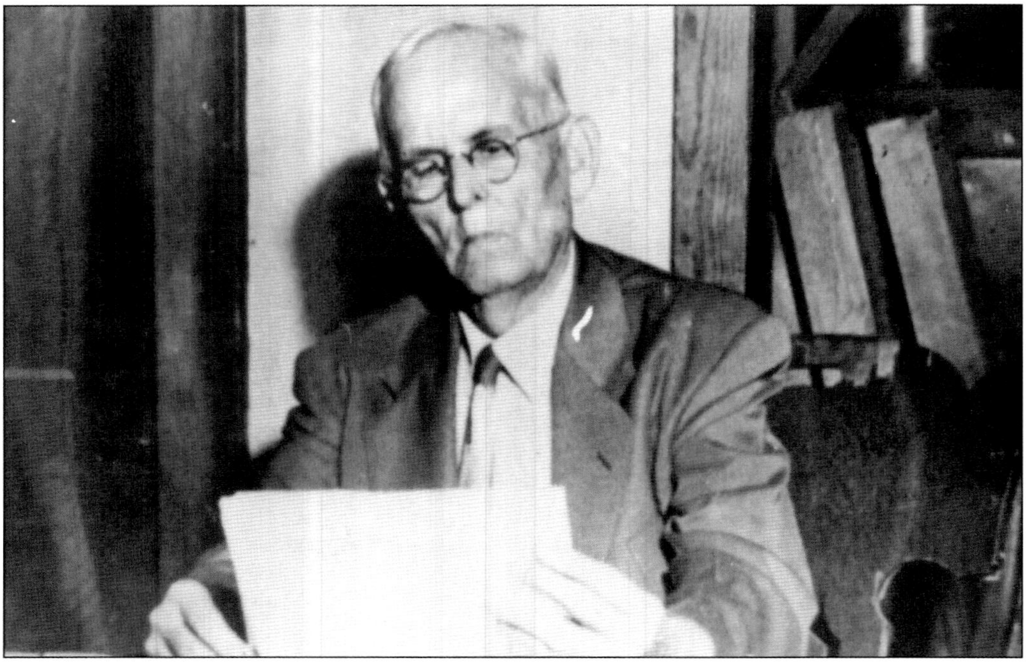

R. L. Savage, shown here around 1960, was elected mayor of San Juan the year it was officially incorporated. He also served San Juan as the justice of the peace, as a judge, and the owner of one of the first general merchandise stores in the area. (Courtesy of Bill Lemen.)

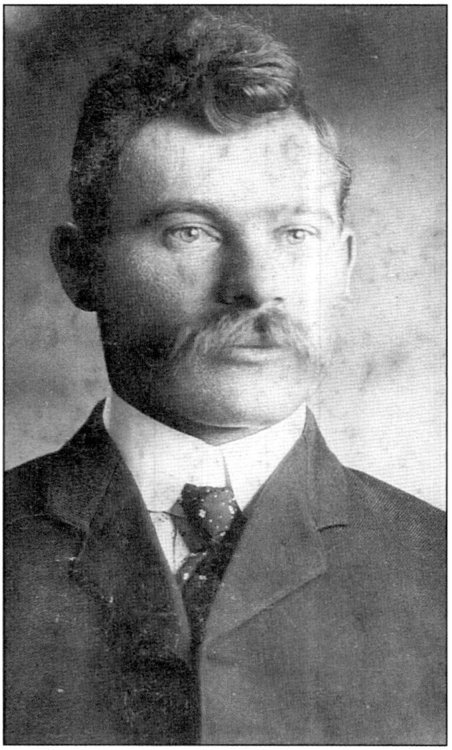

Louis Briedenbach was city commissioner for San Juan from 1929 to 1933. He also was the owner of a small grocery store before becoming owner of the Valley Star Seed and Grain Products Company. His daughter Dorothy Briedenbach Kristek was the oldest living graduate of Pharr-San Juan-Alamo High School but died in October 2009 at 100 years of age. (Courtesy of Robert Kristek.)

Judge W. H. Gossage attends the dedication of the new San Juan United Methodist Church in February 1951. He was the county judge in 1917 who took part in the adoption of the commission, or general law form of government by San Juan, when the town was incorporated in 1917. (Courtesy of San Juan United Methodist Church.)

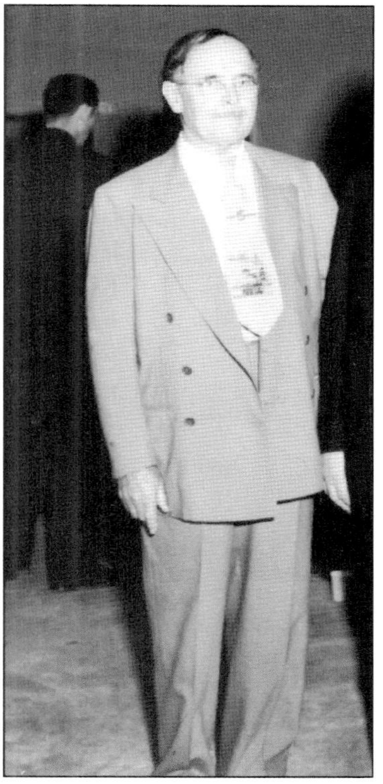

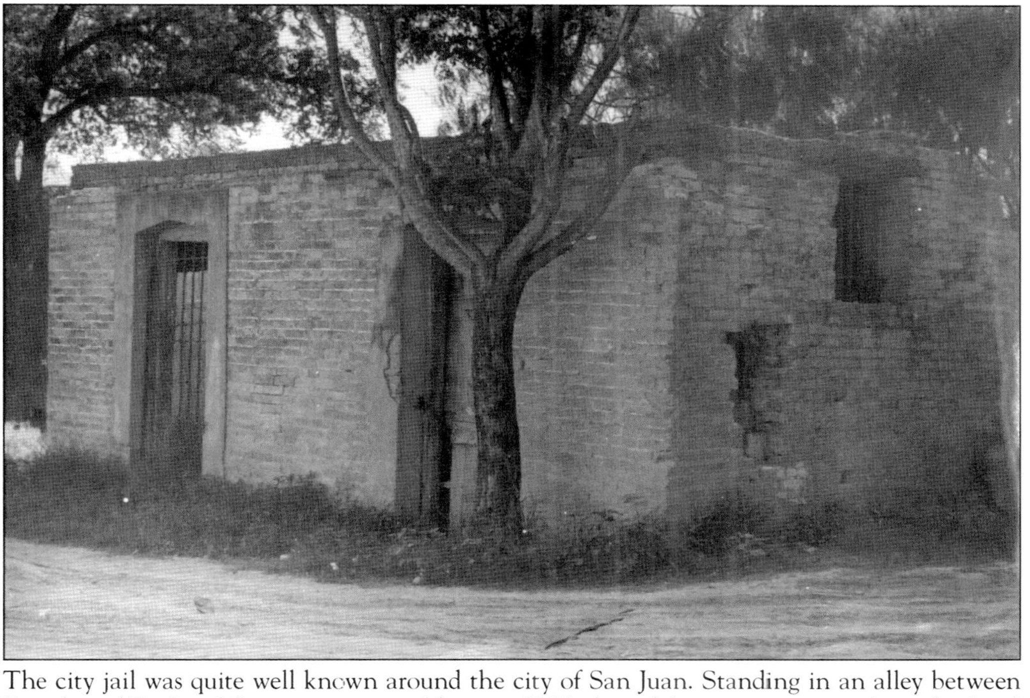

The city jail was quite well known around the city of San Juan. Standing in an alley between Fourth and Railroad Streets as pictured here in 1915, this adobe structure was where the local criminals were held. (Courtesy of Dr. Felipe Alanis.)

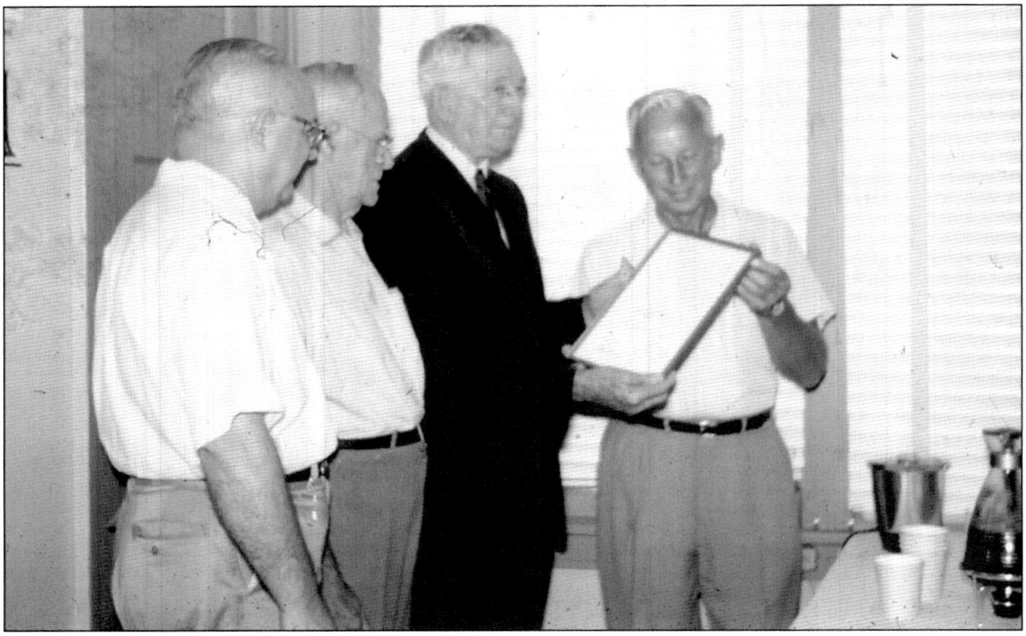

After 23 years of service as San Juan's police officer and city marshal, Tom Mayfield retired in 1962. Mayfield, second from right, accepts a framed resolution thanking him for his service to the community. From left to right are Bill Bormann, A. E. Shearer, Mayfield, and R. E. Coil. (Courtesy of Sue Stevenson.)

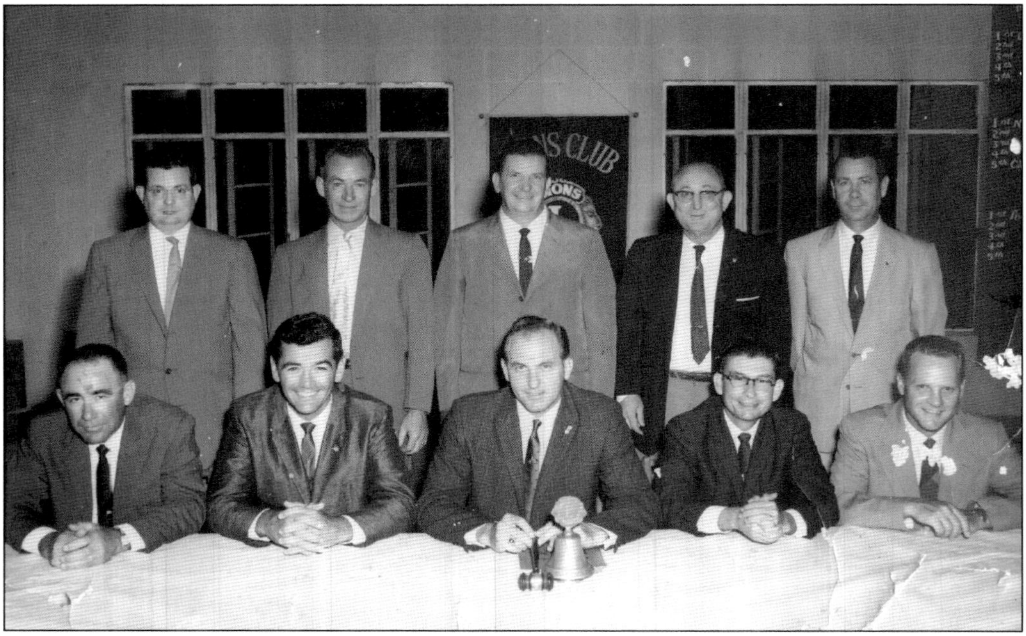

Members of the 1960 San Juan Lions Club are, from left to right, (first row) John Garfield, George Hinkle, Lyle Foster, Bill Lemen, and Dean Bowen; (second row) Dr. Louis Knight, Riley Bethel, Paul Jensen, Max Greenwood, and Jack Marr. The Lions Club has accomplished many community service projects since its inception in San Juan in 1939. (Courtesy of San Juan Lions Club.)

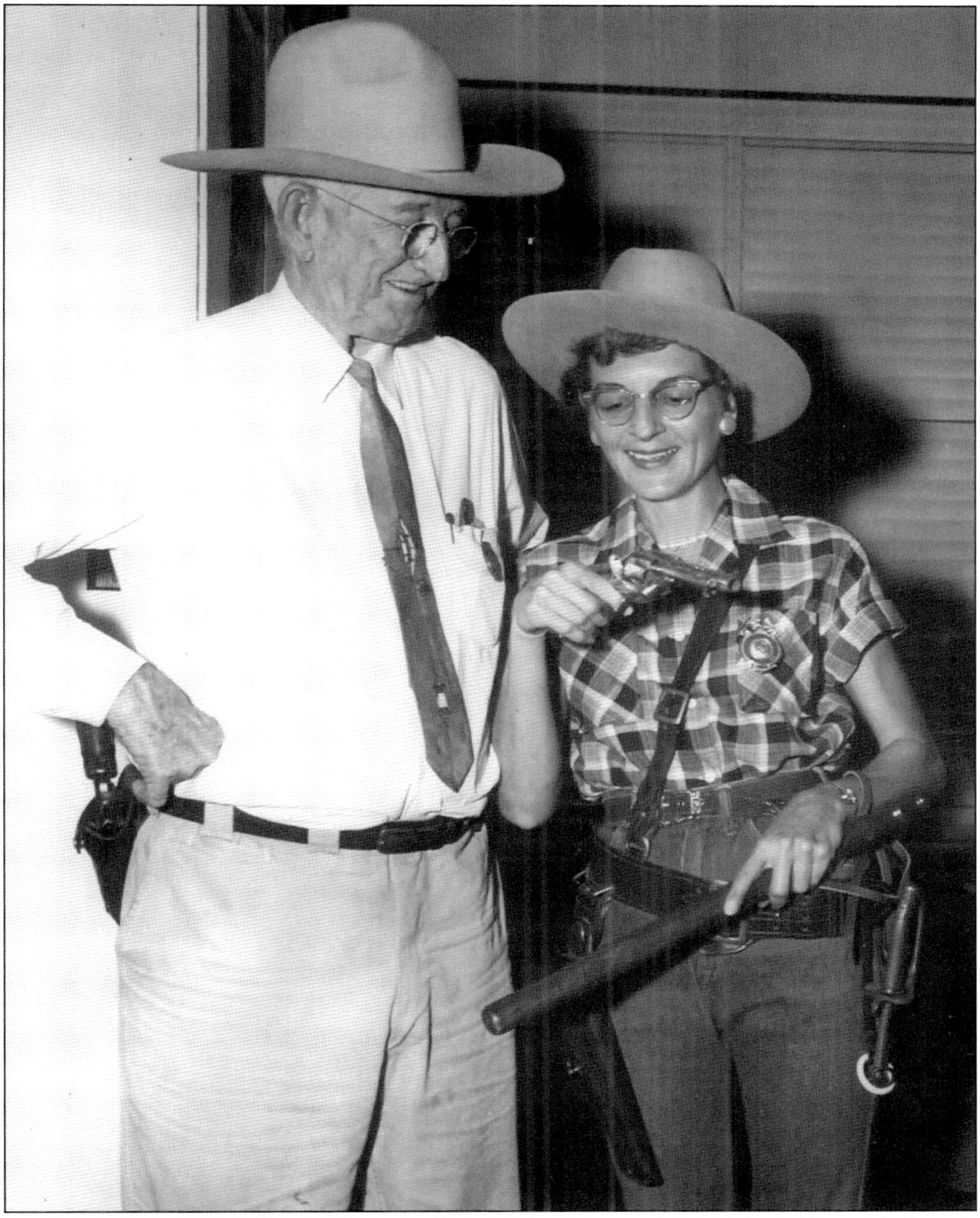

City clerk Mary Lemen examines the tools of law enforcement with Tom Mayfield in 1954. Mayfield was a legendary figure known across the Rio Grande Valley. In 1901, he was the assistant manager of the San Juan Plantation. He also served as Hidalgo County deputy sheriff under A. Y. Baker from 1901 to 1910. Remembered most as a Texas Ranger, Mayfield held various law enforcement positions throughout his life in San Juan. Perhaps his most famous arrest came in 1915 when he apprehended Basilio Ramos while carrying the document called the Plan de San Diego. Also known as "Whispering Tom," his voice was unable to go above a whisper due to a neck injury. Some claimed that Mexican bandits had cut his throat. Others tell of a story of a botched attempt by Mexican bandits to hang Mayfield from a tree after they caught him trying to retrieve stolen horses. (Courtesy of Museum of South Texas History.)

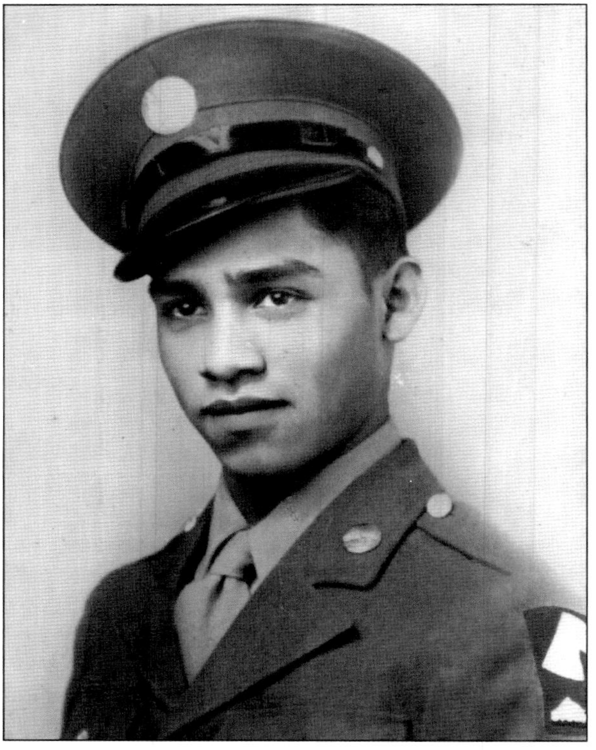

Marin Alonzo made the ultimate sacrifice and died while serving during World War II. Shown here in his military uniform in 1941, he received the distinguished Purple Heart as well as recognition of service from the State of Texas and from Pres. Franklin D. Roosevelt. (Courtesy of Tomas Alonzo Jr.)

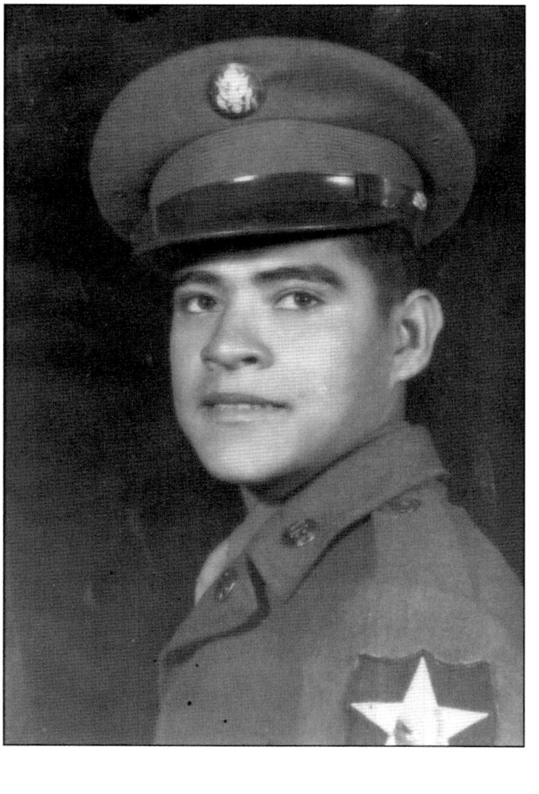

Sgt. Leonel Treviño served as an army infantryman in the Korean War. He was captured in Korea in 1951 and held as a prisoner of war for over two years. He received many honors, including the Bronze Star, two Purple Hearts, the Good Conduct Medal, and the United Nations Service Medal. (Courtesy of Agustin and Elodia Treviño.)

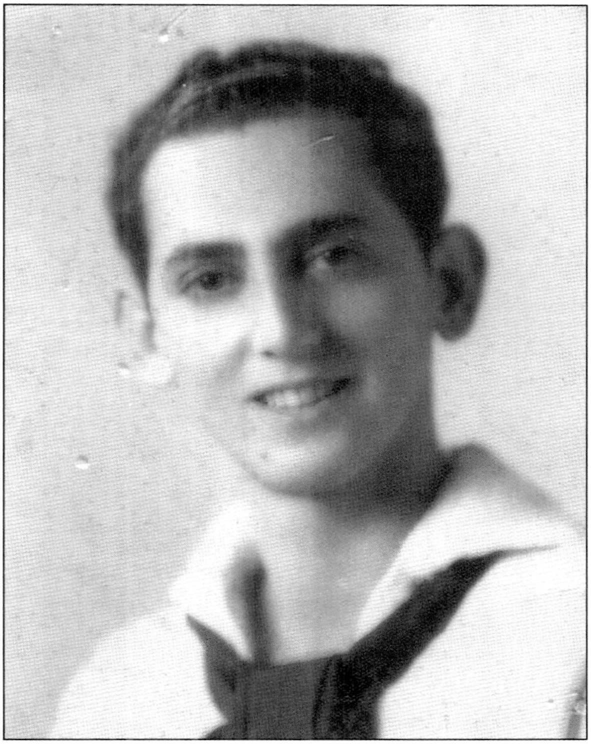

U.S. Navy sailor Alonzo Cantu Villarreal, shown at right in uniform in 1941, survived the attack on Pearl Harbor during World War II. He was on the destroyer USS *Jarvis* in the battle for Guadalcanal in the South Pacific. The *Jarvis* was torpedoed and sank with all its crew on board; 233 sailors perished on that navy ship. Villarreal and the other crew members received Purple Hearts in honor of their service to our country. Below is a letter he sent home to his mother telling her all was well and not to worry about him. (Both courtesy of Sylvia Prado Sandoval.)

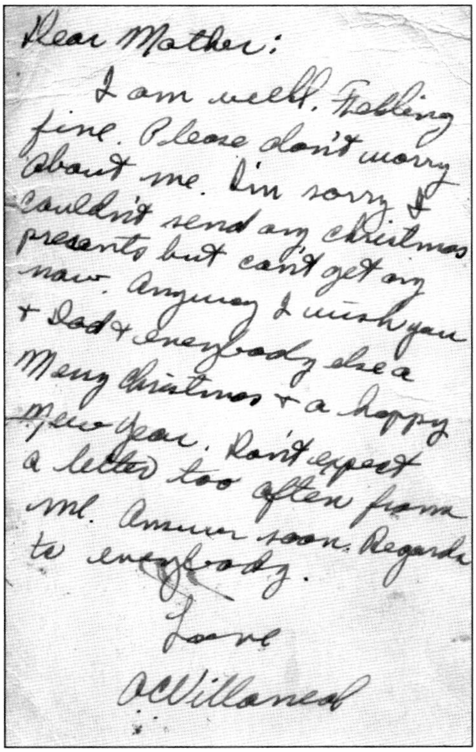

Dear Mother:

I am well. Feeling fine. Please don't worry about me. I'm sorry I couldn't send any Christmas presents but can't get any now. Anyway I wish you & Dad & everybody else a Merry Christmas & a happy New Year. Don't expect a letter too often from me. Answer soon. Regards to everybody.

Love

A C Villarreal

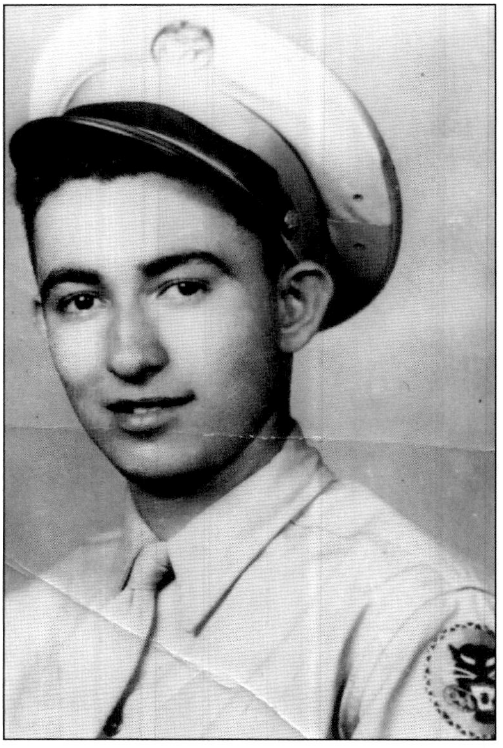

Alfonso Bravo is pictured here in his military uniform. He was a private first class in the 740th Field Artillery Battalion and served in World War II. He was a specialist as a gun crewman and a sharpshooter. He served for three years and returned safely home from the war. (Courtesy of Alfonso Bravo Jr.)

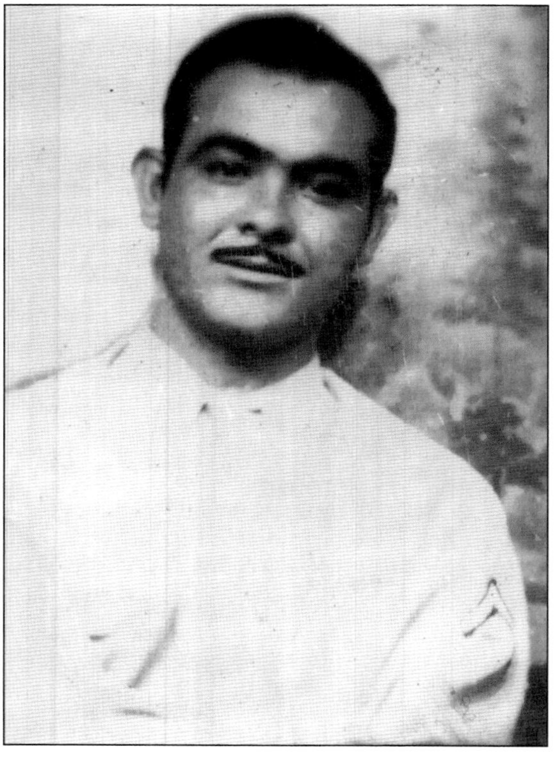

Raul Maldonado as shown here in his 1942 army photograph. He served as a military policeman and a marksman. He earned the American Theater Ribbon, the Asiatic Pacific Theater Ribbon, and was honorably discharged from service in 1945. (Courtesy of Estella Rojas.)

Concepcion "Chon" Aceves, a San Juan native, served his country from 1945 to 1947. An accomplished guitarist, he recorded with Pedro Ayala and Luis Aguilar under the Falcon recording label. He played live on a weekly show on the KURV radio station with Benito Espinoza and played on stage at El Teatro Murillo. His love of music has inspired others. (Courtesy of Romeo Jimenez.)

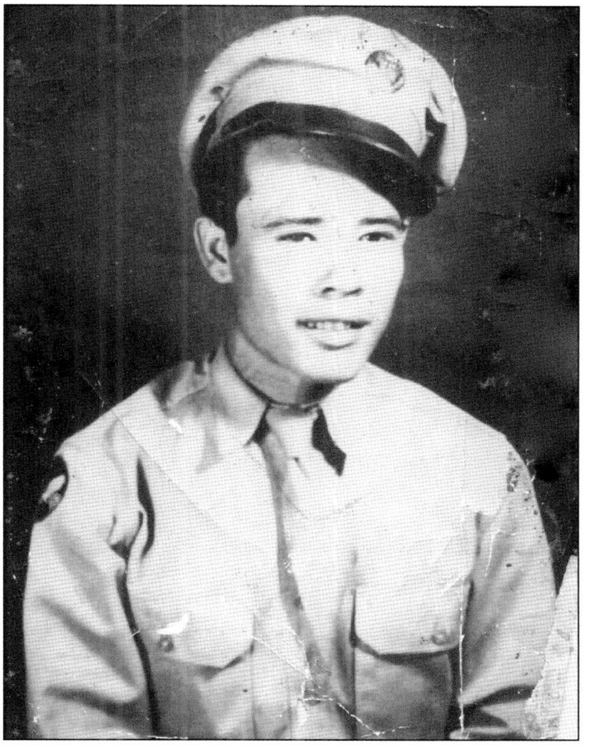

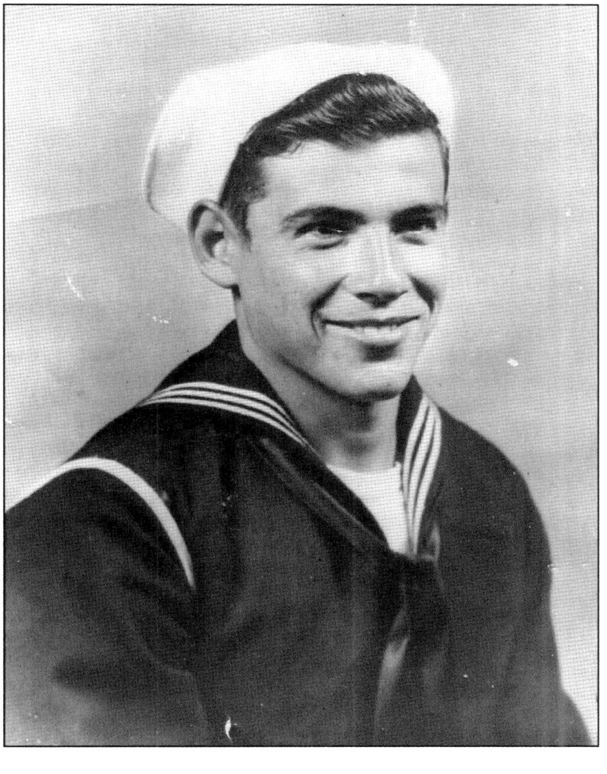

Teodolo "Ted" Guerra served with the Seabees (also known as Construction Battalions) in the U.S. Navy during World War II. (Courtesy of Carlos Salazar.)

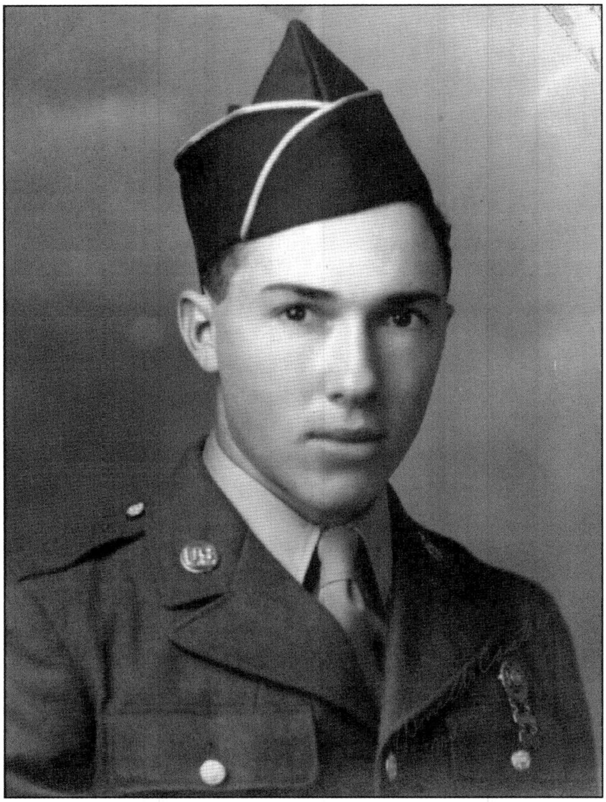

Arnoldo Cantu served in World War II and in Korea. He became a lieutenant colonel in the U.S. Air Force and later went into the reserves. He gave a total of 20 years of service to the military. (Courtesy of Angelita G. Cantu.)

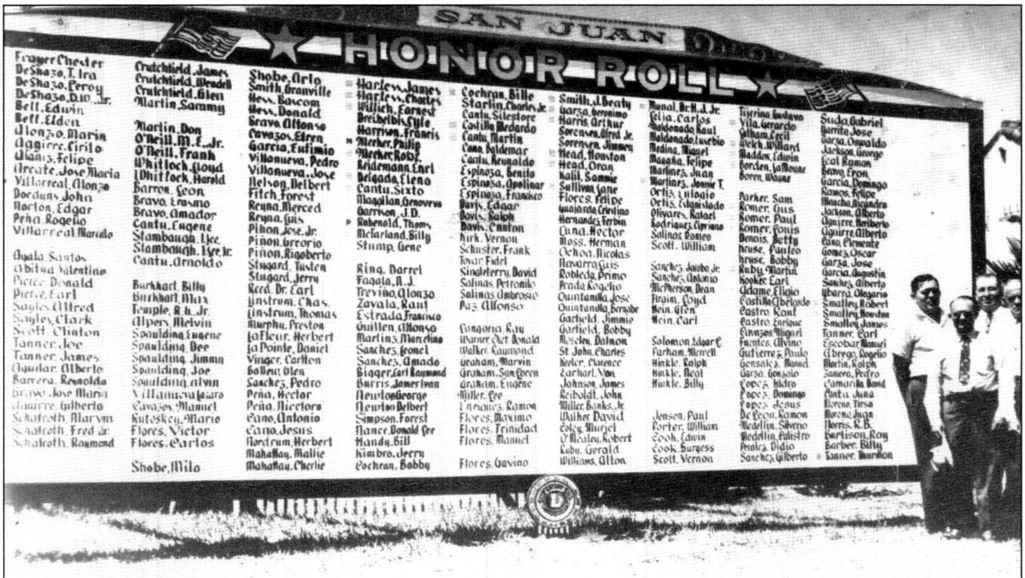

The San Juan Lions Club honor roll of military servicemen from San Juan during World War II was put up in Railroad Park in 1944. It listed approximately 300 names and stood in the park until 1949, when it was taken down due to its state of disrepair. (Courtesy of San Juan Lions Club.)

Six

HISPANIC LEGACY

San Juan has a history rich in cultural development. Many Mexican families settled in San Juan in order to escape the Mexican Revolution, and multiple generations have remained throughout the years. At the time of the Mexican Revolution, the agriculture industry in San Juan had a strong presence and attracted newly arrived families looking for gainful employment. Today's residents remember their families coming here to work with established farming families, some of who are still in business today. Immigrant families recall about their progression into becoming migrant farmworkers. Some discuss their travels by foot from San Juan through Falfurias to Refugio. Others travelled as far north as Michigan to find farmwork to support their families.

As time went on, many of these families had members who were active in the community. Social organizations formed and the Hispanic voice became stronger. Hardworking Hispanics were being elected to local government positions. Civil rights activists were fighting for the rights of local residents as well as for people across the Rio Grande Valley and beyond. Fearless local leaders pushed relentlessly for their voices to be heard via the National Council of La Raza and the Texas Farm Workers Union, which originated in San Juan.

As the demographics of the area changed and the white settlers outnumbered the valley native population, a dividing line emerged within the town. North of Highway 83, Hispanic population lived in *colonias* above the railroad tracks. The white population lived to the south. Lot sizes and city services differed between the two sides, but, as seen in the pages to follow, both sides created businesses, educated their children, and made a difference in people's lives.

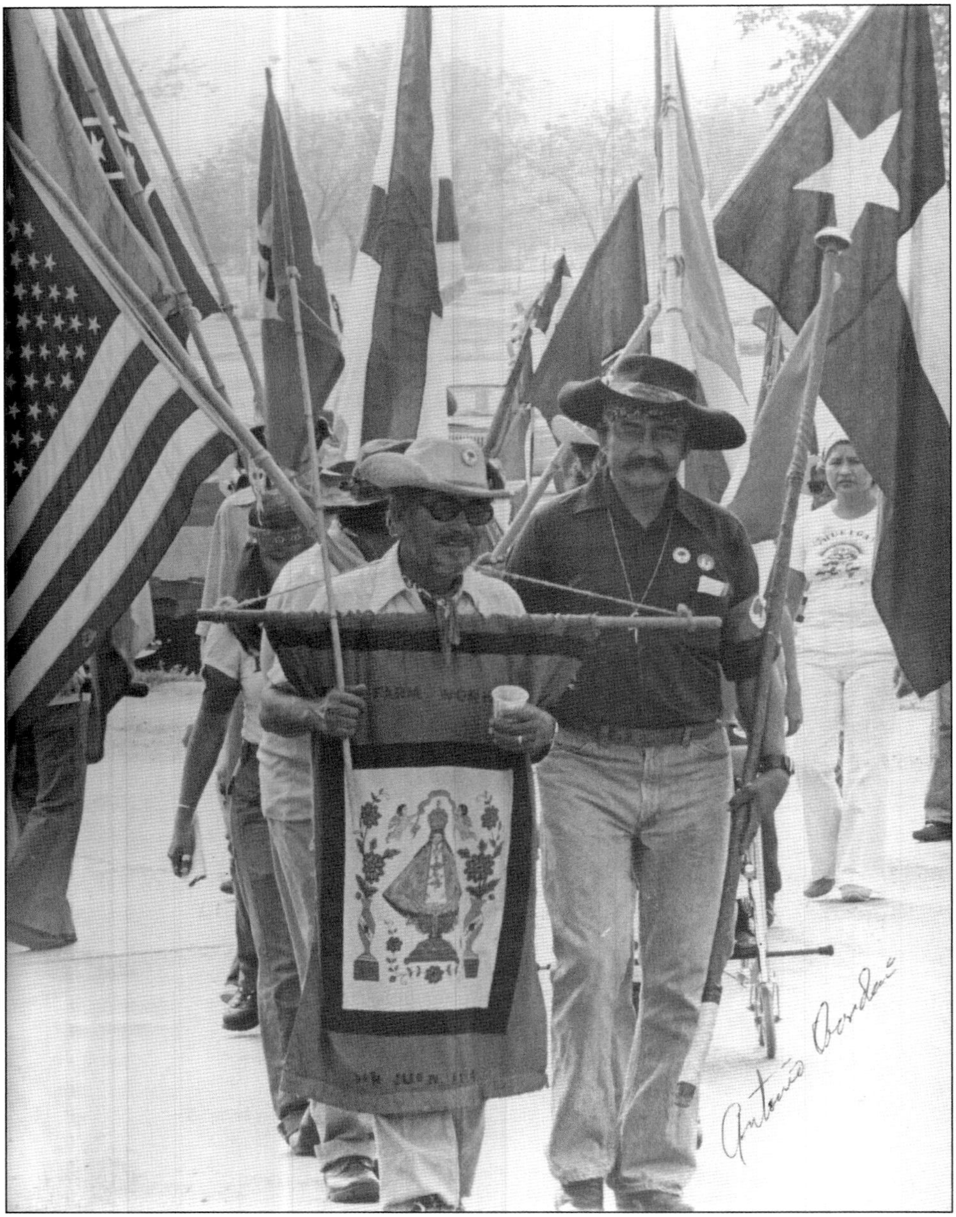

Antonio Orendain (right) and Claudio Ramirez lead the 1977 Texas Farm Workers Union March from San Juan through Austin and onward to Washington, D.C. Sent to Texas in 1966 by César Chávez, Orendain first organized the United Farm Workers Union in South Texas. In 1975, he and his supporters broke away from the UFW and organized the Texas Farm Workers Union. Orendain led the local people in a hard-fought battle for the rights of the migrant farmworkers of Texas. Claudio Ramirez, devoted to the Virgen de San Juan de los Lagos, made a banner with her image and vowed to carry it all the way to Washington. The group marched 15 miles per day between San Juan and Austin. From Austin to Washington, they increased the daily mileage to 20 miles in order to get to the nation's capital in time for Labor Day that year. (Courtesy of Norma Ramirez Aguiñaga.)

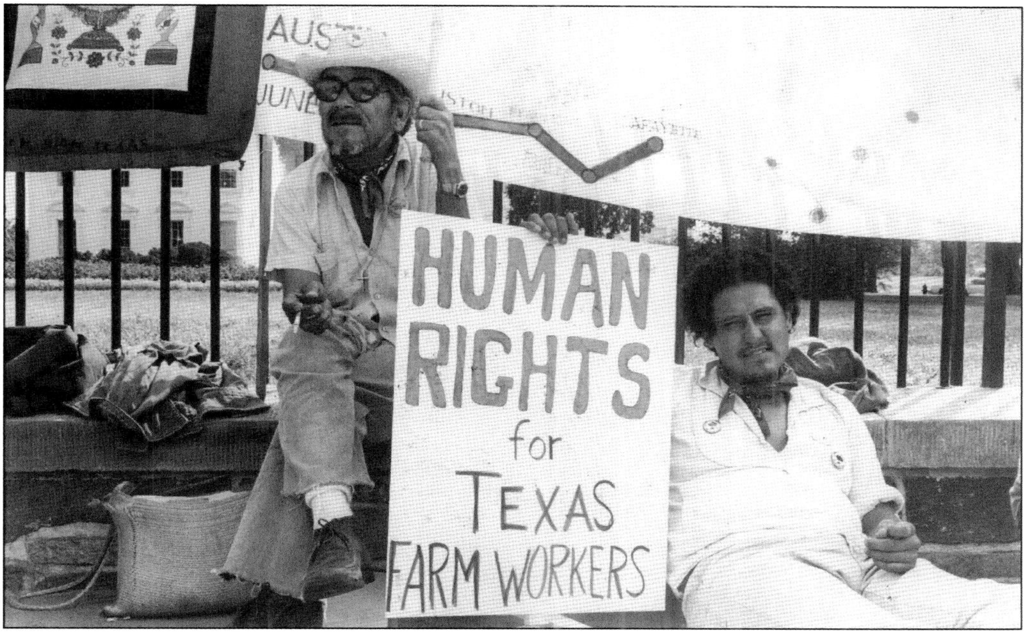

The Texas Farm Workers March began at the Basilica of Our Lady of San Juan Del Valle National Shrine on February 26, 1977, and concluded on the steps of the state capitol in Austin on April 3, 1977. Marchers met with Gov. Dolph Briscoe to discuss their fight to repeal section 14B of the Taft-Hartley Act. Claudio Ramirez is seen here to the left. (Courtesy of Norma Ramirez Aguiñaga.)

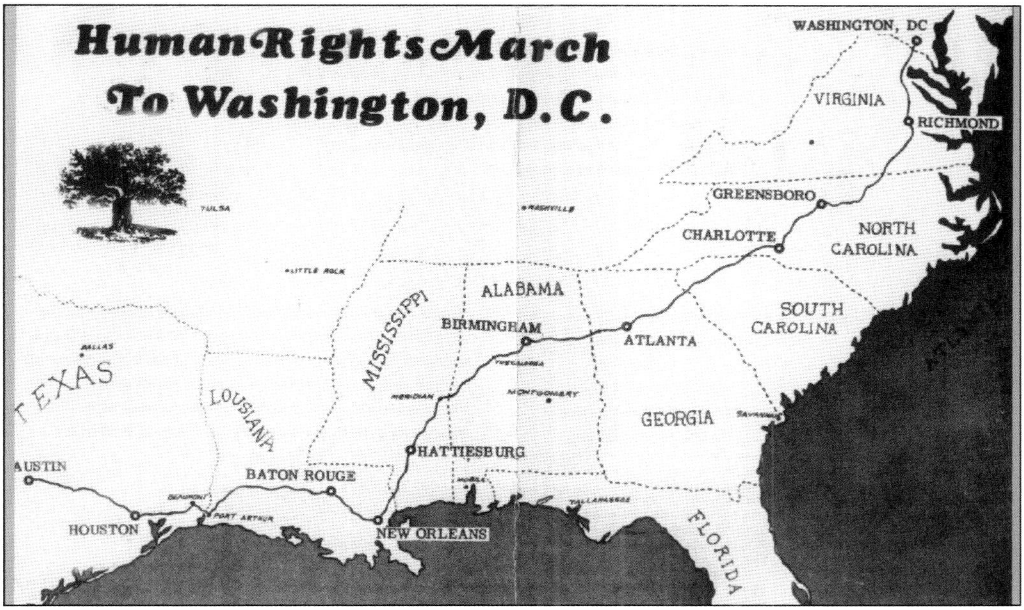

This map of the Texas Farm Workers March route from Austin, Texas, to Washington, D.C., depicts the long road and struggle for farmworkers' rights. This leg of the march began on June 18, 1977, and ended when they arrived at the nation's capital on Labor Day. President Carter would not grant them an audience upon their arrival, and they instead met with Vice President Walter Mondale. (Courtesy of Antonio Orendain.)

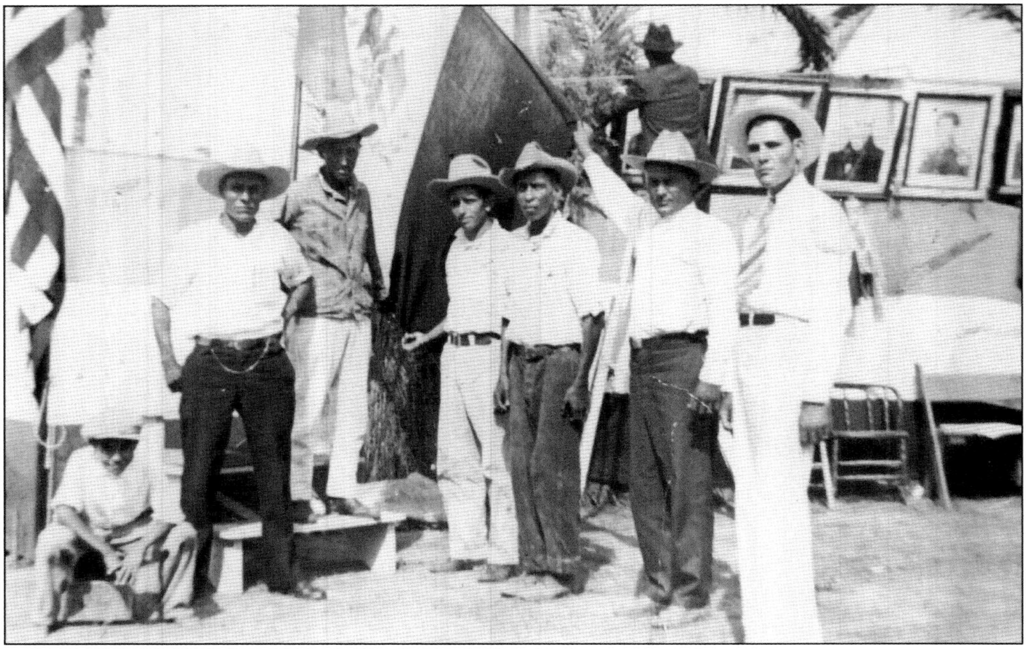

The Sociedad Mutualista Obrera Mexicano, shown here in the late 1930s, met regularly to help their members combat the social, labor, and economic issues of the day. The local Woodmen of the World community organization eventually emerged from this group. Standing from left to right are Jorge Tamez, Abel Tamez, Brother Tamez, Romulo Salazar, Don Rosendo Sosa, and Buenaventura Lopez. (Courtesy of Carlos Salazar.)

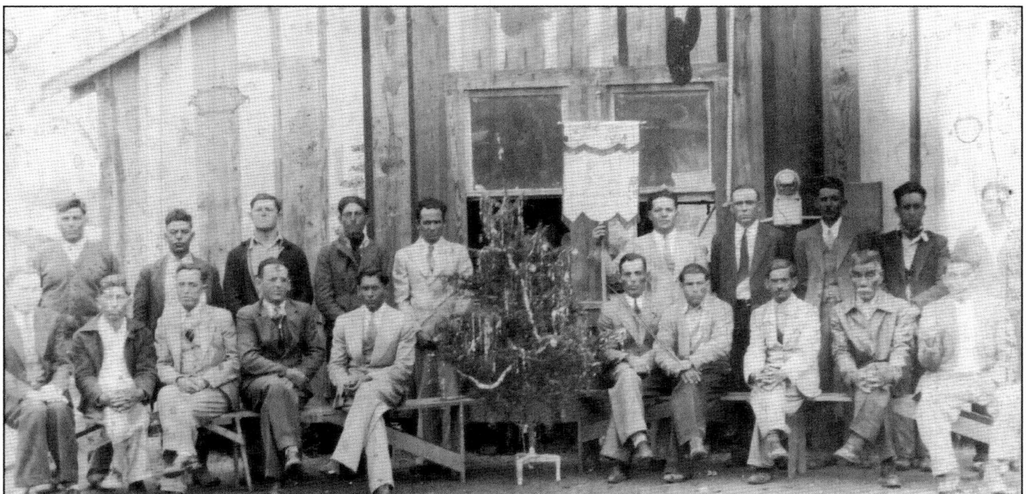

The Sociedad Mutualista Obrera Mexicano celebrates Christmas Day in 1938. The following members, pictured from left to right, are (first row) Antonio Serna, Romulo Salazar, Ramon Serna, Ventura Lopez, Refugio Cano, Leos Cantu, Reyes Aranda, Rosendo Sosa, Leandro Sauceda, and Ismael Zavala; (second row) Lucio Sanchez, Juan Castillo, Cesar Cantu, Rafael DeLeon, Francisco Guerra, Ramiro Cantu, Andres Arcaute, Lucio Gomez, Marcos Zavala, and Socorro Mendoza. (Courtesy of Carlos Salazar.)

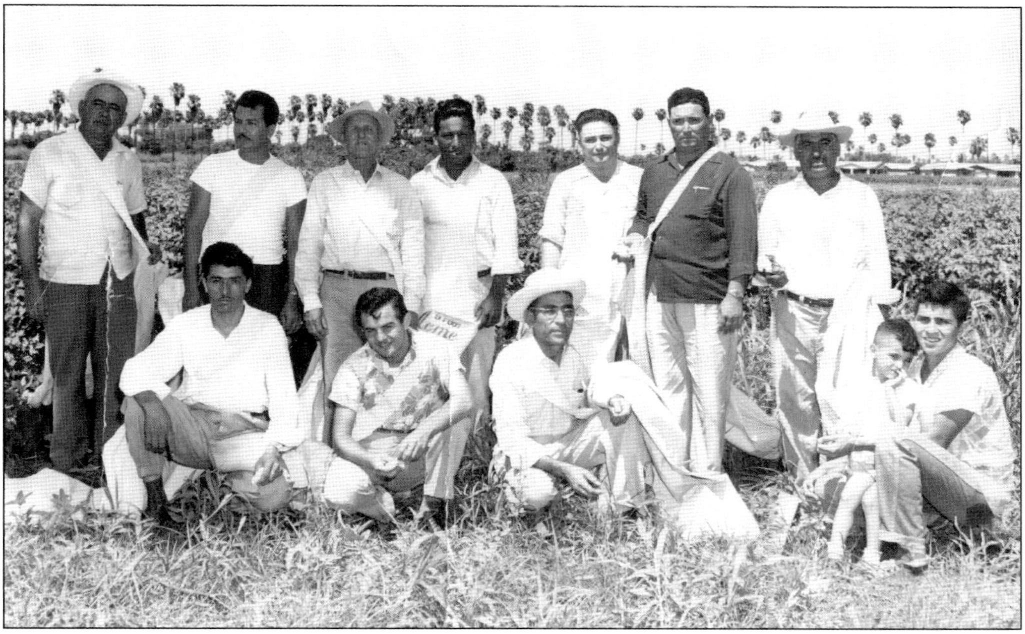

Original members of San Juan's Woodmen of the World are, from left to right, (standing) Andres Arcaute, unknown, Raul Cantu, Apolinar Rodea, Rudolfo Garza Peña, Frutoso DeLeon, and Damacio Rodea; (kneeling) Guadalupe Gonzalez, Arturo Breaux, Lino Pecina, and Adalberto Garza holding his young son Armando. (Courtesy of Juan Maldonado.)

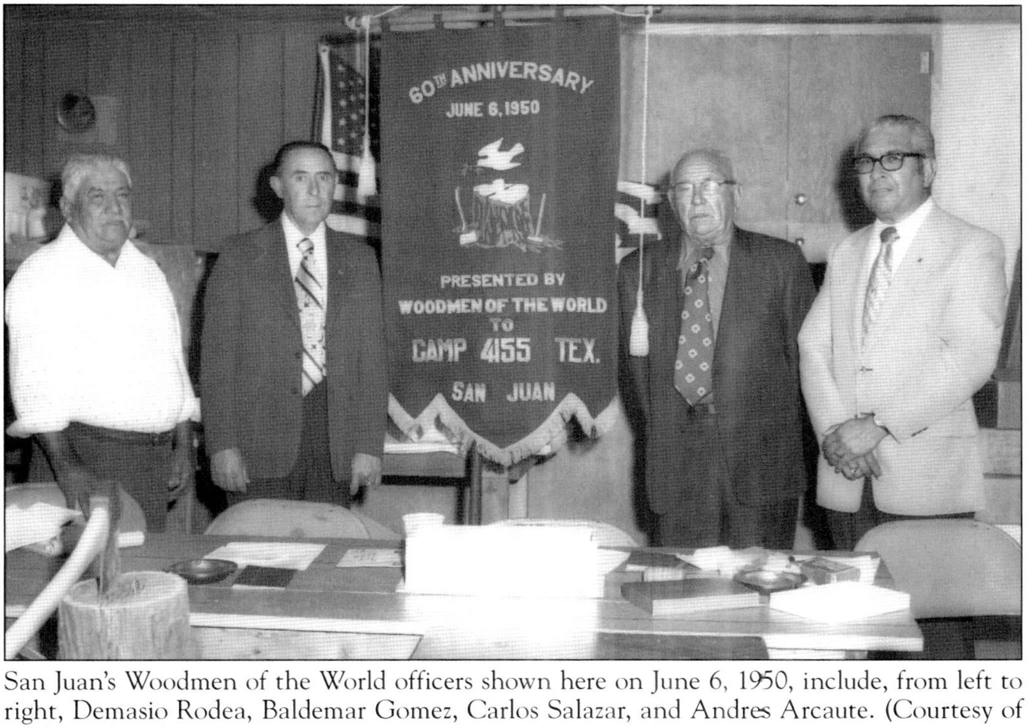

San Juan's Woodmen of the World officers shown here on June 6, 1950, include, from left to right, Demasio Rodea, Baldemar Gomez, Carlos Salazar, and Andres Arcaute. (Courtesy of Carlos Salazar.)

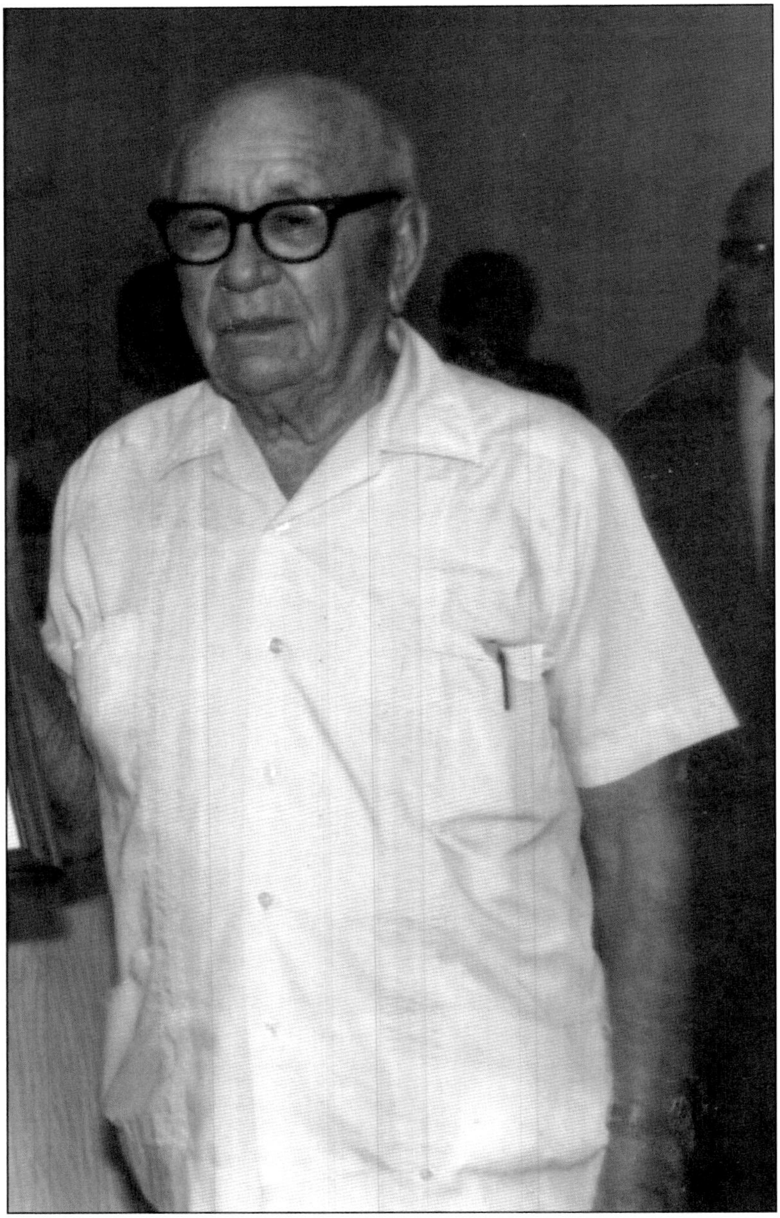

Andres Arcaute moved to San Juan in 1914 from Ciudad Diaz Ordaz, Mexico. He was committed to serving the people of San Juan, and as a charter member of the Woodmen of the World, he served as financial secretary for 40 years. The group honored him by naming their new building after him in the 1970s. He was often asked to accompany young men who went to ask for a woman's hand in marriage, standing up for the honorable status of the young future grooms. A gifted public speaker, he gave eulogies to honor the deceased. Also committed to the Senior Companion Program, Arcaute brought recognition to the group with an honor from Governor White. He was well known in the community and well respected throughout the tri-city area. His son Lalo Arcaute served as San Juan's mayor in the 1970s and his grandson Jorge Arcaute has served as police chief and city manager. (Courtesy of Connie and Lalo Arcaute.)

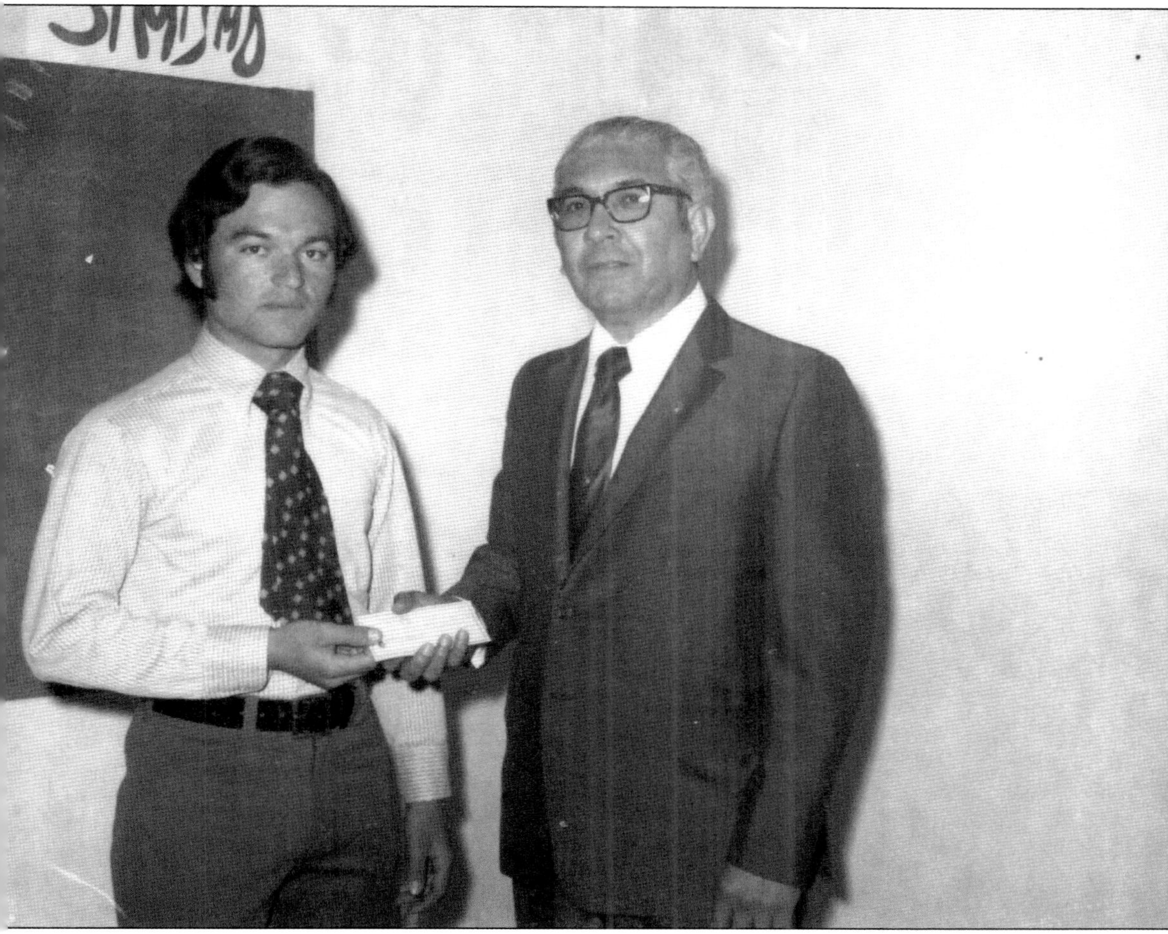

In 1960, Carlos Salazar won the general election for the office as the first Hispanic justice of the peace by defeating a J. F. Crutchfield. During those times, the justice of the peace did not earn a salary but rather $4 per case. In 1964, he was reelected without opposition and remained in office until 1968. Salazar was also the first Hispanic to run on the Democratic ticket for county commissioner, where he lost by only 29 votes. He was one of the charter members of the all-Hispanic Tri-City Lions Club formed in 1971. He had spent many years prior to the founding of this club working with the public, teaching the people how to vote and how to send in their absentee ballots. He has been very successful in pulling a high percentage of people in to the polls. In this photograph, he is awarding Juan Jose Salazar a scholarship on behalf of the Tri-City Lions Club in the 1970s. (Courtesy of Carlos Salazar.)

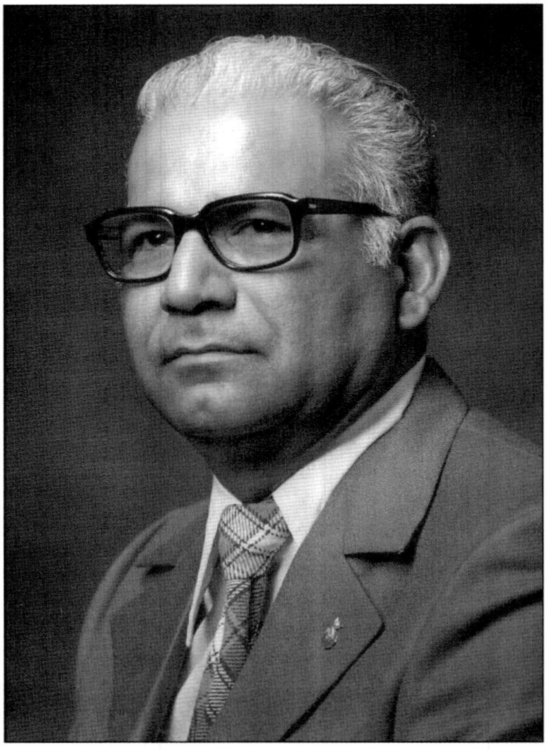

San Juan resident Julian Y. Chapa was one of the founding members of the Hispanic Tri-City Lions Club in 1971. Owner of JY Chapa Oilfield Construction, he served as one of the members of the charter commission that prepared the San Juan City Charter approved by voters on April 5, 1975. His granddaughter serves as the executive director of the San Juan Economic Development Corporation. (Courtesy of Margie McCarthy.)

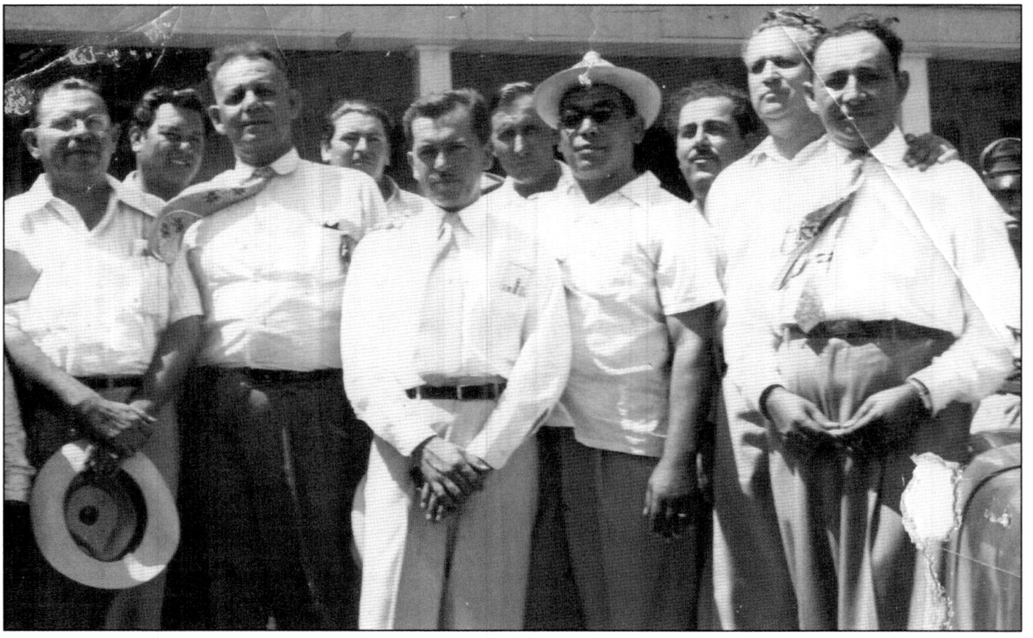

Mexico de Afuera was a group of valley men who kept close ties with their homeland and would often travel to Mexico to be part of ceremonies such as inaugurations. They functioned as an outreach group that raised funds to benefit those in need. Included in this photograph from San Juan are Santiago Alanis (left) and Roque Garza (second from left). (Courtesy of René Alanis.)

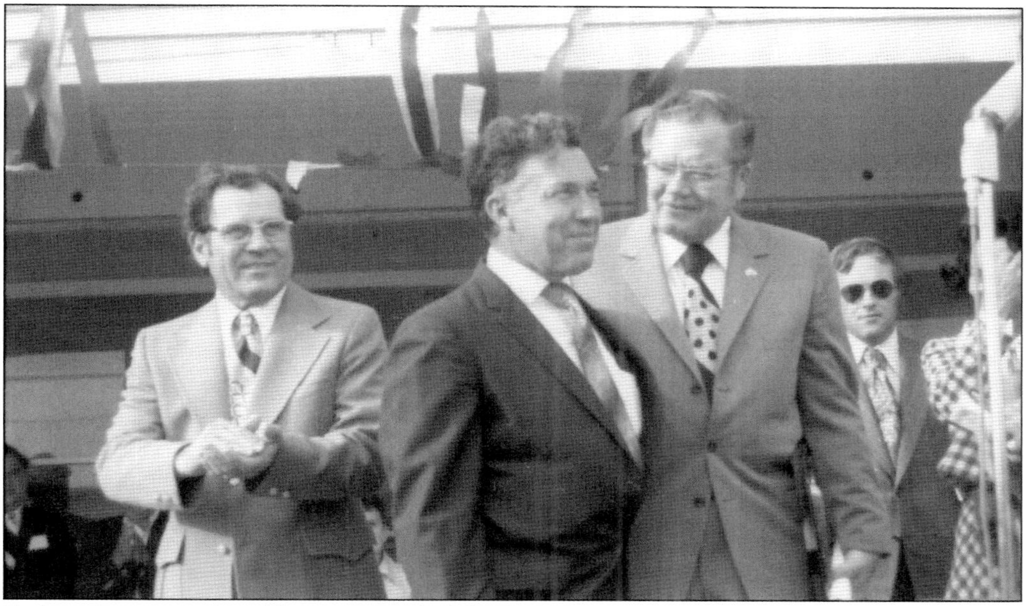

Early in his career, Arnoldo Cantu worked for the Texas Employment Commission placing local people in area jobs. After earning a master's degree, he became a teacher in the Pharr-San Juan-Alamo School District. As an educator of adult basic education within the district, he later became director of the Service Employment and Redevelopment Jobs for Progress program and began to write proposals to obtain funds for job training. Above, Gov. Dolph Briscoe (right) and state senator Raul Longoria (left) honor Cantu (center) for his dedication to Operation SER in the 1970s. Arnoldo and his wife Angelita have been married since 1951 and have six wonderful children. Both have earned the honor of San Juan's Man and Woman of the Year. (Both courtesy of Angelita G. Cantu.)

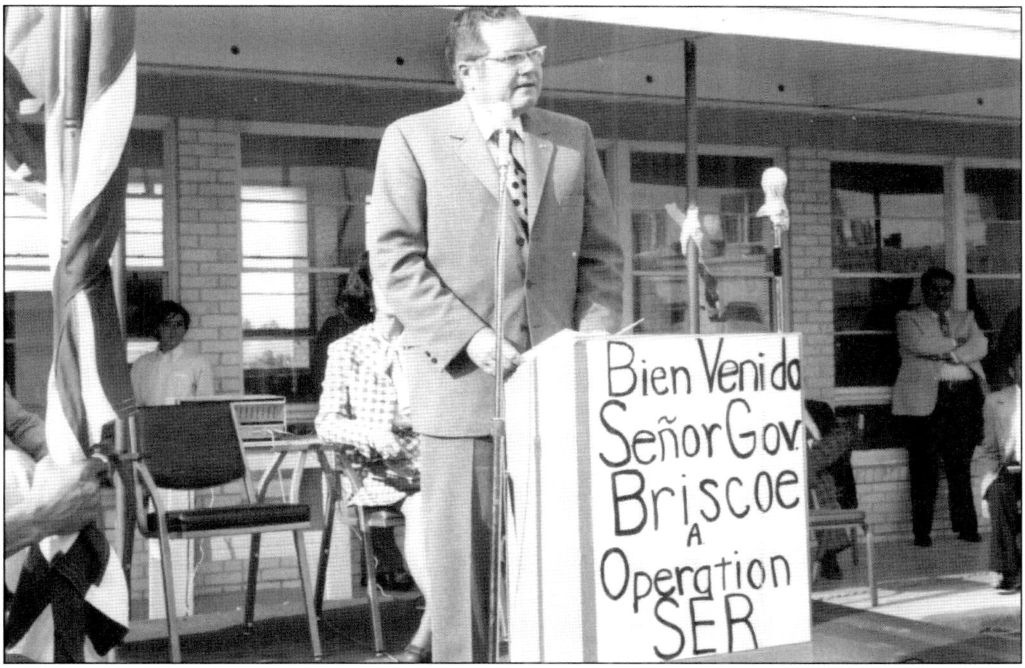

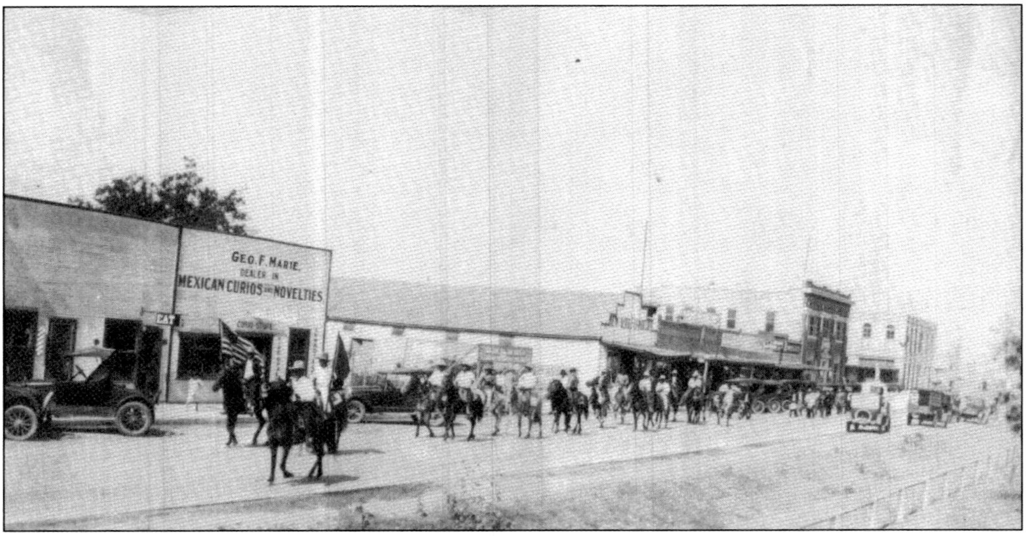

These two photographs from the 1920s represent a parade that celebrated the Mexican Independence Day holiday on the 16th of September. In the photograph below is a group of women dressed completely in white known as the Sociedad de la Cruz Azul (the Society of the Blue Cross). It was a volunteer group that helped the poor and the sick in the community. Standing next to them to the right is Teofilo Treviño. (Both courtesy of Agustin and Elodia Treviño.)

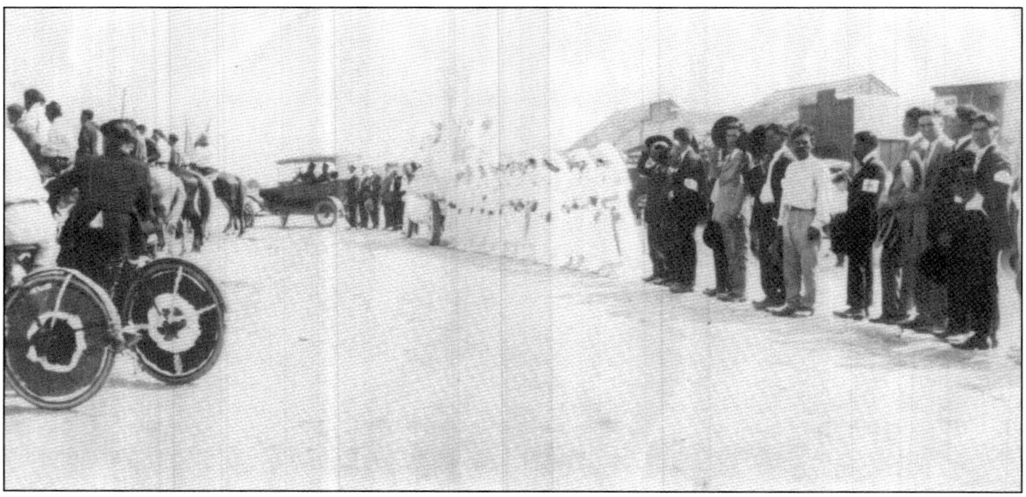

Midwife Aneslma Garza Sloss poses with her granddaughter Estela Garcia Salazar in 1951. The community depended on her services as a *partera*, or midwife, as she was responsible for helping to bring hundreds of San Juan's residents into the world. (Courtesy of Estela Salazar.)

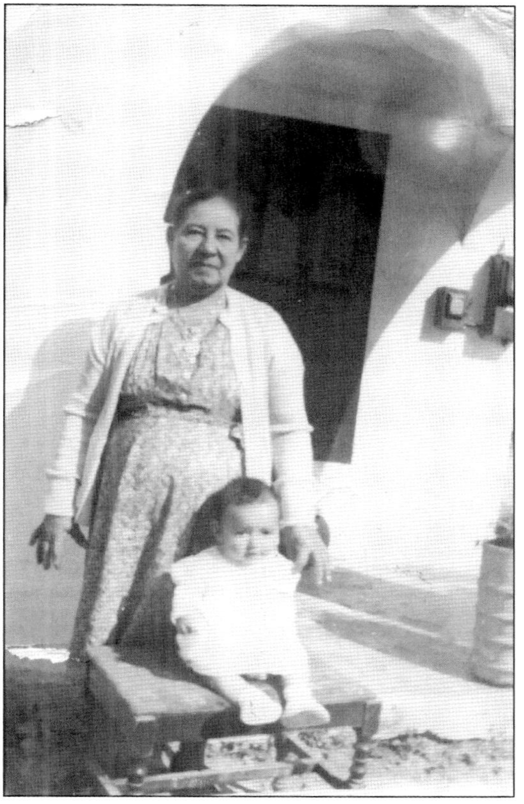

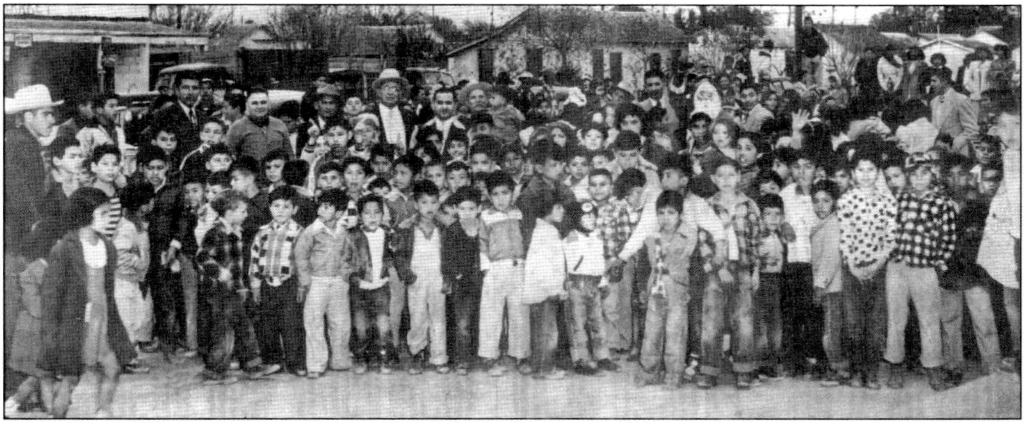

This photograph, taken on Christmas day in 1951, represents a holiday tradition in the neighborhood immediately above the railroad tracks. Local neighborhood merchants would contribute goodies to make gift bags for the kids that included oranges, peanuts, and candies. Some of the adults in the background are Jose Rodriguez, Andres Arcaute, and Nicasio Garza. (Courtesy of Romeo Jimenez.)

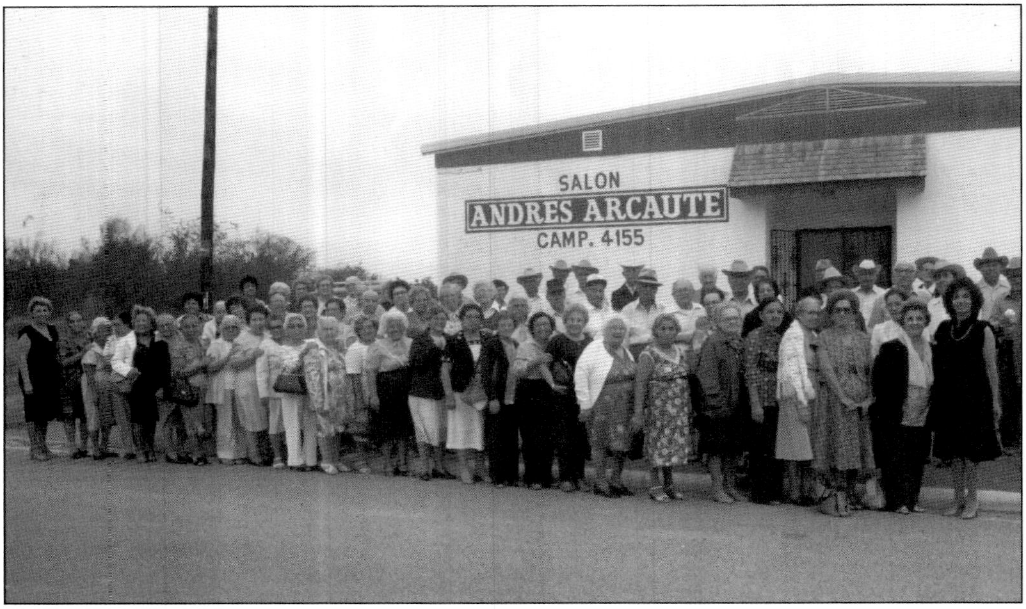

The San Juan Senior Companion Program volunteers pose in front of the Woodmen of the World Building in 1983. Originated by Jesus Ramirez, this program was part of a national network of programs that guided elderly volunteers to help fulfill the needs of the local community. The goal was to enable elderly people to remain independent in their own homes. (Courtesy of Estela Salazar.)

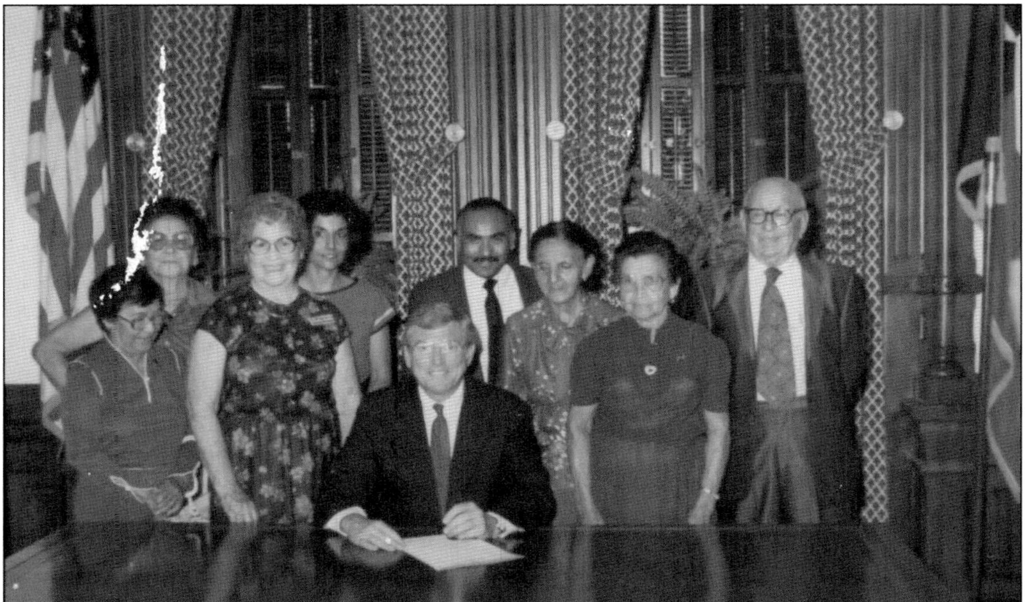

Andres Arcaute, Margarita Lopez, Santos Abrego, Fina Martinez, Aurora Garcia, and other San Juan residents are shown with Gov. Mark White (center) in Austin in the 1980s receiving an honor for their hard work and dedication to the Senior Companion Program. (Courtesy of Estela Salazar.)

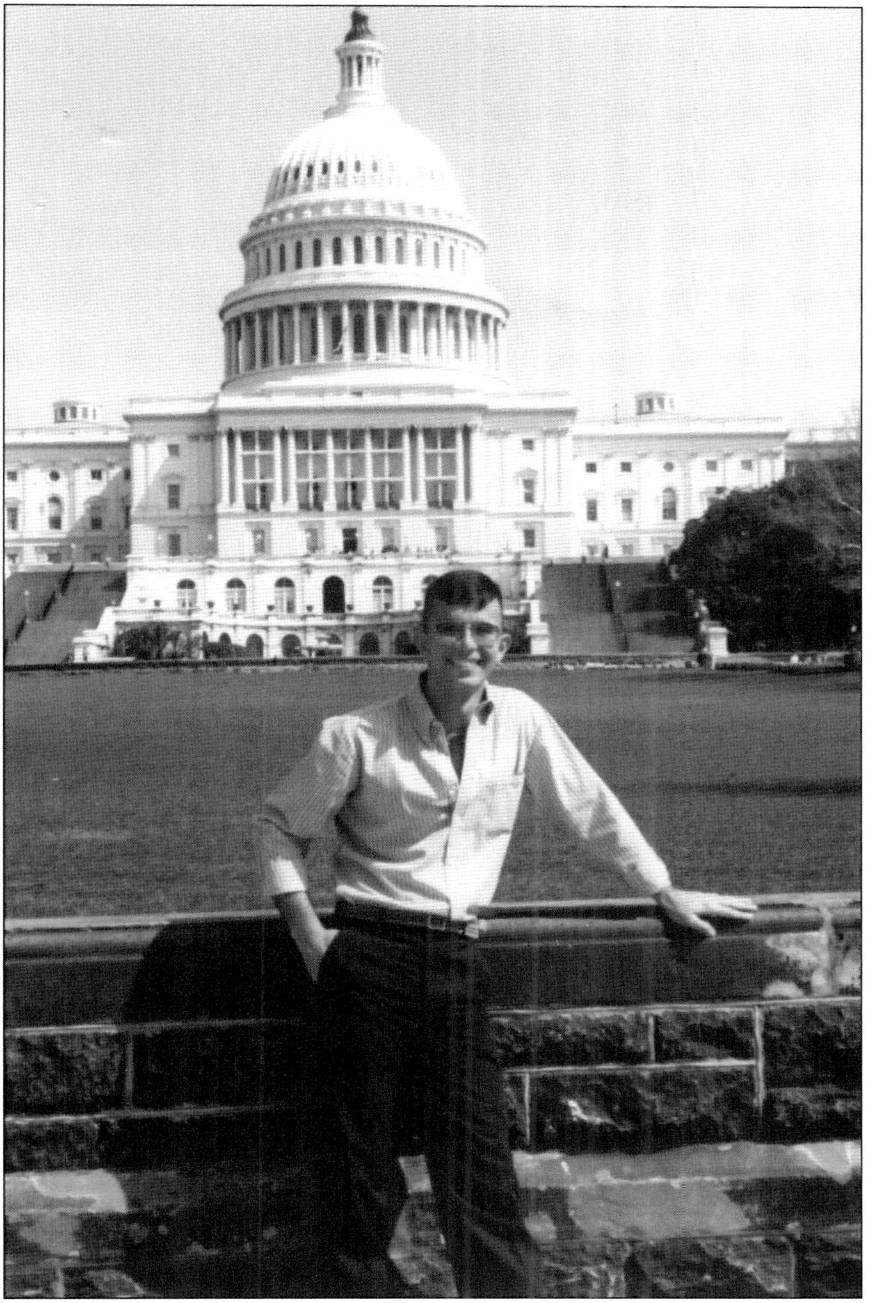

Stationed in Washington, D.C., with the U.S. Marine Corps' security branch, infantry rifleman Johnny Barbosa stands in front of the Capitol in 1983. The Pentagon had commissioned a portrait of the 10 surviving Hispanic Medal of Honor recipients to commemorate Hispanics in the military. As the artist was looking for Hispanic Marines to pose for the portrait, Marine Barbosa was asked to represent his fellow Hispanic servicemen. The portrait hangs in the Hall of Heroes at the Pentagon and was also used for an image on a 20¢ U.S. postage stamp in the 1980s. (Courtesy of Johnny Barbosa.)

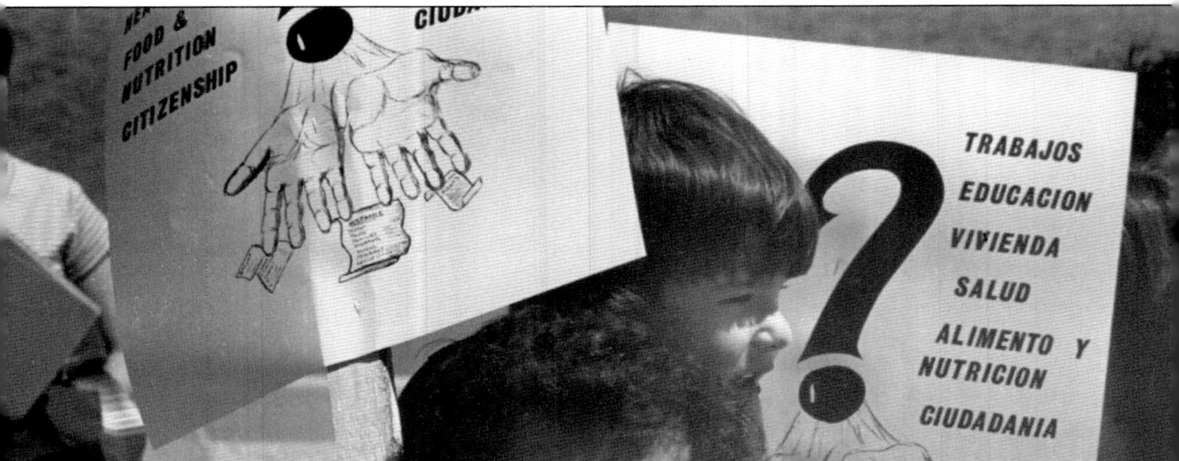

San Juan native Raul Yzaguirre is shown protesting in Washington, D.C., in 1978 with his son Roberto on his shoulders. His goal was to draw attention to the issues facing Hispanics and his disappointment in Pres. Jimmy Carter's leadership as it pertained to the employment, health, and education of the Hispanic population. San Juan holds a special place in Mr. Yzaguirre's heart, and he offered this quote it its residents, "At a more personal level it [San Juan] is a place that became the crucible that shaped my character and exposed me to both the good and the bad in people—lessons that would inspire me to believe in the promise of a better nation." (Courtesy of Raul Yzaguirre.)

Seven

Community Pride

Community and pride are two strong concepts that are present in the city of San Juan. The community's roots run deep into the past, with some citizens tracing their local ancestry to over a century ago. Long-standing traditions continue to be practiced and honored. Hispanic folk dance and costume have adorned local stage, entertaining those who feel it is important to keep in touch with their roots. Eastern European customs found within members of the farming community and midwestern traditions keep the city diverse.

San Juan has a long history of providing various traditional American programs for its residents. Sporting programs, such as Little League and semiprofessional baseball, gave San Juan's athletes opportunities to participate in the great American pastime. Elegant productions, such as the Miss San Juan Beauty Pageant, have presented opportunities for young women to get involved with programs that would benefit them later in life. San Juan can boast of residents who are singers and dancers, artists and actors, inventors and scholars, as well as leaders who not only serve the city but also the county, the state, and the nation. Many gifted and talented people hail from San Juan and have given back to the community that they fondly called home.

The community of San Juan proudly displays five historic markers presented by the Texas Historical Commission. Home to one of three national shrines within the state of Texas, San Juan is well known to global pilgrims who venture to the Basilica of Our Lady of San Juan Del Valle National Shrine throughout the year. The tallest flagpole in South Texas stands in San Juan within Liberty Park, and the largest Bluewood tree recorded in the United States is alive and well, adorning the yard of a San Juan home.

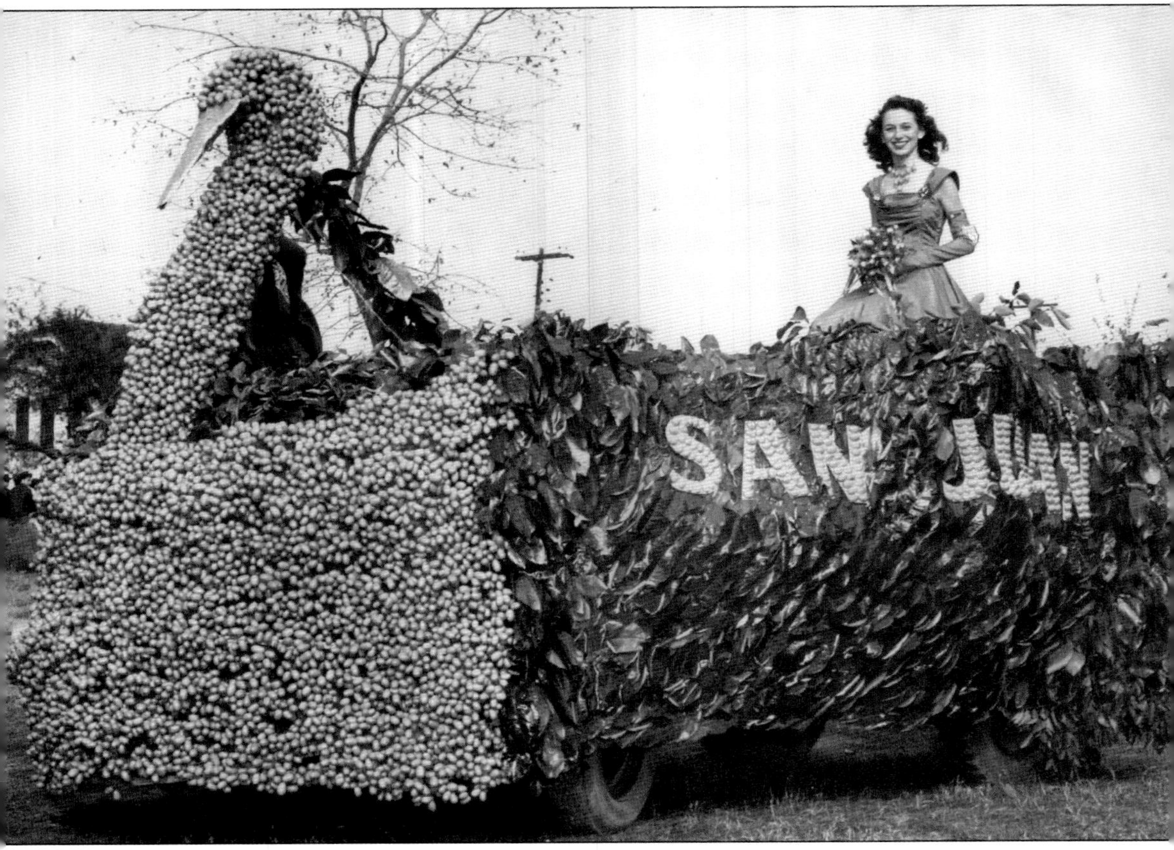

Jane Mellenbruch graces a float as the Duchess of Kumquat in the 1948 Texas Citrus Fiesta. Sponsored by the San Juan Lions Club, her float, in the shape of a swan and covered with kumquats, won first place in the Parade of Oranges. (Courtesy of Jane Mellenbruch Hinkle.)

Olivia Bravo is pictured here in 1944 at 18 years of age while attending a special fiesta for a Mexican holiday. Her dress is a traditional china poblana dress that her sister Juanita painted by hand. (Courtesy of Juanita Flores.)

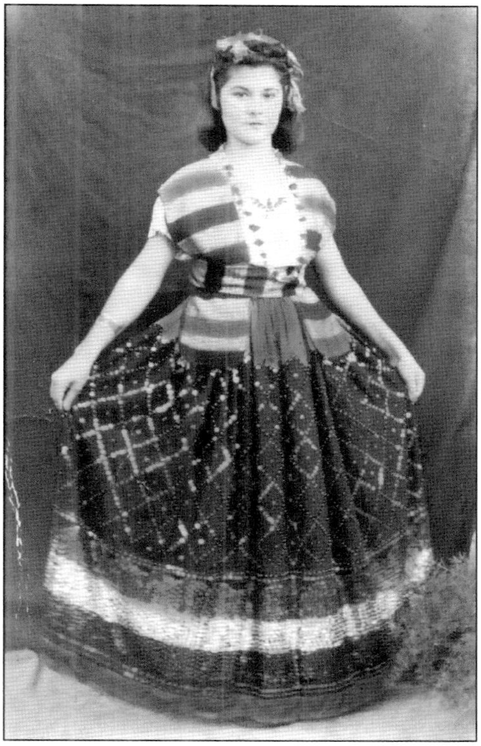

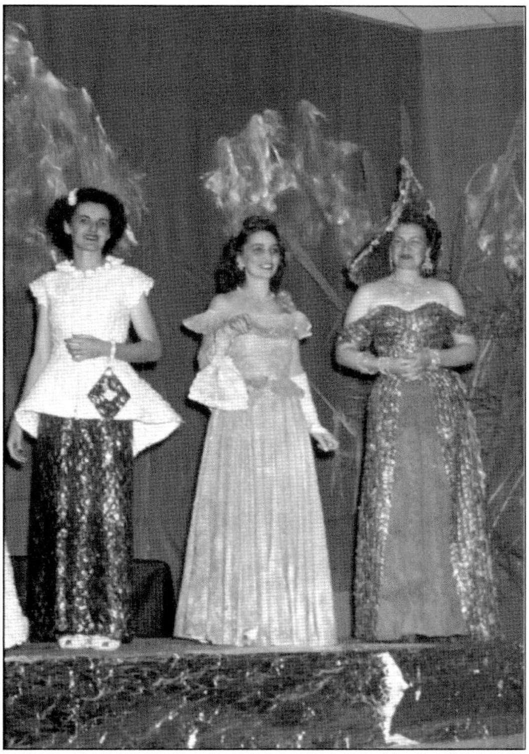

Mrs. J. Randal Hensley of San Juan was the winner of the Lillian Russell costume category in the Texas Citrus Fiesta Style Show in 1948. The dress was made of local fruits and flowers such as dehydrated Meyer lemon peel, ponderosa lemon peel, and pink lemon variegated leaves. (Courtesy of Mission Historical Museum.)

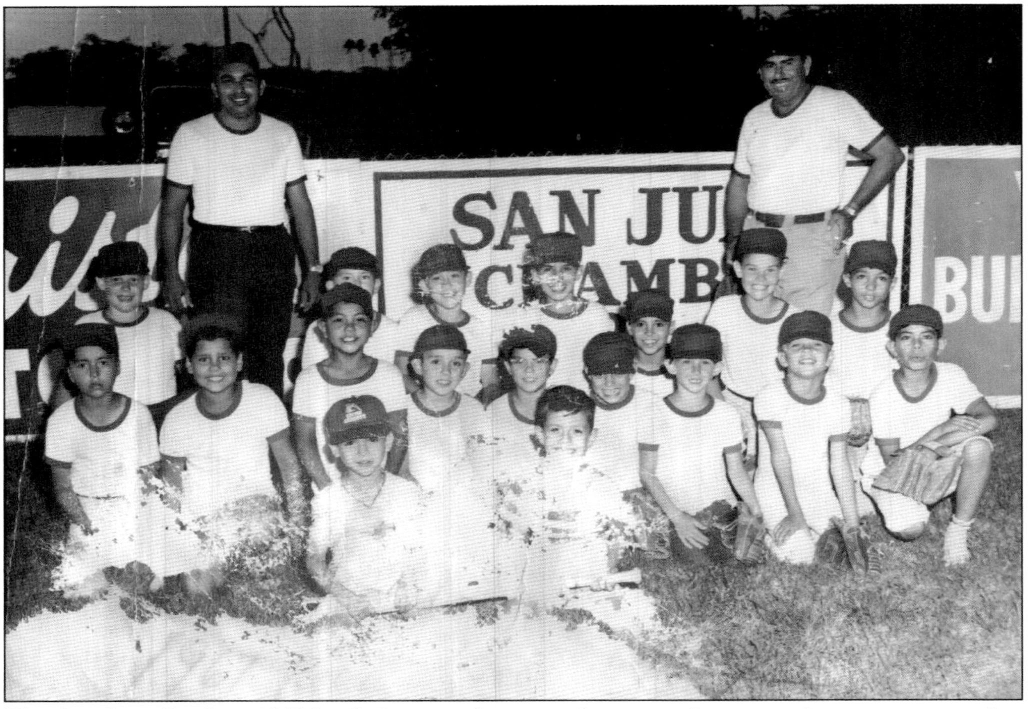

The San Juan Rockets 1967 Little League championship team, beaming their winning smiles, was coached by Octaviano Gonzalez and Erasmo Bravo (back right). (Courtesy of Erasmo Bravo family.)

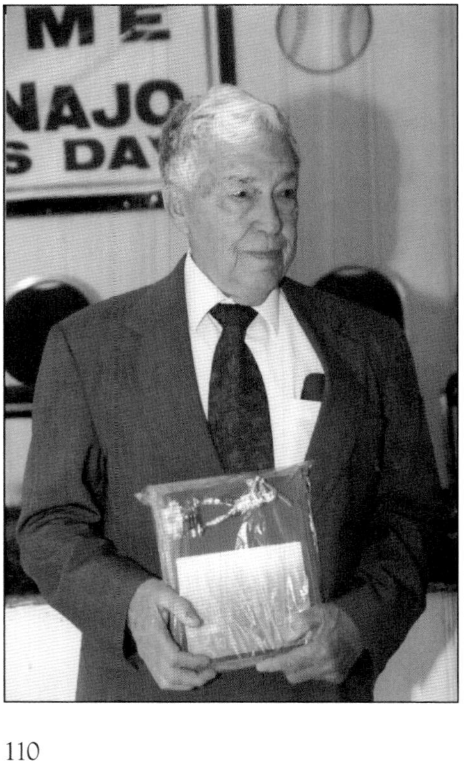

Arnoldo Cantu pitched for the San Juan Pirates semipro baseball team in the 1940s. Here he accepts an award at the 34th annual Leo Najo Day old timer's baseball reunion in Mission in 2005. (Courtesy of Angelita G. Cantu.)

One of San Juan's lifelong residents is racewalking champion Romeo Jimenez. He has won almost every race that he has entered. At right, Jimenez displays his champion medals after he won the 5K racewalk in Temple, Texas, on October 24, 2004, during the state playoff finals. (Courtesy of Romeo Jimenez.)

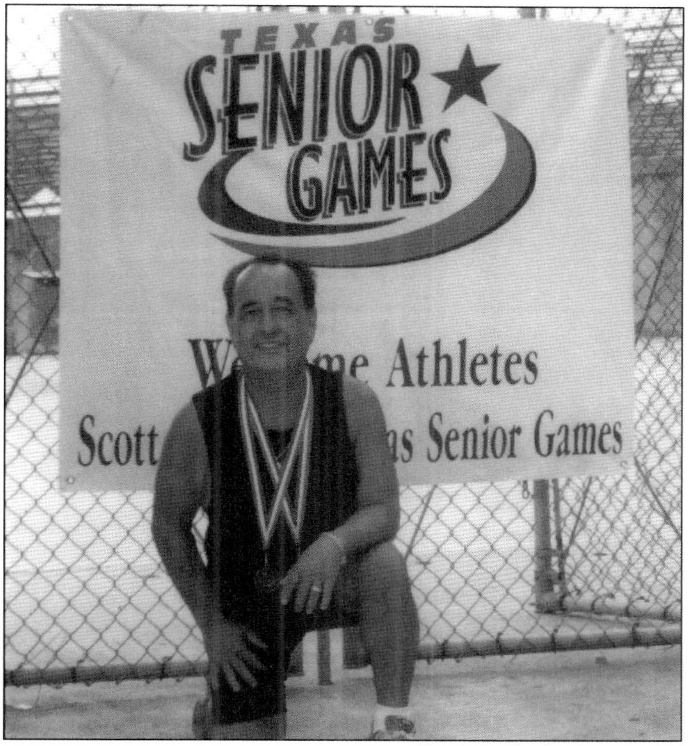

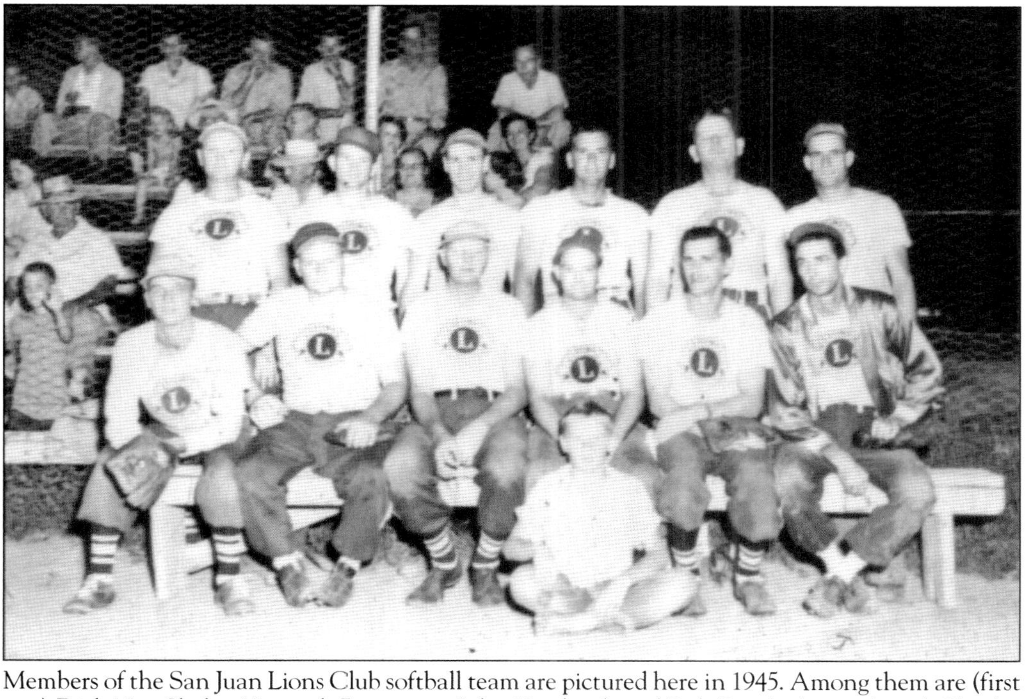

Members of the San Juan Lions Club softball team are pictured here in 1945. Among them are (first row) Dick Van Skyke, Kenneth Browning, John Kimbriel, and Bob Smith; (second row) Charles Kraas, Jimmie Westbrook, Nick Doffing, and Roy Haney. (Courtesy of Kenneth Browning.)

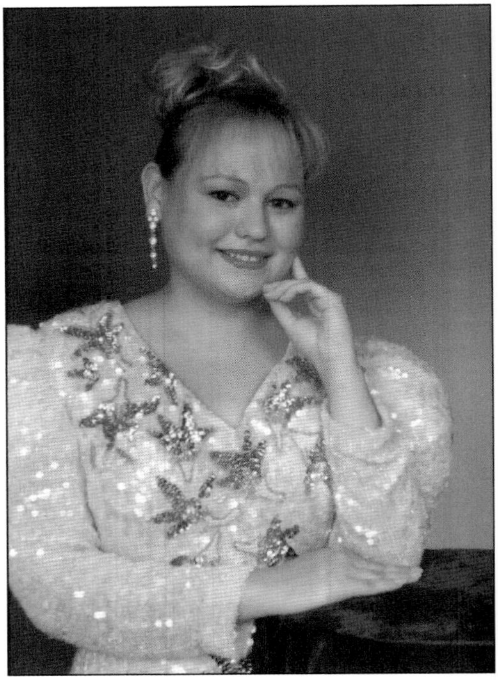

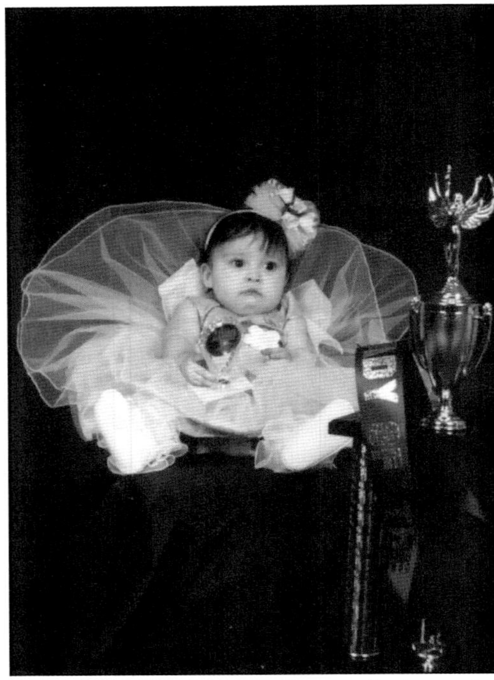

The Salazar family has produced quite a few beauty queens over the years. Laurie (below right) won the Miss San Juan pageant in 1991 and went on to compete in the Miss Texas Pageant. Sylvia (below left) won the Miss San Juan title in 1989 and was Princess Orange Blossom in the Texas Citrus Fiesta. Annie (above left) was a contestant in 1994, and her daughter Kennedy Lee Castillo (above right) won the title of Borderfest Baby in 2000. (All courtesy of Estela Salazar.)

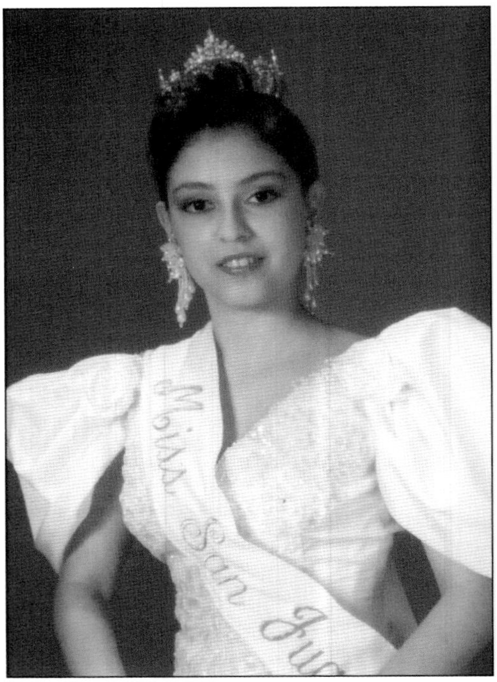

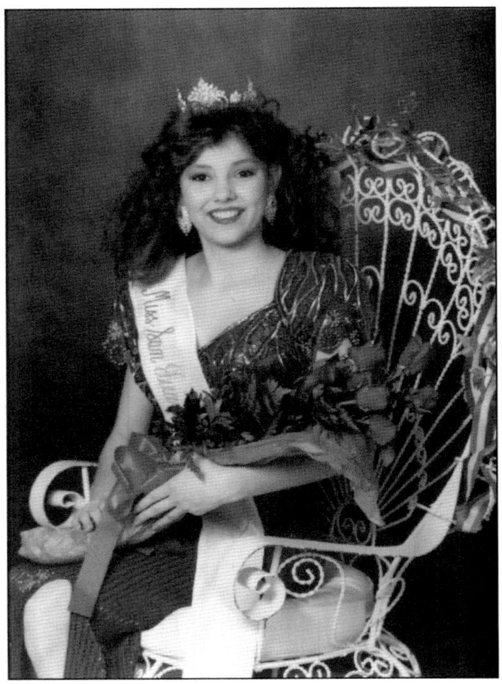

Ruben Rojas Jr. (right) plays the part of an Esparza brother in the production of *Alamo* in 2003. He participated in the Pharr-San Juan-Alamo High School drama program and went to college in Houston to study drama as well. He has also appeared in eight movies, three television specials, and several TV commercials. (Courtesy of Estella Rojas.)

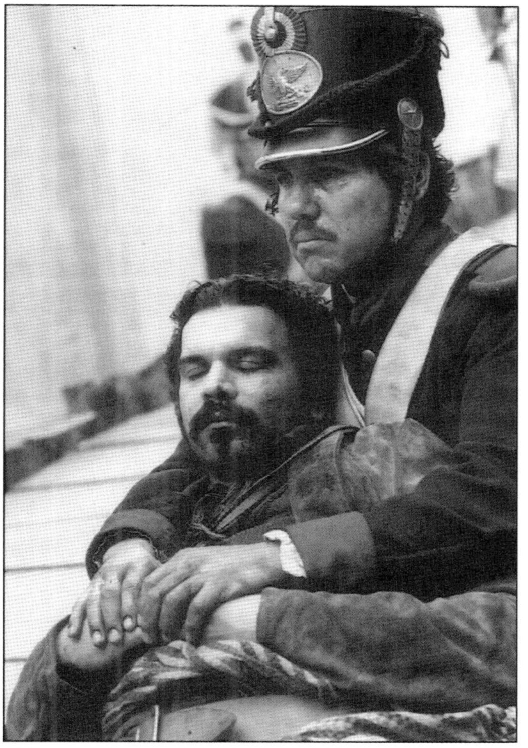

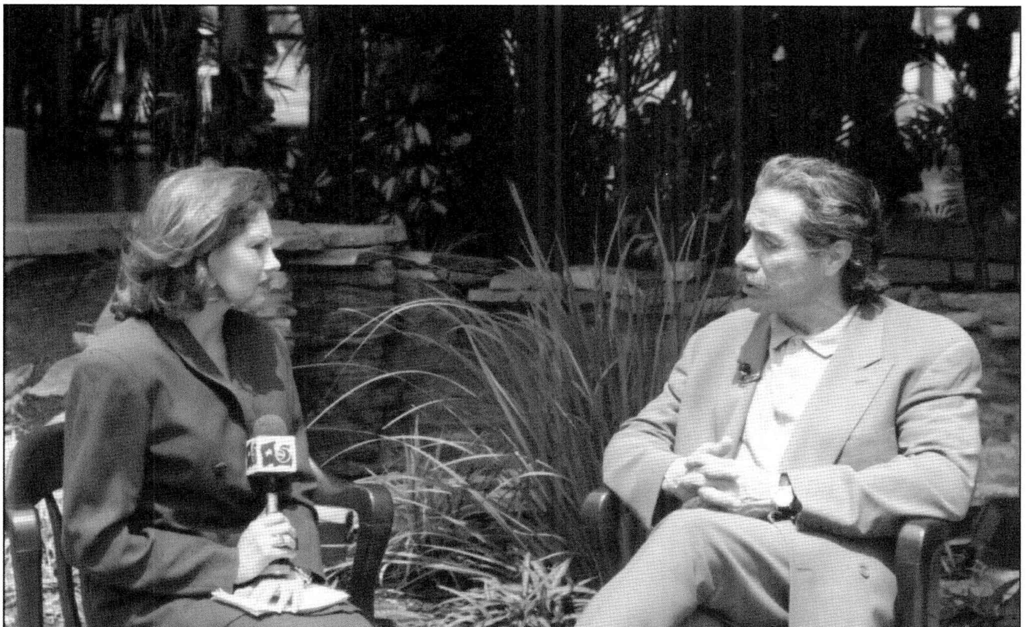

KRGV-TV television anchorwoman Laurie Salazar interviews Edward James Olmos in 1999 after he gave a presentation on gang violence at the campus of University of Texas at Brownsville. (Courtesy of Estela Salazar.)

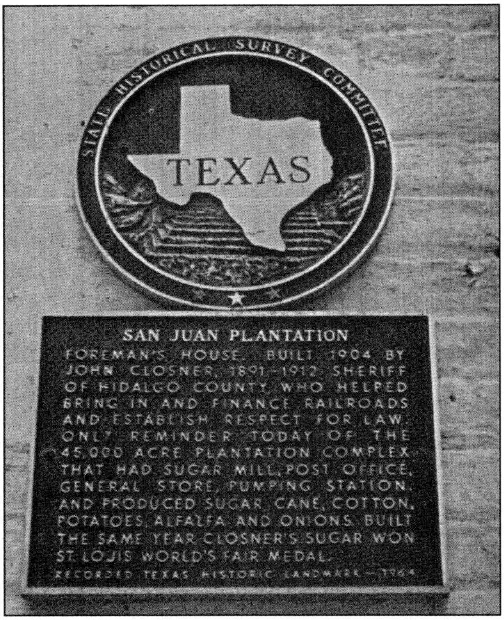

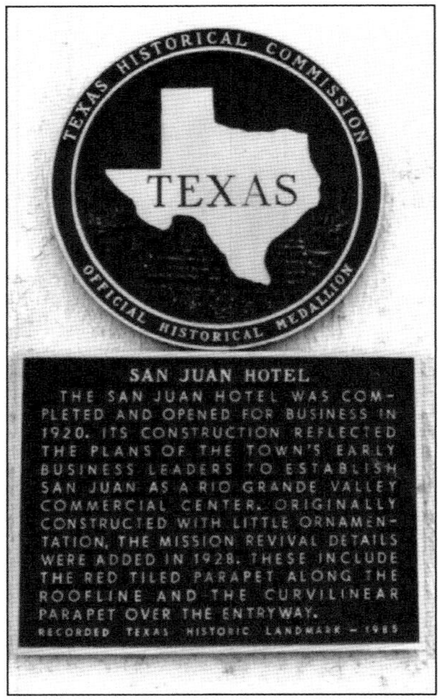

San Juan is home to five Texas Historical Commission historical markers. The San Juan Plantation was honored with a plaque in 1965 and now stands on private property. The San Juan Townsite marker was erected in 1984 and is located at the southwest corner of Standard Avenue and U.S. Highway 83. The San Juan Hotel received this honor in 1986. The hotel is in the process of renovation and is scheduled to reopen for business in the fall of 2010. The Tom Mayfield historical marker was placed on the property of the San Juan Hotel in 1993, as Mayfield had spent his last years living as a resident of this hotel. The San Antonio and Rio Grande Railway "Old Flossie" marker was placed in 1991 along the frontage road between Oblate and Nebraska Streets and can be seen from Expressway 83. (All courtesy of Hildago County Historical Commission.)

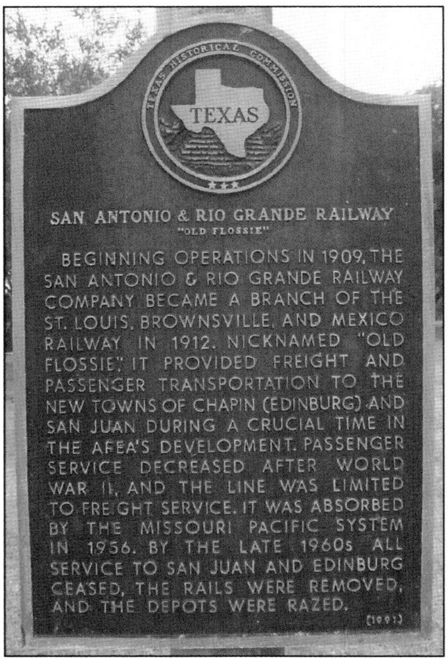

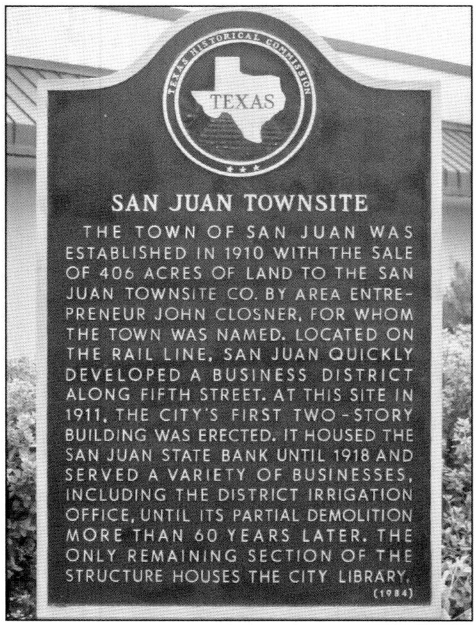

Eight

Family and Friends

San Juan is a place where family, friends, and neighbors have strong bonds and common interests. Local establishments generate fond memories as the senior crowd reflects upon days gone by. Small gestures of kindness, such as bringing dessert to a neighbor's house or speaking eloquently at a funeral, create fond memories and inspire reciprocal acts of kindness. Rites of passage, such as baptisms, graduations, and weddings, offer the community multiple opportunities to gather and celebrate. All of these events were enjoyed with family, friends, and neighbors.

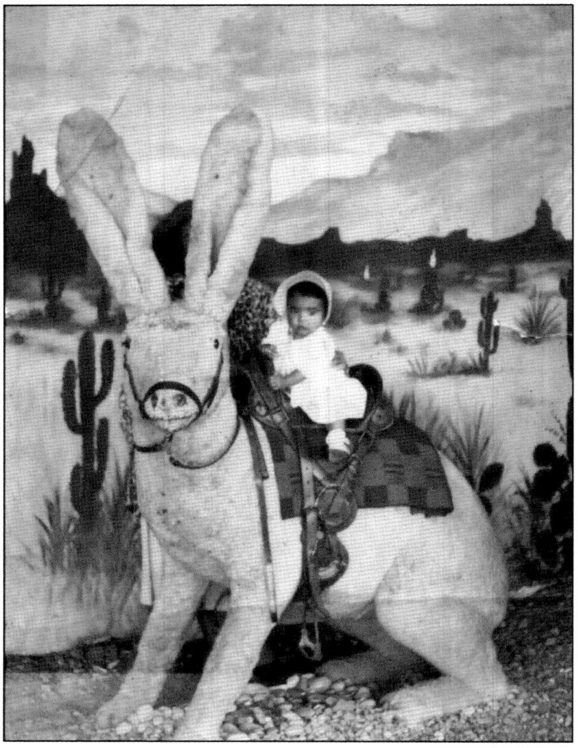

Every year this bunny appeared at the Gulf Station on U.S. Highway 83 west of Standard Avenue. After a month, the bunny moved to another location. Pictured in 1948 is five-month-old Lydia Castillo. (Courtesy of Juanita Flores.)

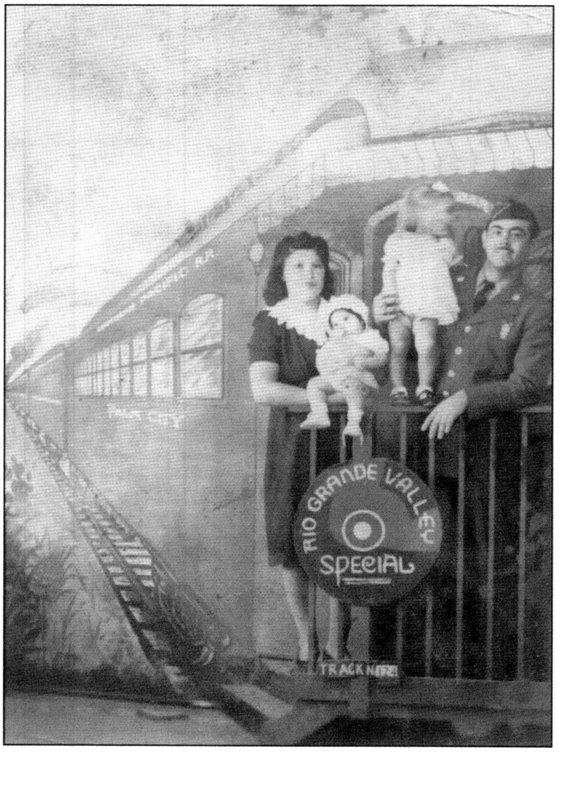

Dolores and Raul Maldonado pose in front of the Rio Grande Valley Special train backdrop in 1944 with daughters Estella, seated, and Susie (Elodia), standing. (Courtesy of Juanita Flores.)

In 1944, 18-year-old Virginia Quintanilla Bravo poses in a dress she sewed herself. Virginia was asked to go to Hollywood by a talent scout at a local café, but, protected by her mother, she remained in San Juan. She married Erasmo C. Bravo, who later became a well-respected lawman. (Courtesy of Erasmo Bravo family.)

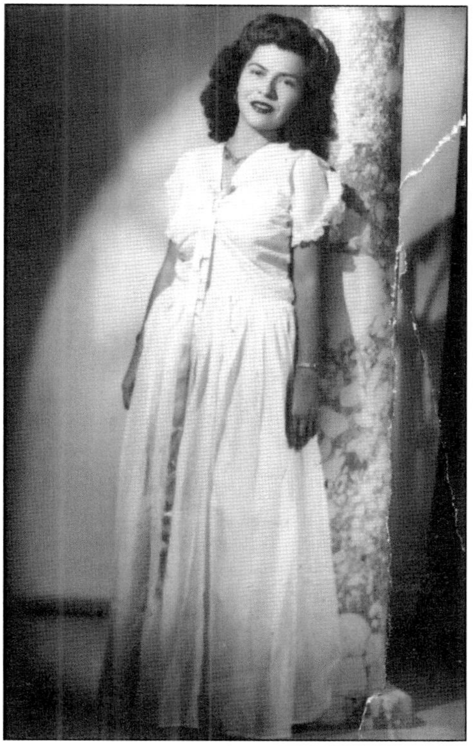

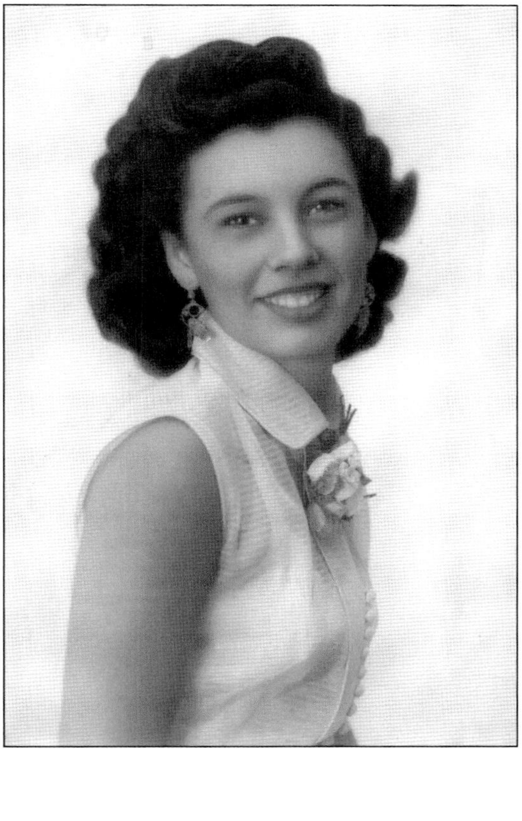

Margie Anaya Chapa, shown in a formal portrait in the 1940s, married Julian Y. Chapa in 1946 soon after his return from World War II. Married for 32 years, they had five children. She became a beautician and opened a beauty salon around 1960 on Sixth Street next door to Stotler Construction and across from what is currently Martin Drug. (Courtesy of Margie McCarthy.)

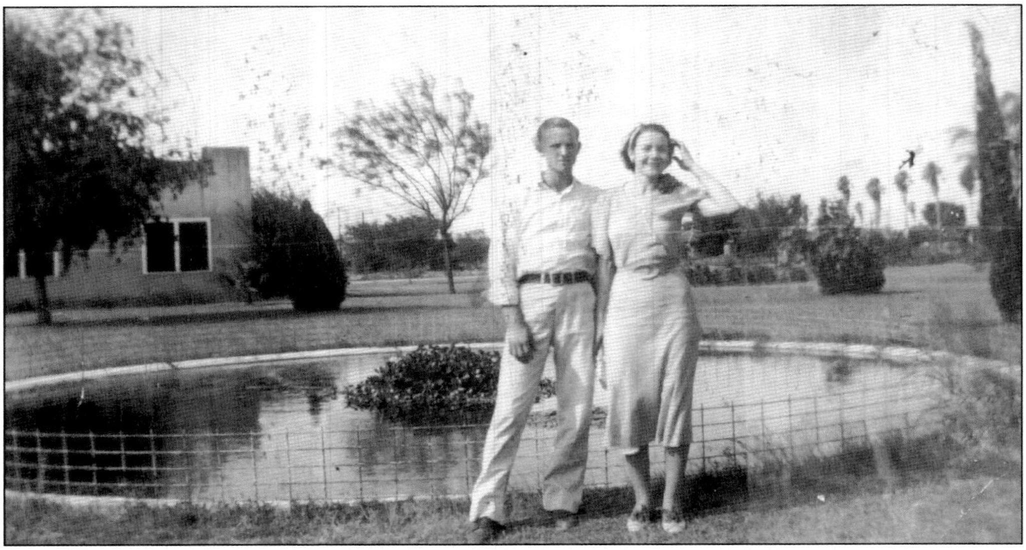

Ralph and Murriel Davis pose in front of the pond at San Juan Park around 1939. Many San Juan residents have fond memories of the pond full of goldfish and the yearly Easter egg hunt. (Courtesy of Sue Stevenson.)

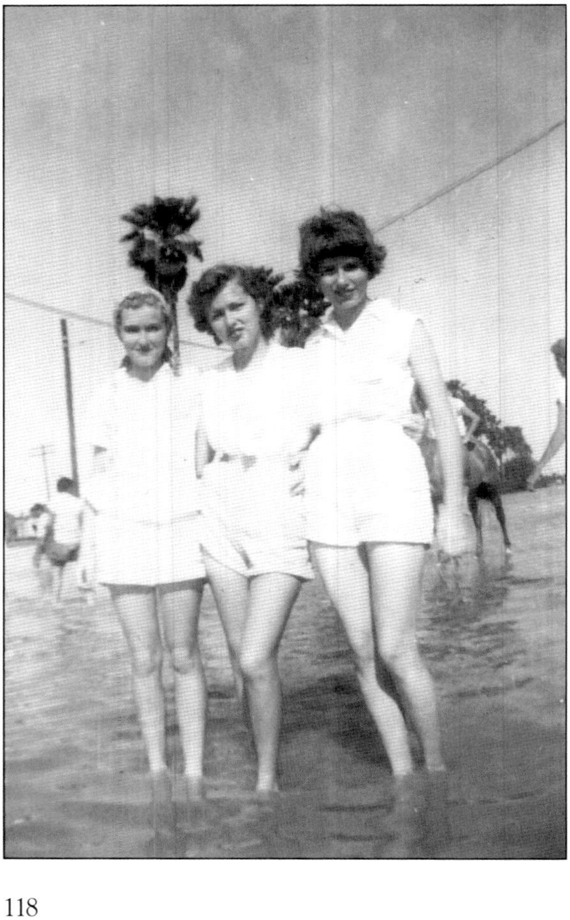

From left to right, Sue Davis, Delores Bartley, and Judy De Mange splash through the floodwaters at the corner of Nebraska Street and Highway 83 after the 1954 hurricane. Sue's future husband, Larry Stevenson, is just visible behind them on horseback, where he had come from McAllen. (Courtesy of Sue Stevenson.)

Sue Davis (center) and her sister Gay pose with neighbor Roy Anderson in 1942. (Courtesy of Sue Stevenson.)

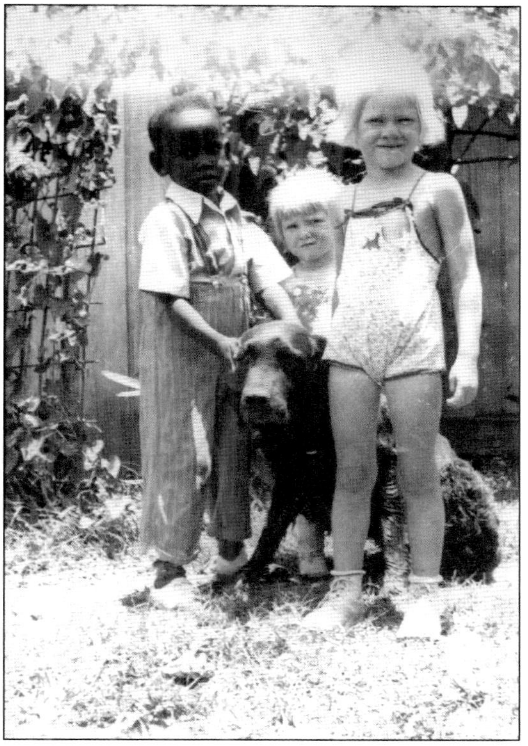

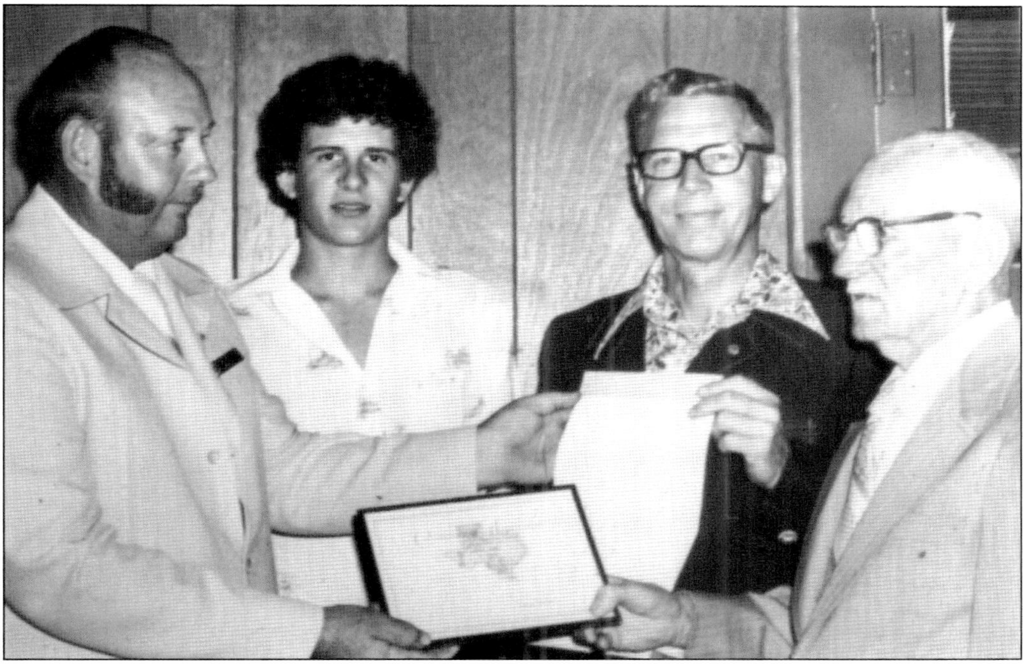

The Lions Club recognized George Bennett, at far right, with the Life Membership Award in 1976. Dr. Robert Norton, second from right, was honored as a Life Member. Also at the presentation are Glen Jewell, at far left, and Steve Smith. (Courtesy of Dr. Robert E. Norton.)

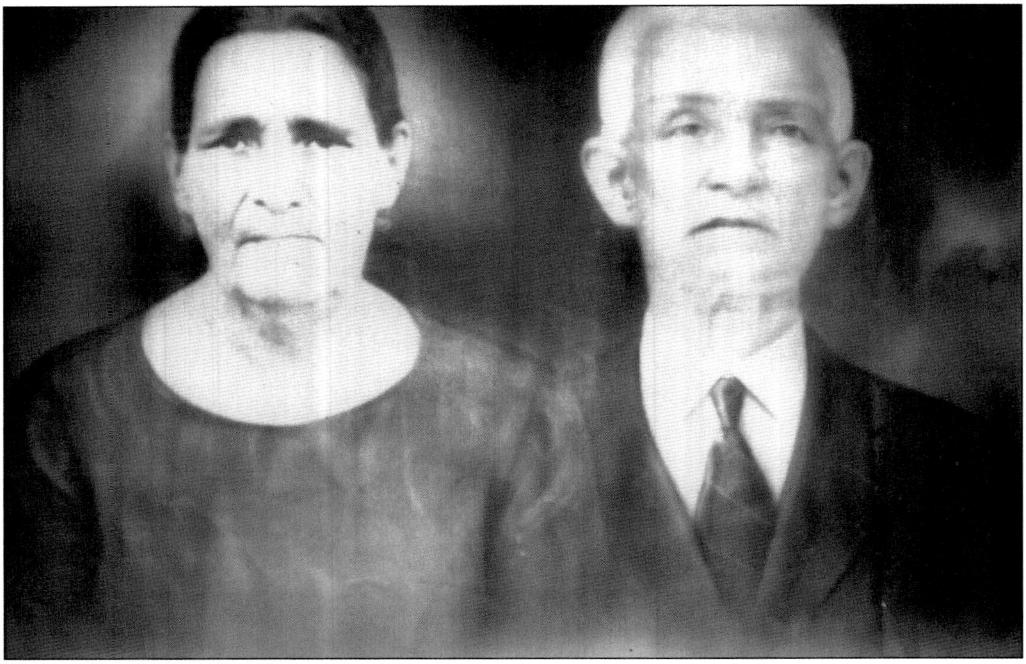

Feliz G. Bravo and Angelita S. Olivarez came to San Juan from Rio Bravo, Mexico. They acquired land north of Railroad Street as well as land south of Military Highway, where many extended family members settled and built a cemetery. (Courtesy of Estella Rojas.)

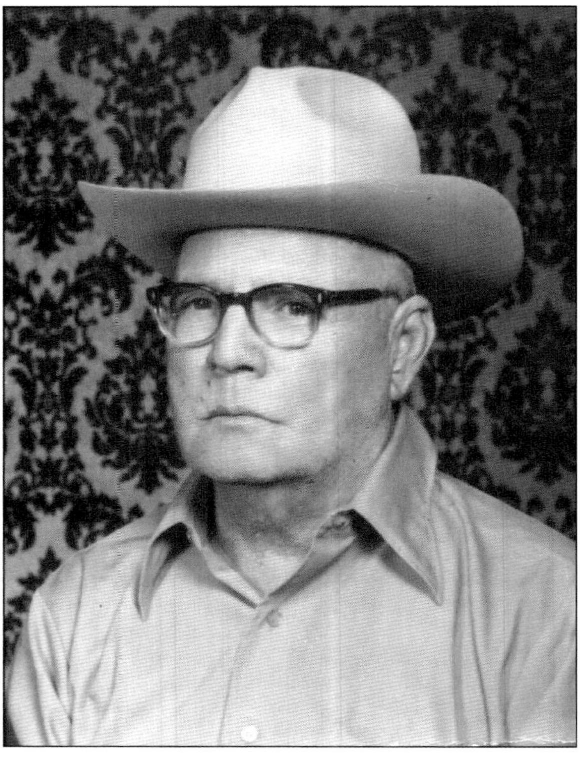

Felix Bravo was born in Reynosa, Tamaulipas, Mexico, in 1902 and moved to San Juan with his family in 1904. The Bravo family settled in San Juan before its founding and set up their homestead on Railroad Street where it crosses Nebraska Street. Felix worked clearing land by using a machine called La Escrapa that cleared the brush and trees to get the land ready for sale. (Courtesy of Estella Rojas.)

Chevo Maldonado is pictured playing his guitar in 1942 at 20 years of age. (Courtesy of Juanita Flores.)

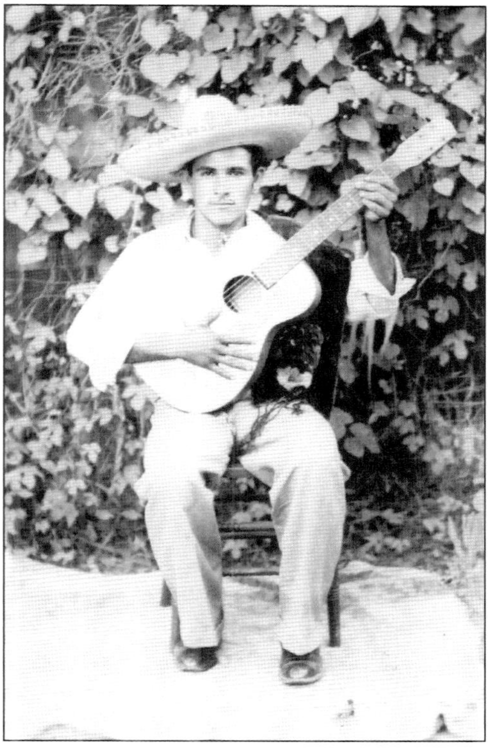

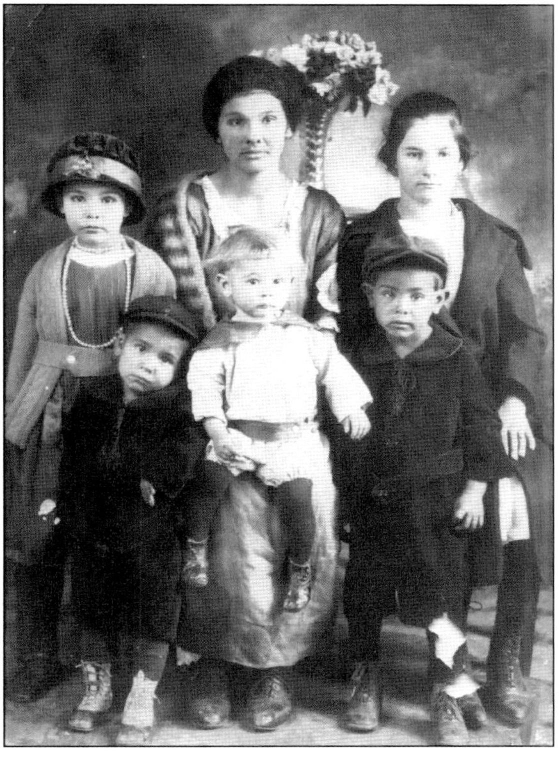

Felicitas Guerra Maldonado poses with her children and their nanny around 1923. They are, from left to right, (first row) Eusebio, Renulfo, and Raul Maldonado; (second row) Juanita Maldonado Flores, Felicitas Guerra Maldonado, and the nanny. (Courtesy of Juanita Flores.)

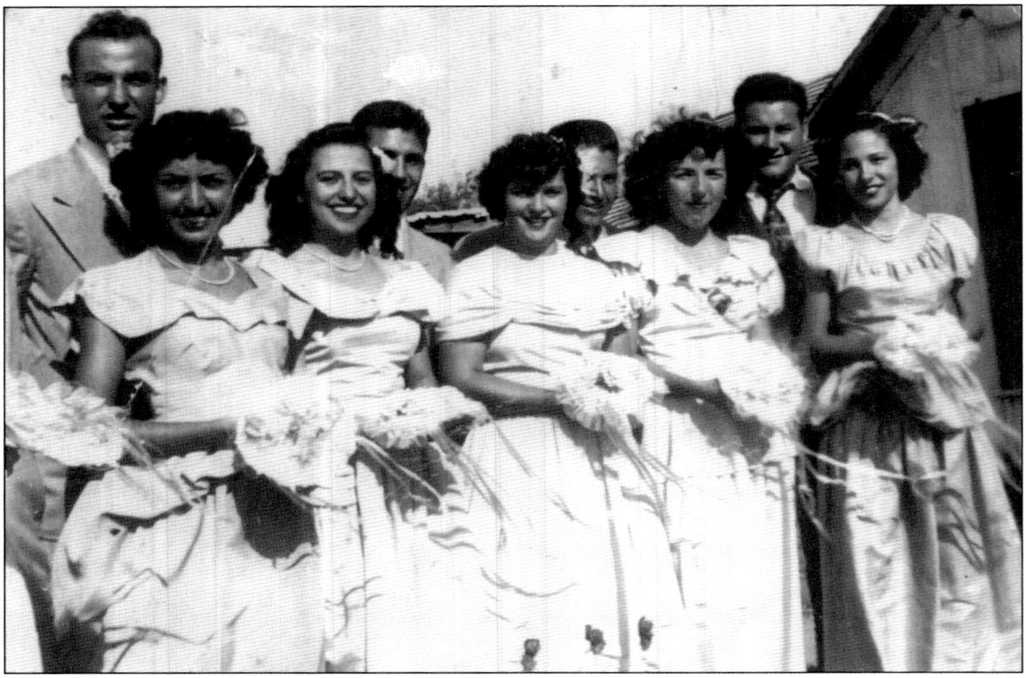

Bridesmaids and groomsmen in the wedding party of Estefana Canales and Gregorio Carrasco in the 1950s include the following, from left to right, (first row) Ofelia Serna, Noelia Cantu (Aguirre), Beatrice Guerra, Raquel Serna, and Angelica Aguirre; (second row) Edward Saenz, Beto Aguirre, Florencio Garza, and Hector Singleterry. (Courtesy of Beto Aguirre.)

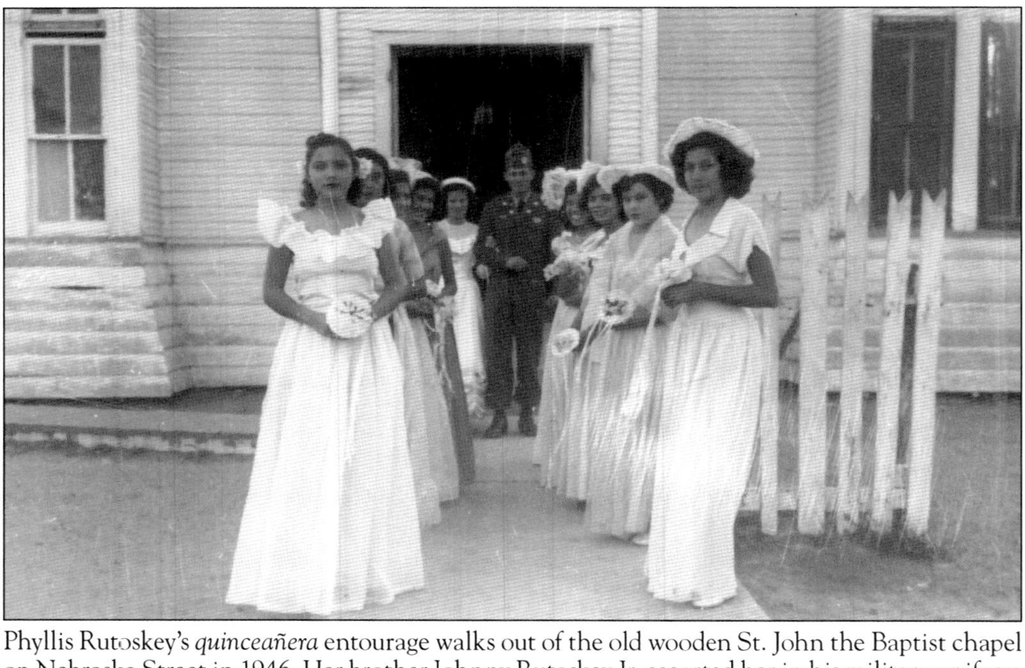

Phyllis Rutoskey's *quinceañera* entourage walks out of the old wooden St. John the Baptist chapel on Nebraska Street in 1946. Her brother Johnny Rutoskey Jr. escorted her in his military uniform surrounded by the *damas*, as is tradition. (Courtesy of Sylvia Prado Sandoval.)

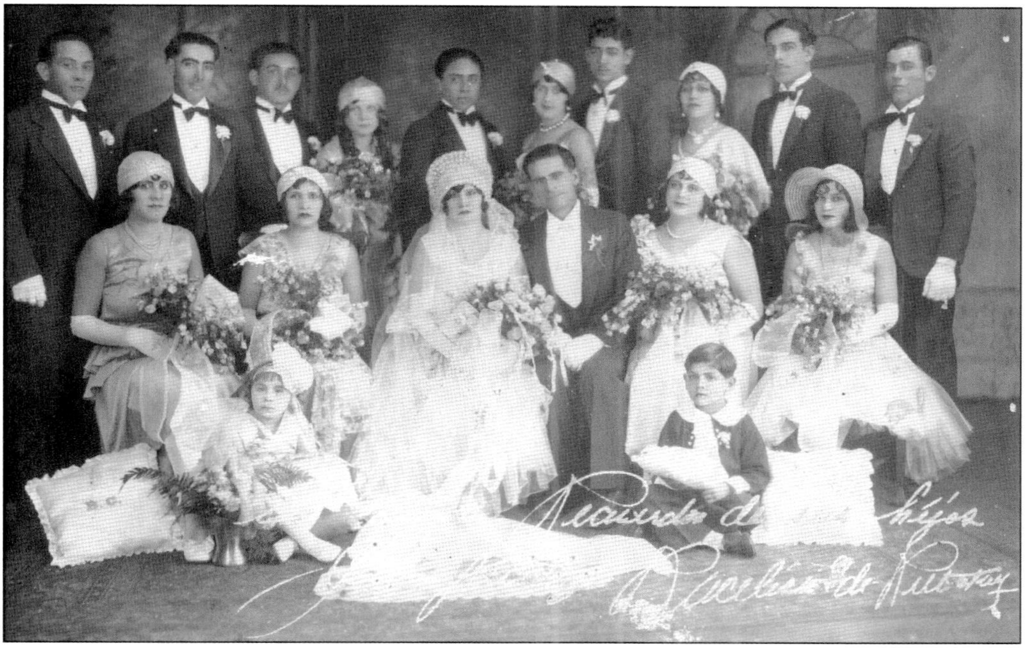

Juan Rutoskey, shown in his wedding photograph, was the son of a Polish stowaway who came to Mexico with his father and uncle to fight in the war with the French. Moving to the United States from their ranch in General Bravo, Mexico, the Rutoskey family settled in San Juan in the 1920s. (Courtesy of Sylvia Prado Sandoval.)

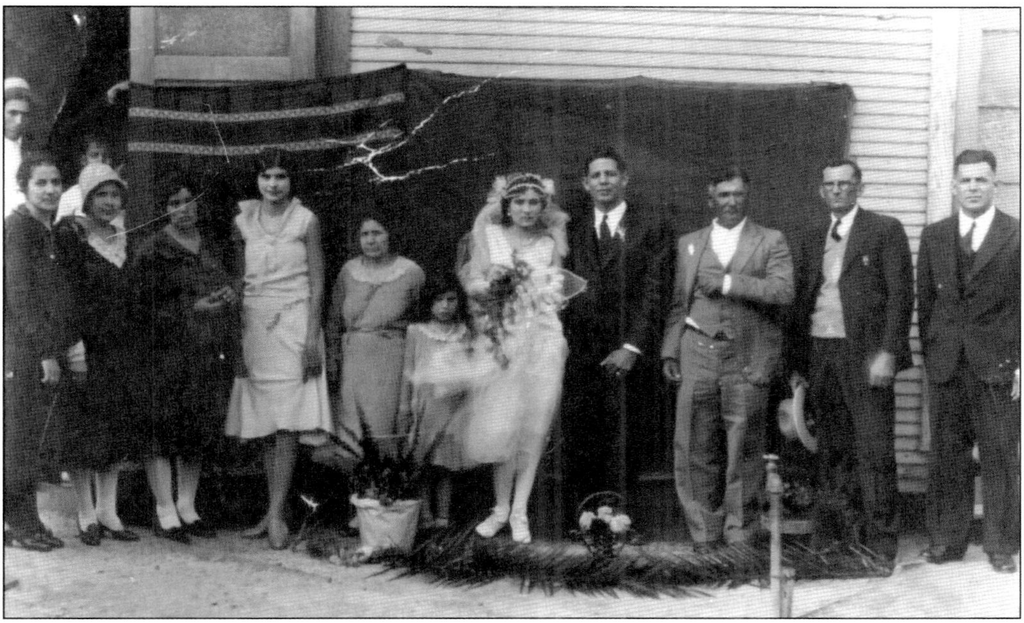

Roque Garza, born in 1904 in Mier, Mexico, and Rafaela Fuentes, born in 1914 in Curias, Mexico, wed in 1931. Roque came to the United States when he was 14 years old through Mercedes, Texas. At first, he worked in the cotton fields but later opened a general merchandise store affectionately called by locals La Gran Tienda Amarilla. (Courtesy of Maruca Longoria.)

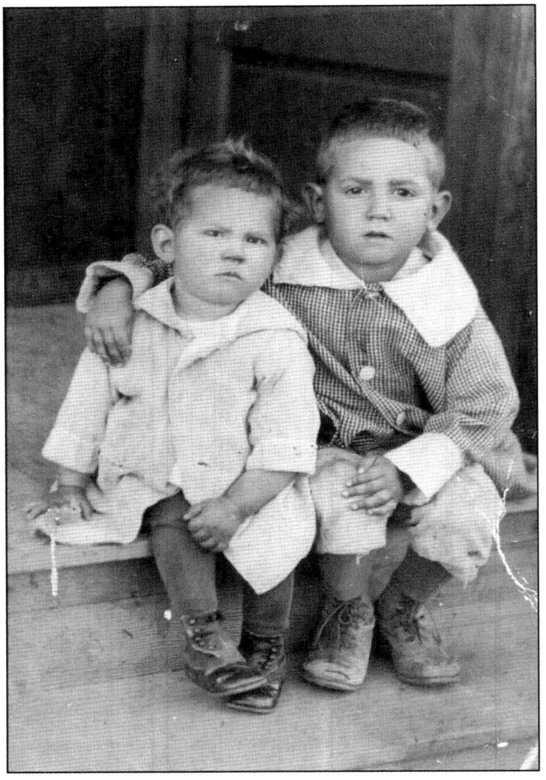

Two-year-old Guadalupe Villarreal Prado is hugged by her brother Alonzo Cantu Villarreal in 1922. Alonzo died a U.S. Navy World War II hero in 1944, surviving Pearl Harbor but became lost at sea among 233 sailors on the *Jarvis* destroyer after being torpedoed in the battle for Guadalcanal. (Courtesy of Sylvia Prado Sandoval.)

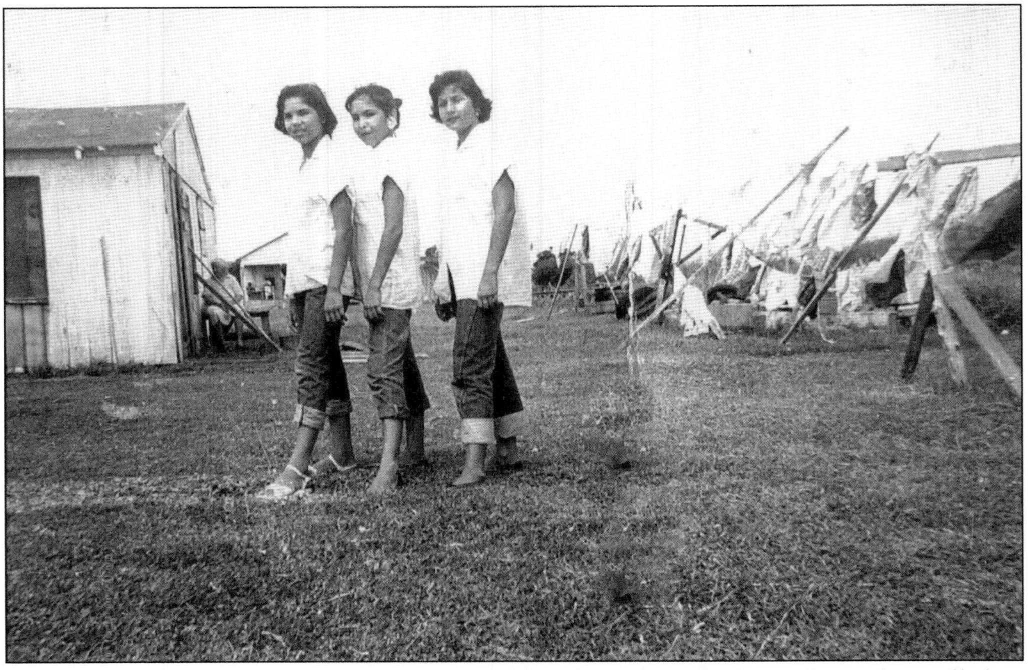

From left to right, Estella Maldonado, Susie Maldonado, and Bertha Bravo flaunt their rolled-up blue jeans in a backyard on Third Street in 1957. (Courtesy of Estella Rojas.)

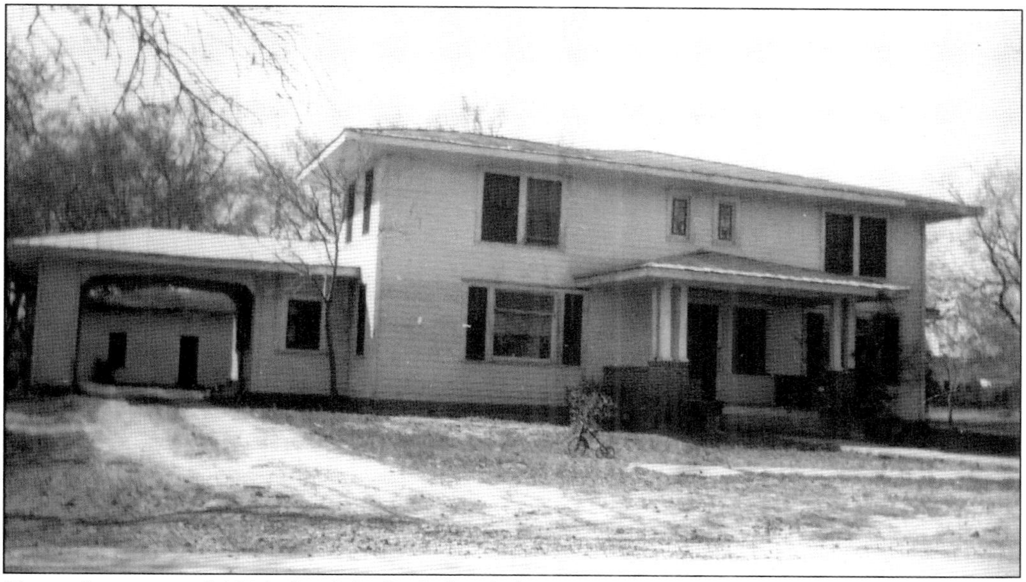

Shown here around 1946, the Schafroth family home at 102 East Ninth Street in San Juan was fondly called the "Big House." It was the home of Fred and Elsie Schafroth, and in later years it became the home of Harold and Myrtle Schafroth. The house was built in 1919 and the Schafroths lived there for 72 years. (Courtesy of Robert D. Schafroth.)

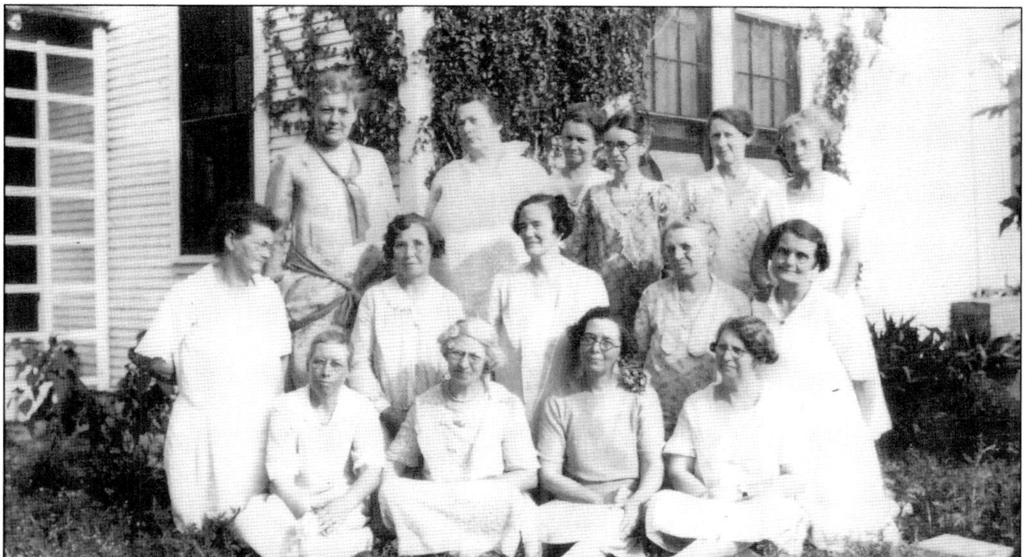

In this 1930s photograph, 44-year-old Elsie Schafroth poses with women from the People's Church. Prominent San Juan ladies shown are Mrs. E. V. Hunt, Mrs. Harris Cron, Mrs. Rice, Mrs. Hancock, Mrs. McCombs, and Mrs. Reichert. (Courtesy of Robert D. Schafroth.)

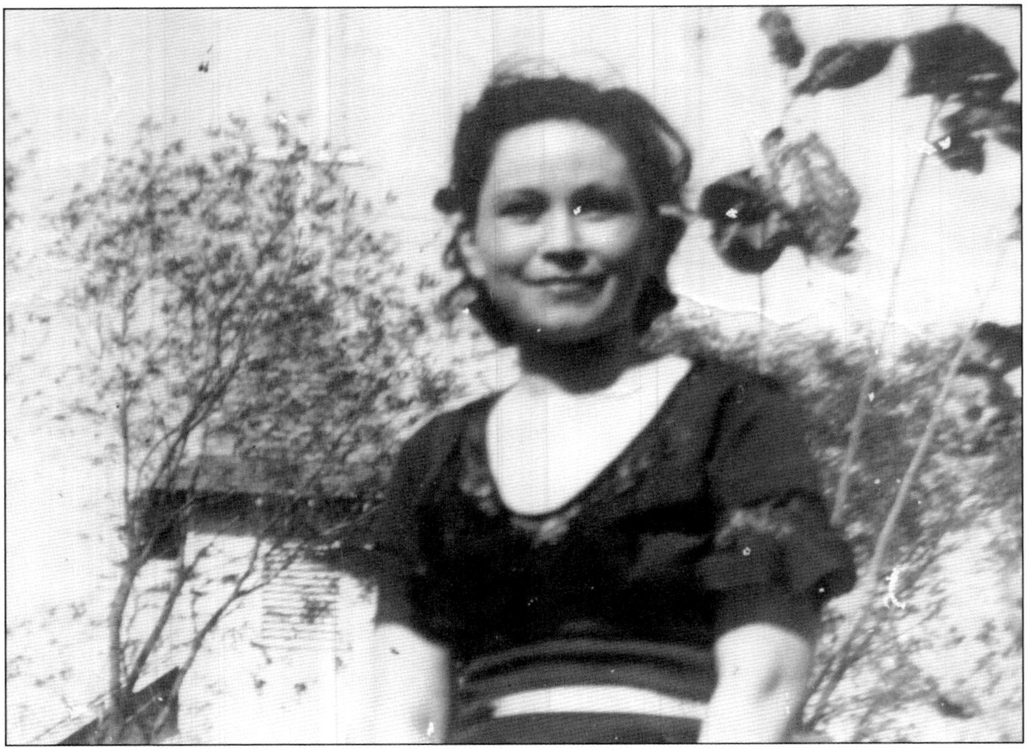

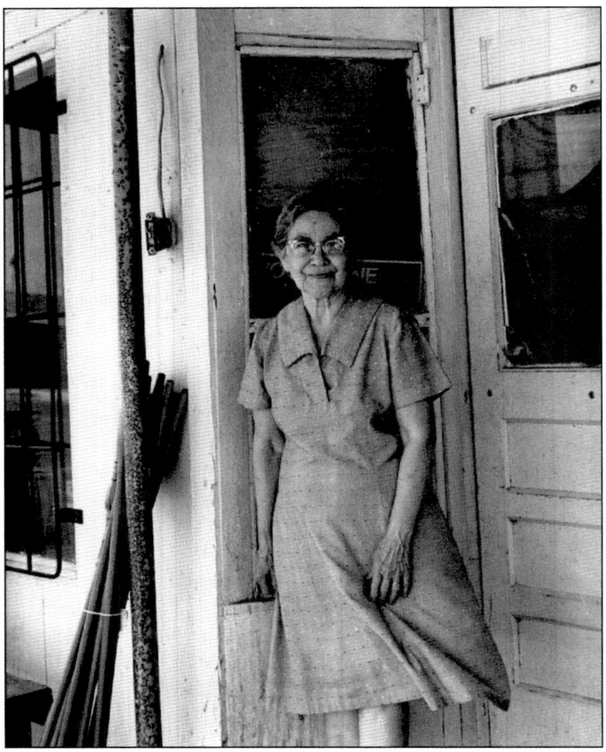

Well known to many in San Juan, Maria Manuela Treviño Alanis is one of its oldest living residents. She and her husband Santiago Alanis used to own a popular store and raised six wonderful children. Born in Donna, Texas, in 1913, she moved to San Juan when she was five years old. Her parents came to the valley from Mendez, Tamaulipas, Mexico, in 1912. Shown above in 1938 wearing a favorite dress and at left in a photograph taken by her granddaughter Arista Alanis in 1984, she has a large extended family that still resides in San Juan and neighboring towns. As one of the first parishioners to celebrate the ritual of confirmation at the Lutheran church in 1924, she has been an active participant in the church as well as in the community throughout her entire life. (Both courtesy of René Alanis.)

Bibliography

Allhands, J. L. *Gringo Builders*. Iowa City: 1931.
Johnson, Marjorie. *Historic Rio Grande Valley*. San Antonio: Historical Publishing Network, 2001.
Krenmueller, Ilse. *Memories 1932–1952*. Self-published.
McAllen, Margaret. *The Heritage Sampler*. Edinburg, TX: New Santander Press/Hidalgo County Historical Museum, 1991.
Pope, Dorothy Lee. *Rainbow Era on the Rio Grande*. Brownsville, TX: Springman-King Co., 1971.
Robertson, Brian. *Rio Grande Heritage: A Pictorial History*. Norfolk, VA: The Donning Company/ Hidalgo County Historical Museum, 1985.
Schafroth, Harold, and Robert Schafroth. *The Biographies of Harold and Myrtle Schafroth: Early Pioneers of the Rio Grande Valley of Texas and Long Time Residents of San Juan, TX*. Self-published, 2000.
Stambaugh, J. Lee, and Lillian J. Stambaugh. *The Lower Rio Grande Valley of Texas*. San Antonio: The Naylor Company, 1954.

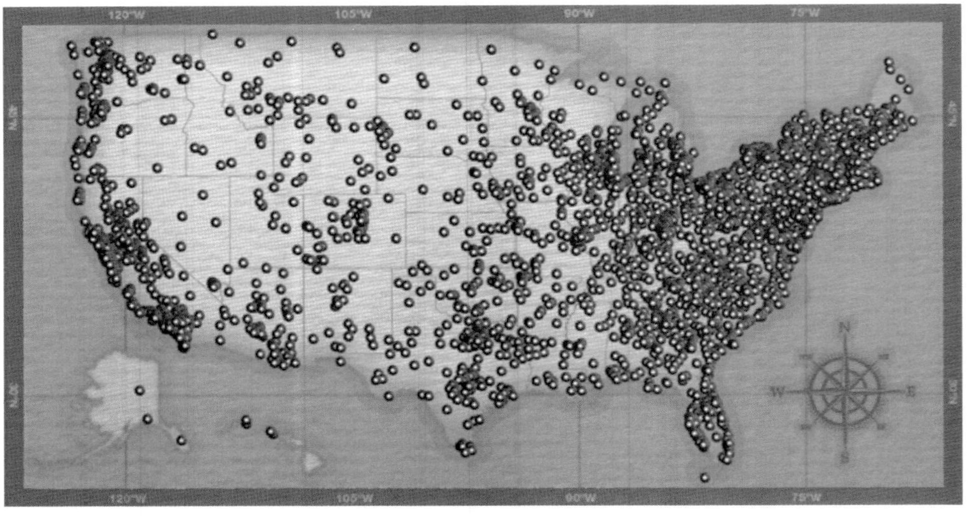